AUTHENTIC INSTRUCTION

 ## AND ONLINE DELIVERY:
Proven Practices in Higher Education

Edited by Kurt D. Kirstein, Judy M. Hinrichs, and Steven G. Olswang

IBSN: 1461051428
ISBN 13: 9781461051428
LCCN: 2011905425

Table of Contents

Preface

This book is a collection of work from a group of faculty members at a single university. City University of Seattle is a small, private, not-for-profit university primarily serving working adults in the Pacific Northwest, with satellite campuses in eleven countries on four continents. Through in-class, online, and hybrid delivery, CityU offers programs in education, management, technology, psychology, and general studies to students worldwide, many of whom would otherwise be denied access to education.

CityU is primarily a teaching institution. It focuses on delivering real-world skills, in an applied manner, that help students achieve professional goals. The vast majority of the university's faculty members are working professionals who are selected to teach what they do for a living. Over the years one of the hallmarks of a CityU education has been the link to real-world applicability that comes from the connections that the university's seven hundred practitioner faculty members bring to their classes.

While the university provides its faculty members with orientations and periodic training, much of what makes these faculty members successful in their classes has come from their own experience, their own proven practices for educating adults. Over the years it has become evident that the university has accumulated a rich collection of valuable educational strategies that can and should be shared with teaching faculty from similar institutions worldwide. This is the driving idea behind this book.

Most of the chapters in this book cover proven practices that have been successful at helping adult students achieve their learning and professional goals. Rather than reporting on educational research and theory, these chapters cover teaching methodologies that CityU faculty members are sharing so that other university instructors can learn from their experiences.

As this book was coming together, a few general themes emerged. The first centered on methods of authentic instruction, or the various ways in which learning can be tied to real-world applicability. These appear in part one. The second theme that emerged was online delivery. As a pioneer in online instruction, CityU faculty members draw upon years of experience as they share proven practices and look toward the future as technology continues to impact the way online education is designed and delivered. These online practices are included in part two. A final part addresses emerging themes in educational assessment and program revision.

If we are to believe that experience is the best teacher, then proven practices, developed through instructor experience, have much to offer both novice and veteran educators. The insights included in this volume are offered with this goal in mind.

Kurt D. Kirstein
Judy M. Hinrichs
Steven G. Olswang

Bellevue, WA
April 2011

PART ONE

AUTHENTIC INSTRUCTION

The goal of authentic instruction is to create learning opportunities that resemble real-world application. In a classroom environment that supports authentic learning, students are able to put new material to immediate use because it is taught in a manner that closely resembles the way it will be used in the real world. Depending on the discipline, many methods are available to facilitate authentic instruction. The chapters that follow make up only a sampling of instructional practices and strategies that can support this style of learning.

Dr. Stephanie Brommer opens this section by discussing a level of constructivism and authenticity that can be achieved in the online classroom through the inclusion of current events. Madeline Crowley reviews the importance of instructor presence in the classroom as it relates to student learning and perceptions of quality. Inquiry learning, as presented by Ryan Gunhold, shows instructors how to utilize this technique to facilitate a truly discovery-based learning process. Drawing parallels to Lincoln's law lectures, Sue Beller sheds light on various aspects of the adult education process, including diligence, cooperation, motivation, and respect for the learner.

Following these, two chapters address self-directed learning. Lana Zaher and Dr. Larissa Chuprina highlight the link between self-reflection and self direction. Doctors Pete Anthony and Gina Smith provide a plan for organizing graduate-level leadership curriculum by respecting the needs of the self-directed learner. Dr. Cheryl Szyarto presents a constructivist technique for teaching students the skills of critical analysis, and Jennifer Diamond presents authentic methods for structuring a classroom, using project management as the descriptive discipline so that it relates more closely to what students experience in the workplace.

This section concludes with five chapters that present specific examples of proven practices used with adult learners in the context of teaching various disciplines. Dr. Kurt Kirstein and Jennifer Diamond discuss the curricular design of a course intended to inspire business students to take action in regard to sustainability issues. George Kelley shares his experiences with leading students involved in service-learning projects within the community. Dr. Robert Brownlow presents the use of crisis management scenarios to challenge project management students. Dr. Judith Gray presents strategies to improve writing among graduate students of education. The final chapter in part one is Nate Kositsky's strategies for involving students in the management of their courses by having them assume a portion of the teaching responsibilities.

Constructivism, Meaning Making, and Breaking News

Stephanie J. Brommer, PhD
City University of Seattle
Division of Arts and Sciences

Abstract

Constructivism and authenticity can be achieved in online classes through the use of current events, including breaking news stories. Used in communications courses, including media and society, intercultural communication, and public relations, this practice is also relevant to social studies, education, psychology, and management courses. Learning through real-world events engages students and faculty alike because they are applying concepts and theories to real topics requiring real solutions, decision-making skills, and ethical and critical thinking. Embedding this practice into pedagogical theory enhances the authenticity of the practice itself.

Introduction

A grassroots revolution unfolded in Egypt, captivating people worldwide through social media as the region faced continued unrest. A nuclear crisis engulfed Japan in addition to the material, human, and economic devastation caused by a 9.0-magnitude earthquake and massive tsunami waves. A 7.0-magnitude earthquake ravaged Haiti. Consumer complaints spurred massive recalls of Toyota vehicles. Plumes of volcanic ash from an Icelandic eruption disrupted air travel, stranding passengers worldwide for days. These topical breaking news events engage students to apply the concepts they are learning in the academic environment to real-life events and controversies. Enhancing critical thinking and civic and social involvement, the incorporation of current news events into the adult learning environment promotes constructivist learning in an authentic way.

Shifting course content to accommodate breaking news events brings contextual relevance into the learning environment. This "event-based learning" is notably appropriate for adult learners. As defined by scholar Sebastian de la Chica (2003), "event-based learning refers to teaching activities that employ either historical or emerging events from the real world to achieve a pre-defined set of learning objectives" (Introduction section, para. 2). However, breaking news and emerging events require nimbleness on the part of both instructor and students to apply knowledge now. This shifting and impromptu analysis of course concepts through breaking news aligns with constructivist learning theory and real-world authentic learning opportunities. In addition it enhances global connections to course content and increases student participation due to topical interest and relevance.

Constructivism and Education

Constructivism, as a theory of knowledge and of learning, is also a teaching practice. A broad term with several strands of thought, constructivism has been viewed as psychological and sociological, although "there has been a trend towards a synthesis of the two, with advocates believing that knowledge is constructed individually but mediated socially" (Felix, 2005, p. 86). Scholars John R. Savery and Thomas M. Duffy (1995) summarize three key tenets of constructivism: "Understanding is in our interactions with the environment;" "Cognitive conflict or puzzlement is the stimulus for learning and determines the organization and nature of what is learned;" and "Knowledge evolves through social negotiation and through the evaluation of the viability of individual understandings" (pp. 31-32, emphasis in original). Thus, constructivism is both a theory and process of knowing, where students are active in meaning making, as noted by educators M. Gail Jones and Laura Brader-Araje (2002). According to Jones and Brader-Araje (2002):

> It is through checking out our understandings and perspectives with others that we develop a sense of the viability of ideas. This process of idea testing can be seen in the classrooms of teachers who value students' ideas and promote the process of critical thinking. (Defining Constructivism section, para. 7)

In sum, the main components of constructivism include meaning making, critical thinking, and the active role of the student.

Vygotsky's social theory of learning contributed to the constructivist philosophy that encompasses interaction between the individual and personal knowledge and experiences and others (Jones & Brader-Araje, 2002; Jaramillo, 1996). Vygotsky's learning theory was directed at children, but the basic principles can be extrapolated to higher education instructional practices. Vygotsky's approach would support experiential learning as well as the instructor facilitating learning in a social environment where students construct meaning, and learning builds on the thinking of others (Jaramillo, 1996). Addressing constructivism at the university level, Lisa Schweitzer and Max Stephenson (2008), both with university professional programs, explained:

> For constructivists, learners are not passive receptors of knowledge provided by an instructor. Instead, students

construct meanings for concepts. These are filtered through the "lens" of their expectations and values. As a result learning is best undertaken in "real-world" contexts in which students may acquire and test concepts. Constructivists argue that instructors teach best by posing meaningful questions—or better still, supporting learners as they discover relevant issues to address. (p. 585)

Many online educators have embraced constructivism as a philosophy for quality online learning and learner-centered focus (Gulati, 2008).

Vygotsky, whose pioneering work took place in the 1920s and 1930s, lived in an era when online learning, let alone the computer, did not exist. Today online classrooms can provide as rich a social interaction as traditional face-to-face classrooms, even with asynchronous discussion forums. Current and breaking news events prompt students to construct new knowledge by incorporating or connecting previous knowledge and/or experience into the analysis and evaluation of social, political, or economic issues and information. This illustrates constructivist teaching and supports constructivist philosophy. Susan Hanley (1994) of the Maryland Collaborative for Teacher Preparation explained:

The goal [in constructivist teaching] is for the learner to play an active role in assimilating knowledge onto his/her existing mental framework. The ability of students to apply their school-learned knowledge to the real world is valued over memorizing bits and pieces of knowledge that may seem unrelated to them. (pp. 8-9)

The value of using mass media in constructivist teaching is that it relies on student interpretation based on prior knowledge, experiences, and beliefs to construct meaning. This aligns with each individual's own practice of information processing during media exposure. According to communications scholar W. James Potter (2009), when a person is confronted with media messages, s/he filters out some messages and pays attention to messages that capture one's attention through key words, sounds, or concepts that trigger one's interest or concern. The individual matches meanings to previously learned or encountered symbols. When the individual has a personal, educational, or professional information goal to "transform messages they take in and create meanings for themselves" (Potter, 2009, p.110), meaning is constructed using one's knowledge, experiences, and beliefs to interpret and evaluate the message. This manner of coping with the deluge of media messages is expanded from the individual's information-processing practice into the constructivist learning environment of meaning making.

Authenticity

Authentic learning is a feature of constructivist tenets. Associated with real-life scenarios and practices, authentic learning also consists of activities and topics that have impacts past the classroom and into the real world (Petraglia, 1998). As active participants in learning, students use their knowledge to engage with real-world problems. According to Australian academic course developers (Stein, Isaacs, & Andrews, 2004) in a case study of authenticity in a university classroom:

> We use the word "authentic" in association with student learning in general, with classroom environments (face-to-face, online, distance, and so on), with learning opportunities, with activities, in relation to the nature of the "real" world beyond the classroom, as well as in relation to student personal meaning making…Authentic classroom practice is, therefore, that which reflects, for the students, a combination of personal meaning and purposefulness within an appropriate social and disciplinary framework. (p. 241)

Authentic Problems, Current Events

Incorporating current events and breaking news into curricular practice supports both constructivist theory and authentic learning. Arguably, the twenty-first century can be characterized as media driven. Students use computers to research and write, and they interact socially via interactive Web tools. Information flows in global networks, and news events are broadcast locally, nationally, and globally immediately, with commentary flying from diverse directions. As a result of the globalization and flow of media, events—from crimes to celebrity follies—are dissected, analyzed, and discussed in-depth in diverse ways and without regard to geography or personal investment.

Examples of current events and breaking news are used to advance critical thinking by applying concepts from the discipline as well as by making connections to issues and experiences outside the classroom. The mass media contribution to constructing social realities, values, and identities makes the articles and broadcasts it produces relevant to exercises in meaning making and problem solving. Using these media texts to develop discussions on the course Discussion Board, as well as topics of journal or blog entries, promotes constructivist meaning making, critical thinking, student involvement, and real-world value.

Although using current events or emerging news stories to facilitate learning communications, business, psychology, or social studies concepts does reflect constructivist learning, reflecting and commenting on current events or emerging news stories through blogs and/or journals cements its position in constructivist practice. In effect, this is event-based learning since real-world events are used to achieve learning objectives and key concepts.

When the Virginia Tech massacre occurred in spring 2007, the instructor of a media and society class shifted content to look at the coverage of the event. Students took the breaking news story of the college shootings and discussed news vis à vis construction, context, balance, and perspective. When radio personality Don Imus used racially derogatory comments about the Rutgers women's basketball team in spring 2007, students engaged in discussions about racial and gender stereotypes, emotional intelligence, free speech, and knowledge structures. These stories required shifting the discussions and applying concepts to current topics. The discussions met course learning objectives, including the need to apply skills to critically analyze media construction and content, and to analyze and recognize diverse subject positions interpreting media representations as well as those reflected in media representations. At the end of the course, a student commented, "As unfortunate as the events were, I feel that the Imus and Virginia Tech stories were perfectly timed and great for this class. To me I learned more from attaching our readings to these than I did the rest of the questions" (personal communication, June 15, 2007). Another student wrote, "Modifying the course structure to incorporate breaking news events that helped learning was fun" (personal communication, June 15, 2007).

An introductory anthropology class looked at the unfolding Haiti earthquake in January 2010 and addressed the following anthropological queries: How do power and wealth impact disaster recovery? How do cultures remember natural disasters? What are the effects of displacement from one's space, place, home, and community (all that help define one's identity)? What cultural attitudes and beliefs do relief agencies need to take into account as they provide aid? What are the coping mechanisms supported by a culture? What is the traditional knowledge of the environment and medicine? With these questions students were encouraged to think critically about their own and other cultures' beliefs and practices and to examine and explore cultural differences, all of which are course learning objectives.

These topical, current events touched students' lives, and raising the topic in discussion forums prompted a high percentage of participation as well as in-depth discussion. Students in an intercultural communication class jumped at the opportunity to analyze civil disobedience, online activism, and government shuttering of Internet access in Egypt in early 2011 as well as the health, economic, technological, and cultural reactions to the triple disaster that hit Japan in March 2011. One student wrote in his journal, "I find it strangely appropriate that we're studying the interaction of media and technology with intercultural communication in the same week that the world is watching the disaster recovery efforts under way in Japan" (personal communication, March 12, 2011), and he proceeded to analyze the images and communications coming from the epicenter of the disaster. Another student wrote about this class discussion as well as class study of cultural parenting and family structure based on a newly released contro-versial book about a self-proclaimed Chinese "Tiger Mom" with strict, authoritarian parenting behavior: "The Japanese earthquake and the cultural behaviors seem very relevant to our book knowl-edge we gained this quarter. The Tiger Mom discussion question was a good example of using a current event on the discussion board" (personal communication, March 15, 2011).

Other examples can include using the massive recall of Toyota vehicles in 2010 to evaluate public relations practices and utilizing articles regarding annual salary surveys in math and statistics cours-es. The 2010 eruption of Eyjafjallajökull in Iceland, which spread ash and disrupted air travel across western and northern Europe, can become an impromptu business and public relations case study. A hurricane's wrath, such as Hurricane Katrina, can be introduced into meteorology curriculum, and "while this event-based approach to teaching science may result in less curriculum coverage, students will be more likely to remember the scientific concepts addressed and to remember enjoying the study of science" (de la Chica, 2003, Event-based Science section, para. 1). De la Chica (2003) also dis-cusses disaster coverage in event-based learning:

> These activities match the qualifications of *constructivism* because the student extends his/her knowledge through self-directed exploration and manipulation of the relevant disaster scientific data. This account makes explicit refer-ences to students not only achieving the level of com-prehension of the natural disaster but also reaching the level of *evaluation* of media reports related to the studied natural disaster as an educational goal. (Idealized Science Education section, para. 1, italics in original)

Using current events to illustrate societal relevance of particular disciplines focuses "on learners becoming accom-plished analysts of domain-specific articles in the news as a result of individual research and collaborative group discus-sion activities" (de la Chica, 2003, Archetype Characterization section, para. 3). Real-world events, illustrated through break-ing news, can also "serve as entry points into specific curriculum topics and to stimulate learner's interest on the related subject matter" (de la Chica, 2003, Archetype Characterization section, para. 4).

Using social forms of media, such as blogs and journals, enhances student satisfaction and connection with course concepts. Both journals and blogs have been used in an intercultural communications class, where reflection on current events and life experiences is based on artifacts, including those addressing current events. Wrote a student after the course, "I viewed the journal as a personal journey to a better understanding of not only the world around me but of my own self and history as well" (personal communication, Sept. 15, 2010). In their journals and blogs, students pulled articles about the 2010 story of the trapped Chilean miners to think critically and reflexively about culture as well as discuss challenges in intercultural interaction. Project management students could focus on international cooperation and problem-solving skills, assessing risk, and leadership style.

According to instructional developer Joyce Seitzinger (2006), "one of the most obvious ways to use blogs in constructive learning is as an online learning journal in which students reflect on their perceptions of the learning materials and on their own learning process" (p. 6). Seitzinger (2006) wrote the following about blogs, but it can also apply to active discussion forums:

> It is almost impossible to be a passive learner when reading comments on your own posts and responding in comments to others' blog posts. It forces learners to engage higher cognitive skills. You cannot just browse; you need to ponder, formulate an opinion about what's read, and then effectively articulate those thoughts; in other words be an active learner. (p. 8)

Conclusion

Constructivism is applicable to adult education since its basic tenets involve flexibility, relevance, and learner ownership.

Meaning construction, as a basic information-processing task during media exposure, is relevant in constructivism as "the mass media allow[s] for and even demand[s] the divergence of meaning across audience members" (Potter, 2009, p. 176). Discussion forums, blogs, and journals used to respond to current events and breaking news by applying course concepts are tools for constructivist learning and meaning making. They are problem-based in real-world events, learner centered in a social context, and authentic learning activities due to the critical investigation of real-world cultural and social contexts in practice. The immediacy of information dissemination makes this a particularly successful practice in the online course. The online discussion forum, blogs, and journals enable an interactive, learner-centered approach since the formative activities inherent in the forums, blogs, and journals are readily and quickly adaptable to incorporating topical discussion opportunities. The challenge for instructors and students alike is the sudden shift from a scheduled set of discussion questions and possible reordering of topics. But the benefits of relevance and critical thinking outweigh the extra time required to rethink course organization while the course is in session.

References

de la Chica, S. (2003). Event-based learning: Educational and technological perspectives. *University of Colorado, Boulder Learning Technologies Research Group Technical Reports.* Retrieved from https://webfiles.colorado.edu/delachic/www/publications/EventBasedLearning.pdf

Felix, U. (2005). E-learning pedagogy in the third millennium: The need for combining social and cognitive constructivist approaches. *ReCALL, 17* (1), 85-100.

Gulati, S. (2008). Compulsory participation in online discussions: Is this constructivism or normalisation of learning? *Innovations in Education and Teaching International, 45*(2), 183-192.

Hanley, S. (1994). On constructivism. *Maryland Collaborative for Teacher Preparation*. Retrieved from http://www.towson.edu/csme/mctp/Essays/Constructivism.txt

Jaramillo, J. A. (1996). Vygotsky's sociocultural theory and contributions to the development of constructivist curricula. *Education, 117*(1), 133-143.

Jones, M. G., & Brader-Araje, L. (2002). The impact of constructivism on education: Language, discourse, and meaning. *American Communication Journal, 5*(3). Retrieved from http://acjournal.org/holdings/vol5/iss3/

Petraglia, J. (1998). *Reality by design: The rhetoric and technology of authenticity in education*. Mahwah, NJ: Lawrence Erlbaum Associates, Inc.

Potter, W. J. (2009). *Arguing for a general framework for mass media scholarship*. Thousand Oaks, CA: Sage Publications.

Savery, J. R., & Duffy, T. M. (1995). Problem based learning: An instructional model and its constructivist framework. *Educational Technology, 35*, 31-38.

Schweitzer, L., & Stephenson, M. (2008). Charting the challenges and paradoxes of constructivism: A view from professional education. *Teaching in Higher Education, 13*(5), 583-593.

Seitzinger, J. (2006, July 31). Be constructive: Blogs, podcasts, and wikis as constructivist learning tools. *Learning Solutions E-magazine*. Retrieved from http://www.elearningguild.com

Stein, S. J., Isaacs, G., & Andrews, T. (2004). Incorporating authentic learning experiences within a university course. *Studies in Higher Education, 29*(2), 239-258.

Presence & Engagement: Best Practices for the Online Text-based Classroom

Madeline Crowley, MA
City University of Seattle
Division of Arts and Sciences

Abstract

Instructor presence is vital for students to become engaged in their courses. Literature from distance learning journals, student interviews, and an ethnographic study show that how present and involved an instructor is in a text-based online course influences both student perceptions and the quality of learning. This chapter begins by reviewing the literature in the field that offers support for the ideas on best practices that follow. It also includes student interviews regarding instructor presence that have had the greatest impact on them, both positive and negative, including what has engaged or disengaged them during a course. Also detailed are best practices gleaned from teaching online courses.

Introduction

It is often said that what makes teaching worthwhile is having an impact on students, providing encouragement, and inspiring them to pursue their individual ambitions. This is no less true of online teaching. While this teaching medium may seem to be less involved as there is no required face-time, it is especially important for instructors to impress upon students their presence by being accessible, committed to the material, and interested in the students. It may be even more important to establish this feeling of "presence" than in a traditional classroom. This chapter will share some communicative practices that increased a sense of instructor presence that benefited students.

Background

The confusing thing about online courses is that they seem at first glance to require less time and effort for both students and instructors, seemingly making instructor presence less important. In fact, studies indicate the reverse is true if a course is to be effective and result in deep learning. Literature in the distance education field discussing online learning has focused on "social presence" or the impression a teacher's input makes upon students in the course. Research by Kehrwald (2008) defines this as social presence which "is an individual's ability to demonstrate his/her state of being in a virtual environment and to signal his/her availability for interpersonal transactions" (p. 94). These interpersonal exchanges are how an instructor can provide a tangible social presence in a course which has significant effects not only on student morale and engagement; it creates an atmosphere conducive to involvement and true learning. Garrison and Cleveland-Innes's (2005) study on the subject states, "It appears that teaching presence contributes to the adoption of a deep approach to learning…" (p. 140). Wu and Hiltz argue that "…the instructor's role is crucial to effective online discussions and considerable time devotion is required for instructors" (as cited by Garrison & Cleveland-Innes, 2005, p. 136).

When a considerable time investment is not made by the instructor, student distress often results. This has an impact on learning, on overall satisfaction with the course, and on students' impression of the education they're receiving. Due to the traditional power relations between students and teachers, that distress is often not apparent to instructors. Hara & Kling's (2000) study *Student Distress in Web-based Distance Education* reveals that "Part of the reason for the instructor's misperception resulted from students' reluctance to express their anxieties, frustrations and confusions…to the instructor" (p. 22). Instructors may be unaware of how much students require of them, as students often don't directly communicate their needs or dissatisfactions to instructors, fearing retribution.

Perhaps as important are the effects on the type of learning inspired by competent and constant instructor presence in the online classroom. As Garrison and Cleveland-Innes (2005) note, "There is considerable literature pointing to the relationship between teaching presence and perceived learning" (p. 136). In other words without a strong instructor presence, students can believe they learned yet accomplished little from having taken the course.

In an interview one student clarified the effect this has by stating, "A key thing that has given me tremendous staying power in the online learning atmosphere has been student-instructor communications during Blackboard discussions. Instructor feedback is priceless as far as I'm concerned" (S. Jenny, personal communication, December 2, 2010). Along similar lines a student gives some specifics, saying, "I stay most engaged when I get consistent, constructive, weekly feedback and questions from the instructors. It pushes me to do more than the bare minimum" (K. Spas, personal communication, November 29, 2010). Students seem to require more feedback in the online classroom perhaps because they are operating in comparative isolation in relation to their experience with traditional classrooms. Time is not always available to address all student needs for feedback, but with a greater awareness of the needs, instructors can develop ways to address these efficiently.

Practices—Creating Presence through Availability and Accessibility

Student Introductions

Instructor presence can be enhanced from the start of a course. Many online courses begin with rounds of introductions; this gives instructors two opportunities, first to introduce themselves and second to get to know the students. It is an opportunity to ask "telling" questions that reveal students' motivations and interests, not just relative to the course but also to their educational goals. Referring back to student introduction pieces periodically allows an instructor to develop familiarity with the students but also to tailor responses to those interests. In so doing the instructor can create a feeling of "being seen"; generally when we believe we've been "seen" we feel that we are of interest and therefore of value. From a student interview, "I feel it is conducive to student engagement to have actual honest, interested conversations with the instructor in the discussion forum" (D. Brown, personal communication, November 29, 2010). The perception of instructor presence through the discussion can translate into immediate student engagement and a better classroom experience for the entire class.

Create a Safe Learning Environment

Instructors should strive to establish presence through open and welcoming communications. This is especially important when faced with a discussion forum post with which they disagree. Ideally responses should be moderated in friendly but concrete terms. When a post revolves around an interpretation that can be seen as disagreeable, it is best to express that disagreement in the mildest terms possible, something like, "That's interesting, I hadn't thought about it like that. I'd generally regarded this as ___ instead." Students notice the tenor of the exchange and feel that they too can express perhaps unpopular but honest opinions, which makes for more interesting discussions. One student remarked, "I appreciate the even-tempered approach when an instructor negotiates the different attitudes and reactions of students within a class discussion" (S. Williams, personal communication, November 29, 2010).

When an answer is wrong, this too can be handled diplomatically with a gentle correction along the lines of, "That's a common misconception; research shows that…" This can de-personalize the answer so that the student doesn't feel singled out and allows the entire class to feel exchanges can be enjoyed without fear of embarrassment.

This constant demonstration of presence by respectful openness allows for more frank discussion from all participants. In rare instances when a student is aggressive to another student in a post, the instructor needs to respond in two ways, one private and one public. First a private e-mail sent to the aggressor, and another to the victim addressing the problem clearly. In the discussion forum, the issue should be addressed very diplomatically and in terms of appropriate discussion "etiquette." A relatively neutral posture here is generally effective. Instructors could use something like: "Written communications are easily misunderstood and while you probably only meant to state your position clearly, it could have been misinterpreted as aggressive." Acknowledging the ambiguities in written communication allows the saving of face and ideally creates less resistance to change. From a student interview, "I became disengaged in a course when the instructor used the Discussion area of Blackboard as a "public whipping post" to tear apart a student for views held or a misplaced punctuation. This is antithetical to the mission of building engaged and critically thinking students" (D. Larsen, personal communication, December 10, 2010).

Framing Communications

Instructor presence can continually be asserted whenever there may be questions about a topic, procedure, or assignment; it takes only a moment to append a statement asking for questions. Students are sometimes reluctant to appear uncomprehending, and this allows them to ask rather than to stew or complain to their classmates.

The instructor could send private e-mails to students to provide additional clarification when there seems to be confusion; this is generally greatly appreciated. Using e-mail to expand further on topics a student brings up in the discussion or to mention what they're doing well also assists in establishing a strong presence.

Establishing Connection

Presence is best established by creating connections to the students. When possible, instructors can look for opportunities in the Discussion forums to open avenues for further discovering students' interests and ambitions. "It is important to relate material to real life. Theory is well and fine but being able to relate it to something within our experience is crucial to online students" (D. Brown, personal communication, November 29, 2010). E-mail in response to posts allows instructors to reinforce presence by reaching out to students individually by encouraging, offering advice (when appropriate), and by providing clarification or corrections. Taking advantage of all means of communication available in the online environment allows instructors to draw students out or to note how specific skills bode well for their goals and/ or ambitions. "If an instructor forces me to look at things deeper (I tend to skim the surface) or from a different angle, critically, I appreciate it very much and tend to learn a lot that way. It also stays with me" (K. Spas, personal communication, November 29, 2010).

Create a Challenging Environment

The presentation of challenging material is another way to enhance instructor presence. Generally students respond well to intellectual stimulation. Certainly instructors can easily increase the level of challenge by changing discussion questions from text-based answers to answers requiring thought and application of concepts. One student explains the profound effect of instructor presence: "What engaged me was a competent, enthusiastic and engaged instructor. Competency was important, obviously, because it helped instructors to inform and guide discussions and pose probing questions that forced students to think beyond their sphere of influence" (D. Larsen, personal communication, December 10, 2010). Another asserts, "The best courses were the ones where the instructor would respond to posts with additional questions and thoughts for us to really think through the concepts" (J. Upegui, personal communication, December 3, 2010).

One method to engage key performers is to e-mail and let them know early in the course that their efforts are appreciated, and that they seem to be "raising the bar" for the discourse in the Discussion Forum. This not only gives them their due; it helps keep them engaged and encourages them to provide leadership throughout the course.

When practical, instructors should include discussion questions in the Forum as much as possible in terms of application of the material or interpretation of the material rather than finding an answer in the text. One student shares, "I realize that part of our weekly assignments must be regurgitating information from the text, but it's difficult to comment when everyone is saying the same thing in the discussion. I really appreciate it when we have to take that information and apply it somehow" (K. Spas, personal communication, November 29, 2010). Asking about ramifications or implications of course concepts creates a deeper level of thinking about the material and a higher level of engagement from the students while reinforcing instructor presence as an authority.

Once initial posts are made by students, it is often helpful to ask questions about their posts to encourage deeper, more complex thinking about the material. On occasion it is helpful for the instructor to use student posts to jump into deeper levels or implications of the material from their broader knowledge of the material. "Anytime an instructor can display their expertise and knowledge rather than just facilitate the course, I feel I learn more and tend to be more involved in the class" (K. Spas, personal communication, November 29, 2010). When an instructor shares his/her extensive knowledge of the subject and related issues, it reveals instructor competence and reassures the students that they're receiving a quality education.

Create a Coherent Learning Environment

It is very important that instructors prepare a clear organization of the online course. Without this clear organization, the perception by students of the instructor and his/her presence suffers dramatically. "Organization in course structure and correspondences between students and instructor was grease in the bearings of the online classroom. Without organization the entire operation would melt down and the entire class would be less motivated to participate in a meaningful way" (D. Larsen, personal communication, November 29, 2010). Another student is even more specific: "To enable and facilitate the students' learning is to ensure the syllabi and assignments are synced. When a course is poorly organized, it is obviously distracting to the student and distressing as well. In one badly organized course I no longer gave a damn and just wanted to finish the course" (D. Brown, personal communication, November 29, 2010). Hara and Kling (2000) noted that student distress due to ambiguous or confusing course instructions impeded learning and led to a feeling that expectations for the course were not being adequately met.

Convey Enthusiasm and Interest in the Subject Matter

Perhaps the best way to enhance instructor presence is in the attitude to the material and to the course itself. Instructors have to dig deep to inject fresh appreciation for a subject taught over a long period of time. Still, it is possible to convey presence and interest by giving further details on facets of the subject or topic, especially in relation to student posts. Sometimes a simple question like, "That's interesting, how did you arrive at that answer or conclusion?" can elicit some very interesting discussions not only from the queried student but also from the cohort. Students long for a commitment and passion from their instructors regarding the subject: "I felt unengaged in courses when an instructor demonstrated a lack of interest in the subject matter or in the success of students" (D. Larsen, personal communication, December 10, 2010). Students experience distress when they believe they don't have an involved instructor presence.

Comments on Papers

An ideal way to establish a strong, useful instructor presence is in the comments given on student papers. First, if at all possible, students should submit papers to Smarthinking.com or the University's Writing Center to catch small errors. That frees the instructor to focus on logical flaws, fallacies, and other significant problems in student writing. If time allows, rather than simply attaching a short comment like, "logical flaw", explain what the student has gotten wrong and briefly explain how to fix it so that the student feels guided or led rather than "wrong." When possible comments are a chance to offer needed personal tutoring on writing (however, it must be said that in very large classes this may be more difficult). Students do consider comments absolutely vital to their learning and are deeply disappointed when they get routine, short comments or none at all: "The most tarnishing experience was when an instructor gave zero feedback on a paper. Without that priceless feedback I had nothing to base my learning or progress on; I need to see my errors to correct myself" (S. Jenny, personal communication, December 2, 2010). In addition to offering more extensive comments, when possible give students a general idea of how they're doing relative to others, and if there's a sufficient display of skills or ability, encourage the student to consider further education.

Future Research

Information for this paper came from an informal study involving a small sample of students (six) who were contacted via e-mail.

Students were selected from prior courses in two departments due to their general availability and willingness to speak freely. Many are still enrolled at the university while a few have graduated.

Further research could include a much broader sample, using either ethnographic or experimental methodologies, in order to test individual best practices. Also it would be ideal to have more formal qualitative research performed in a variety of ways, including observation, ethnography, teacher interviews, etc. This sample was very small—six students—and a larger sample would give much more information.

Conclusion

This essay has used distance learning literature, personal experience, and student interviews to argue for a set of distance-learning best practices to enhance instructor presence in online courses. While instructor presence cannot always be precisely quantified, it is viewed as indispensable and valuable by students.

One unspoken benefit of online courses is the participation requirement. Unlike in a traditional classroom, no one can silently hang back and simply listen. Every student is generally required to participate in online courses that have a Discussion Forum, giving them a presence in the classroom that may be unique. Sometimes the most silent students are the most interesting thinkers, and often for the first time in a classroom setting, they have the chance to shine before their peers. In many traditional classrooms, shy students will not ask questions or directly communicate with the instructor; in an online venue instructors have the chance to connect and communicate with students in a variety of ways.

In just that one sense, online classrooms can be transformational to students. Students remember and value classes from an instructor who is in command of the material and communicates a true interest in individual students. An inspiring teacher presence can encourage ambitions and dreams in ways that might not be available in a traditional classroom. It is a time investment worth making both for instructor satisfaction and for better student learning outcomes.

References

Garrison, R., & Cleveland-Innes, M. (2005). Facilitating cognitive presence in online learning: Interaction is not enough. *American Journal of Distance Education, 19*(3), 133-148. Retrieved from http://www.informaworld.com/smpp/content~db=all~content=a783721031~frm=abslink

Hara, N., & Kling, R. (2000). *Students' distress with a web-based distance education course: An ethnographic study of participants' experiences* (No. WP 00-01-B1). Bloomington, IN: Center for Social Informatics. Retrieved from http://rkcsi.indiana.edu/archive/CSI/WP/wp00-01B.html

Kehrwald, B. (2008). Understanding social presence in text-based online learning environments. *Distance Education, 29*(1), 89-106. Retrieved from www.eric.ed.gov/ERICWebPortal/recordDetail?accno=EJ799371

Inquiry Learning in Higher Education

Ryan Gunhold, MAL
City University of Seattle
Gordon Albright School of Education

Abstract

Acknowledgment of Inquiry Learning, sometimes known as Open Learning, Guided Investigation, or Learning Discovery, began in the early 1960s. Since its initial use in science labs, inquiry learning can be found in use across several professional arenas, including education, business, and civic learning.

It is useful to understand the origins and benefits of inquiry learning, examine its use in higher education classrooms, and describe basic fundamentals in how to run, moderate, or facilitate an inquiry learning experience. Additionally, action learning, the emerging learning approach in the workplace which uses many of the same learning elements as inquiry learning, demonstrates how these innovative learning approaches better prepare students for the skills necessary in today's workplace.

27

Introduction

Inquiry learning is an effective instructional tool which, when skillfully designed and applied, can be a dynamic learning tool to enhance the learning experience. Inquiry learning accomplishes this through increasing engagement and allowing the learner to explore and increase self-autonomy and self-mastery of skills desired.

The *National Science Education Standards* (National Committee on Science Education Standards and Assessment, 1996) defines scientific inquiry as "the diverse ways in which scientists study the natural world and propose explanations based on the evidence derived from their work. Scientific inquiry also refers to the activities through which students develop knowledge and understanding of scientific ideas as well as an understanding of how scientists study the natural world" (p.23).

Scientific inquiry reflects how scientists come to understand the natural world and it is at the heart of how many students learn. From a very early age, children interact with their environment, ask questions, and seek ways to answer those questions. The understanding of content and methods is significantly enhanced when ideas are anchored to inquiry experiences. Although this definition is centric to science, it really can be applied across all schools of thought and learning methods.

Despite the demonstrated effectiveness of inquiry learning, it is still commonplace to find the traditional "stand and deliver" approach in most universities though inquiry learning strategies are more effective than traditional approaches. Inquiry learning better prepares students for their own professional learning experiences once they get into the workplace.

The Rise of Inquiry Learning

Inquiry learning had its roots in science labs prior to its emergence in science education classrooms during the 1970s. The development of such tools as Marshall Herron's scale for evaluating the amount of inquiry in science lab experiences allowed for science students to engage with and explore science concepts in more meaningful ways (Herron, 1971). Also around this time, similar strategies which encouraged quality questioning, constructivist ideas, and student exploration emerged in many science museums.

One of the most well-known examples of these museums was the Exploratorium in the San Francisco Bay area (Oppenheimer, 1972). The Exploratorium was developed in 1969 by Frank Oppenheimer, a well-known scientist who observed the impact that hands-on learning had with his own high school students. Like many other science museums that followed, inquiry learning allowed for student exploration or informal learning to be at the center of exhibits. These experiences provided further validation of constructivist theories and the important role they played in shaping one's own thought process to better understand the world and the connectedness within it.

Hands-on learning, or the idea of allowing students greater autonomy in their use of the scientific method, also emerged during this period. With hands-on learning arriving in the classroom, the teacher could now explore its impact throughout the entire school curriculum. The National Science Teachers Association (NSTA) has created the most extensive evidence of inquiry learning's impact on the classroom learner and further provided the framework for implementing inquiry learning effectively.

As noted from the NSTA website (NSTA Board of Directors, 2004), numerous declarations must be in place to support inquiry learning as a successful learning approach. These declarations are as follows:

- Planning an inquiry-based program by developing both short- and long-term goals that incorporate appropriate content knowledge.
- Implementing approaches to teaching that cause students to question and explore and to use those experiences to raise and answer questions about the natural world. The learning-cycle approach is one of many effective strategies for bringing explorations and questions into the classroom.

- Guiding and facilitating learning using inquiry by selecting teaching strategies that nurture and assess students' developing understandings and abilities.
- Designing and managing learning environments that provide students with the time, space, and resources needed for learning science through inquiry.
- Receiving adequate administrative support for the pursuit of science as inquiry in the classroom. Support can take the form of professional development on how to teach scientific inquiry, content, and the nature of science; the allocation of time to do scientific inquiry effectively; and the availability of necessary materials and equipment.
- Experiencing science as inquiry as a part of students' preparation program. Preparation should include learning how to develop questioning strategies, writing plans that promote abilities and understanding of scientific inquiry, and analyzing instructional materials to determine whether they promote scientific inquiry.

NSTA's declarations on inquiry learning support the effectiveness of inquiry learning in both the higher education learning environment and in the workplace. These elements are also found in City University of Seattle's (2011) Academic Model as well as those of other institutions which emphasize practical learning applications for students. The elements of such a model are as follows:

A Focus on Student Learning—When students participate in well-designed inquiry learning, student learning should increase.

Reflective Practitioner Faculty—Inquiry learning allows one to step back from the traditional direct instruction process, observe student learning, and offer coaching to those who might need further tools to reach learning outcomes. In the coaching process, the ability to teach new skills or reinforce old ones rises to the top, allowing the instructor to provide important one-on-one assistance as needed.

Relevance to the Workplace—Inquiry learning, when structured around real-life experiences, ends up becoming a more realistic experience in replicating workplace environments and therefore is more relevant to lifelong learning.

Service to Students and Responsiveness—Students will become more autonomous learners when inquiry learning is introduced because they will have a greater stake in the learning process. Essentially inquiry learning allows the learners to take control of their learning experiences with a greater sense of self-motivation and mastery.

The rise of inquiry learning in schools also saw a parallel emergence in the business workplace. According to observations of action learning at Cisco (Lamoureux, 2009), action learning in the workplace is a way of simultaneously conducting action and inquiry as a disciplined leadership practice that increases the wider effectiveness of actions. Such action helps individuals, teams, organizations, and institutions become more capable of self-transformation and thus more creative, more aware, more just, and more sustainable.

The Connection to Action Inquiry in the Workplace

As Bill Tolbert (2004) points out in his book *The Promise and the Power of Action Inquiry: The Secret of Timely and Transforming Leadership*, "In principle, no matter how much or little positional power you have, anyone in any family or organization can become more effectively and transformationally powerful by practicing action inquiry" (p. 1).

Tolbert (2004) continues to note, "Action inquiry is a lifelong process of transformational learning that individuals, teams, and whole organizations can undertake if they wish to become:

- Increasingly capable of making future visions come true
- Increasingly alert to the dangers and opportunities of the present moment
- Increasingly capable of performing in effective and transformational ways" (p.1).

The increase of action inquiry learning in organizations gives rise to a number of improved learning opportunities during an employee's career. Examples of these learning experiences include workplace simulations and new approaches to e-learning as noted in Clark Aldrich's (2004) book *Simulations and the Future of Learning: An Innovative (and Perhaps Revolutionary) Approach to e-Learning*. Such examples are also found throughout City University's courses.

To clarify the pedagogical shift associated with inquiry, it is useful to see how the three Rs of the past have become the seven Cs of the present. The three Rs, reading, writing, and arithmetic, have been referred to as the old framework of learning. Meanwhile, the 21st Century Skills Project has given rise to the new seven Cs of learning, which include critical thinking and problem solving; creativity and innovation; collaboration, teamwork, and leadership; cross-cultural understanding; communications, information, and media literacy; computing, and ICT literacy; and career and learning self-reliance. All of these skills are addressed better through active inquiry learning and, over time, several skills are enhanced with its correct use, implementation, and facilitation (Lawson, 2009).

Due to the need for these new skills, new methods of learning are needed to prepare the twenty-first century learner. This is especially true in technology-driven learning environments where students or employees are required to interact using technology (Jacobson & Spiro, 1995). In cases such as these, active learning better serves individuals and groups by creating greater autonomy, mastery, and self purpose. As Daniel Pink (2009) has already noted in his book *Drive*, these are the primary means by which we are all motivated.

Whether it is learning in the classroom or in the workplace, the ability to remain motivated and master new skills is far better served with inquiry and inquiry action learning. Thus, to ensure that the adoption of this work is successful, one need contemplate numerous considerations.

Inquiry Learning in Higher Education

Inquiry learning has had many useful applications both in the classroom and the workplace. Highlighting basic fundamentals of inquiry learning in the classroom will promote a simple implementation strategy for those wanting to further investigate inquiry learning within a higher education setting.

Numerous benefits to students can be explored, but the most profound reason for using inquiry learning in higher education is that when given greater autonomy, students are able to reach their own mastery of skills and content faster and, thus, give rise to a greater sense of purpose and ownership in their work (Pink, 2009). As a result many students who learn how to design and test their own thinking are far better prepared for real-life scenarios which arise most commonly in the workplace (Raelin, 2008). In fact, this was precisely the intention of inquiry learning in the first place. However, instead of inquiry learning helping students better understand science, as has been the case in the past, it is now helping students to better prepare themselves to handle real-life learning situations which occur more commonly in the workplace.

Students coming from traditional learning environments may take longer to grasp learning that occurs through inquiry because they are not prepared or accustomed to having the "driver's wheel" approach to learning. To be implemented effectively, inquiry learning requires greater discipline by the learner (Black & Deci, 2000). As a result students who have not experienced inquiry learning in the past may need to work together to support one another through this process or have a means of accessing mentor or coaching programs to support it. Support programs, such as Stanford's School of Business Volunteer Program, have shown to have tremendous success in this past decade in the higher education setting (Marquardt, 2004).

Some further best practices to consider when implementing inquiry learning in higher education classrooms include the following:

> Provide greater student success through student "coaching" or "teaming." In using this approach, faculty will observe students reaching learning outcomes with greater success due to increased engagement (Datar, Garvin, & Cullen, 2010).

Faculty may need assistance in learning inquiry methods and how to facilitate inquiry learning well. A way to do this is to train instructors how to modify current syllabi into an effective inquiry-learning model of instruction. Faculty can learn how to conceptually design an inquiry course and use instructional strategies based on this model.

For inquiry design to be done well, the learner needs additional time to explore the core concepts being taught, and faculty need time to better align how the integration of new knowledge and approaches can be transferred into real-world situations and work-world scenarios.

Faculty can browse resources to learn more about inquiry design, but the best means to learn about inquiry is to gain actual experience with it. Having a focus on inquiry learning within faculty development at universities would provide the opportunity for faculty to experience the strategies they would need to implement in their own courses.

Moreover, the approach of integrating inquiry learning through faculty development allows for the evolution of current curricula into an ever more relevant and cross-dimensional study in the future. Having greater flexibility with curricula allows instructors to be more agile in educational delivery and thus works to ensure that higher education development remains on the cutting edge of innovation (Datar et al., 2010).

Future Research Directions

Many rich opportunities to support the improvement of the use of inquiry learning in higher education are available through relevant research efforts. Following are some areas that may benefit from such examination:

Real-time learning or "gaming" simulation models are examples of inquiry learning and are becoming a more popular means of learning in the workplace and for students in the classroom, as described by Aldrich (2004). Expanding the research around virtual learning simulations would allow instructors to develop and use better models for reenacting business situations and environments than was previously possible. In such situations it would be interesting to see how the inquiry process could be enhanced through simulations, especially for project-based learning.

The focus of engagement as a student motivational tool is another emerging area of research which has strong roots in inquiry and active inquiry learning (Salmon, 2002). As noted previously by Pink (2009), engagement, or the means by which the organization and individual interact, will better serve student needs through the increased options provided by inquiry learning methods as compared to traditional learning (Pink, 2009). Experience and research are needed to find ways for students or employees to explore their own ideas.

Investigating how technology can help to support inquiry learning in the higher education classroom would provide additional strategies of value to students. More research is needed on how faculty can learn to diversify their skill sets to include inquiry learning in their repertoire of teaching strategies.

Conclusion

With new and diverging skills needed in the workplace, the higher education classroom should be a place for innovation in learning strategies. With greater understanding and experience, with inquiry learning, and with documentation of its effectiveness in the classroom, instructors should be able to improve student learning. Inquiry learning must be further developed at higher educational institutions that seek to provide real-world learning experiences. Not only will it serve the future of higher education well, it will work to prepare a more motivated, autonomous, and successful workforce for the future.

References

Aldrich, C. (2004). *Simulations and the future of learning: An innovative (and perhaps revolutionary) approach to e-learning.* San Francisco, CA: Pfeiffer.

Black, A. E., & Deci, E. L. (2000). The effects of instructors' autonomy support and students' autonomous motivation on learning organic chemistry: A self-determination theory perspective. *Science Education, 84,* 740-756.City University of Seattle (2011). *Academic model.* Retrieved from http://www.cityu.edu/about/profile/academic_model.aspx

Datar, S. M., Garvin, D. A., & Cullen, P. G. (2010). *Rethinking the MBA: Business education at a crossroads.* Watertown, MA: Harvard Business Press.

Herron, M. (1971). The nature of scientific enquiry. *Educational Psychologist, 79*(2), 171–212.

Lamoureux, K. (2009, October). *Action learning facilitates business growth: A look inside Cisco's progressive executive development approach.* Oakland, CA: Bersin & Associates.

Lawson, K. (2009). *The trainer's handbook.* San Francisco, CA: Pfeiffer Publishing.

Marquardt, M. J. (2004). *Optimizing the power of action learning: Solving problems and building leaders in real time.* Mountain View, CA: Davies-Black Publishing.

Jacobson, M. J., & Spiro, R. J. (1995). Hypertext learning environments, cognitive flexibility, and the transfer of complex knowledge: An empirical investigation. *Journal of Educational Computing Research, 12*(4), 301-333.

National Committee on Science Education Standards and Assessment (1996). *National science education standards.* Washington DC: National Research Council.

NSTA Board of Directors (2004). *NSTA position statement: Scientific inquiry.* Retrieved from http://www.nsta.org/about/positions/inquiry.aspx

Oppenheimer, F. (1972). The Exploratorium: A playful museum combines perception and art in science education. *American Journal of Physics, 40*(6), 978.

Pink, D. (2009). *Drive: The surprising truth about what motivates us.* New York, NY: Riverhead Books.

Raelin, J. (2008). *Work-based learning: Bridging knowledge and action in the workplace.* Hoboken, NJ: Jossey-Bass.

Salmon, G. (2002). *E-tivities: The key to active online learning.* New York, NY: Routledge.

Tolbert, W. (2004). *The promise and the power of action inquiry: The secret of timely and transforming leadership.* San Francisco, CA: Berrett-Hoehler Publishers.

The Lincoln Paradigm: An Educational Vision for the Future

Susan Mendoza Beller, JD, LLM
City University of Seattle
School of Management

Abstract

Drawing on lessons included in Abraham Lincoln's works can help inform adult education practices. This chapter utilizes excerpts from one of Lincoln's law lectures to highlight points that are important in the delivery, development, and evaluation of adult education. Throughout the chapter, quotations from Lincoln are used to set the context for best practices in adult education. Each of these practices is then further described along with its relevance to an overall educational vision for adults.

Introduction

The rapidly evolving classroom impacts both learning and performance. Technology enhances increased dissemination of knowledge, but the essence of adult learning remains the development of marketable skills and competencies for application in real-world scenarios.

Abraham Lincoln certainly never touched a computer, but his advice to prospective lawyers creates the perfect guideline for successfully facilitating communication and learning. He proposes a combination of diligence, honesty, and a proactive facilitative approach outlining a clear purpose that helps everyone succeed.

With Abraham Lincoln as mentor and guide throughout, this chapter proposes a "teachable vision," a vision for the future that acknowledges differences and overcomes barriers through honesty, diligence, and a willingness to both listen and learn. Lincoln proposed a vision for the future that everyone can understand, work toward, and accomplish together.

Diligence and the Adult Learner

In Abraham Lincoln's Notes for a Law Lecture (July 1, 1850) he states,

> *I am not an accomplished lawyer. I find quite as much material for a lecture in those points wherein I have failed, as in those wherein I have been moderately successful. The leading rule for the lawyer, as for the man of every other calling, is diligence. Leave nothing for tomorrow which can be done today. Never let your correspondence fall behind. Whatever piece of business you have in hand, before stopping, do all the labor pertaining to it which can be done…*

Diligence requires a solid foundation predicated on an adult-oriented education system encompassing essential processes, including creative thinking, problem solving, brainstorming, and follow-through. The cornerstone of this foundation is the realization that teaching adult learners is a vastly different process than teaching children or adolescents. Pedagogy refers to the teaching of children where the teacher is the focal point of learning. Andragogy is the process of teaching adults and is based on "informed professional opinion; philosophical assumptions associated with humanistic psychology and progressive education; and a growing body of research and theory on adult learning, development, and socialization" (Beder & Darkenwald, 1982, p. 143).

Essentially andragogy shifts the focus from the educator to the learner. This creates a learning environment whereby the learner has substantial self-direction and control over the process. For example, the educator should:

- Determine learner interests and motivation for enrollment in the course. Course goals and objectives can thereby be modified to accommodate learner needs (Cranton, 1996).
- Facilitate an environment where students can learn from each other. Peer Learning Groups, including online Discussion Forums, create a support system for self-directed learning, information exchange, the stimulation of new ideas, and the allocation of relevant resources (Brookfield, 1986).
- Encourage periodic learner feedback, including discussion of the quality, sequence, and pace of the activities (Cranton, 1996).
- Provide access to additional resources and learning materials reflecting varying viewpoints are valuable tools (Cranton, 1996).
- Value and encourage participation and acknowledge the accumulated experience of adult learners as an important educational resource (Brookfield, 1986).

Ultimately, the success of the learning process depends on the instructor's ability to listen. Every adult learner is different, and everyone learns at his/her own pace, taking into account variables such as cognitive style, culture, and personality. Studies have shown that implementation of andragogy itself may require a modified teaching style when dealing with cross-cultural issues

(Ziegahn, 2001). Examples of cross-cultural concerns requiring acknowledgment and accommodation are as follows:

- Tradition vs. Modernism: andragogy emphasizes progress and a future-oriented perspective; more traditional cultural perspectives emphasize historical status quo.
- Andragogical vs. Pedagogical: individuals may be comfortable with the familiar passive role of the pedagogical learner and uncomfortable with the concept of independent learning.
- Egalitarianism vs. Collectivism: andragogy supports equal access and individual reward; traditional cultures may value hierarchy and social status.

Adults are inherently diverse in their life experiences as well as diverse in their motivations for enrolling in a particular class. Although it is important for every instructor to consider his/her students as individuals, three common motivators encompass the majority of adult learners (Merriam & Caffarella, 1991). Most adult learners are:

- Goal oriented: classes are taken to reach a pragmatic goal, such as career advancement.
- Activity oriented: social interaction is an important component of the learning process.
- Learning oriented: the seeking of topic specific knowledge.

Because of this motivational diversity as well as the underlying cultural diversity of adult learners, open dialogue is essential to facilitate the incorporation of new facts and skills into experience. Remembering that every new skill takes time to learn, it is important for instructors to encourage participation and opposing viewpoints while maintaining a civil and respectful atmosphere.

Creation of an organized, timely, and positive learning environment is essential. Instructions should be clear, concise, and part of an ongoing communication process throughout the term. Although the andragogical framework emphasizes learner self-direction and control, it is the educator's responsibility to present the information in a format that will encourage learning. The goal is to create an environment whereby learners will acquire and retain knowledge (cognitive), increase their awareness (affective), and develop new skills (behavioral).

The classic evaluation model for organizational training programs is applicable to the classroom as well as the business environment (Kirkpatrick, 1994). The Kirkpatrick model creates four evaluation levels:

- Reaction: learner overall satisfaction with the course, taking into account diverse learning styles.
- Learning: evaluation through the use of tests, written assignments, observations, discussions, and interviews to determine cognitive impact.
- Behavior: learner development and application of new skills.
- Results: In the business environment, this evaluation measures the economic impact of training. Economic impact can be evaluated in academics in terms of student retention.

Providing guidance and encouragement is essential to the educator's role. New skills and the assimilation of new knowledge take time and effort. Learners who quickly acquire information may appear impressive, but the real test is retention and application of skills. Speed at the cost of retention is ill advised, and detailed developmental feedback can provide a valuable learning tool. Successful teaching balances a variety of active learning techniques as well as cognitive, behavioral, and affective learning.

From Lectures to Learning

…Extemporaneous speaking should be practiced and cultivated. It is the lawyer's avenue to the public. However able and faithful he may be in other respects, people are slow to bring him business if he cannot make a speech. And yet there is not a more fatal error to young lawyers than relying too much on speech-making. If anyone, upon his rare powers of speaking, shall claim exemption from the drudgery of the law, his case is a failure in advance.—Lincoln

The traditional pedagogical lecture has been supplanted by the active learning andragogical model. However, lectures can be memorable and dynamic (Reinsmith, 1994) as well as an effective tool for teaching inexperienced active learners. Studies show that adult learners with limited active learning experience feel uncomfortable forming their own opinions and judgments and have a structured educational expectation (Tice, 1997).

Diverse expectations and learning styles can be accommodated through structuring and modifying the andragogical model. For example, instructors can consider using:

- Knowledge Hunt: rather than supplying knowledge in a lecture format, create small teams to search for the information.
- Question Generation: each team member creates a question relevant to the course materials, and the group researches the answer.
- Summation: learners review course materials and summarize the information.
- Group Review: divide the course materials into study segments assigned to each team. The teams will then present their area of knowledge to the class as a whole.

Adult learners in active learning classes and their counterparts in strictly lecture courses received similar grades on knowledge tests. However, active learning participants scored substantially higher on tests measuring the relationship of theory to practice, the ability to understand multiple perspectives, and the ability to self-correct (Wright, Miller, & Kosciuk, 1997).

Cooperation over Conflict

Discourage litigation. Persuade your neighbors to compromise whenever you can. Point out to them how the nominal winner is often a real loser in fees, expenses, and waste of time. As a peacemaker, the lawyer has a superior opportunity of being a good man. There will still be business enough.—Lincoln

It is the responsibility of the educator to be a role model for class discussion, interaction, and inclusiveness. When conflicts occur, resolution involves calm discussion to mediate misunderstandings in a timely fashion to prevent escalation. The classroom is the perfect environment to practice tolerance and inclusion. Instructors need to pay attention to the quality and tone of learner questions and responses and give developmental feedback when appropriate. Troubling behaviors should not be ignored. Problems will not resolve themselves, and learners should be made aware of their inappropriate behavior.

Cooperative learning, defined as "the instructional use of small groups so that students work together to maximize their own and each other's learning" (Johnson, Johnson, & Smith, 1991, pp. 147-148), used in conjunction with the andragogical framework, will help to alleviate the need for conflict resolution. Group learning provides a practice environment introduction to real-world project teams and self-directed work groups.

Studies indicate that cooperative learning creates higher achievement, positive learner relationships, and improved psychological adjustments as opposed to individual learning (Johnson et al., 1991). Cooperation and compromise are encouraged through interdependence resolving conflict and encouraging change.

From Mistakes to Motivation

Never stir up litigation. A worse man can scarcely be found than one who does this. Who can be more nearly a fiend than he who habitually overhauls the register of deeds in search of defects in titles, whereon to stir up strife, and put money in his pocket? A moral tone ought to be infused into the profession which should drive such men out of it.—Lincoln

People make mistakes. When this occurs instructors should acknowledge the mistake, find an acceptable solution, and move on. Otherwise an environment of denial and blame will be created, with participants so frightened to be wrong that it becomes impossible to learn from mistakes and move forward.

One way to learn from mistakes within the andragogical framework is to learn skills within the context of problem solving. This concept of practical application, the idea of doing while learning, is the key difference between the traditional and the active teaching styles (Vella, 1994). When the learner is actively involved, knowledge retention and practical application increase.

The andragogical model assumes that adult learners are problem centered in their orientation and that problem solving provides the most beneficial educational opportunity. Further assumptions include adults self-direct; life experience is a valuable learning resource; and adults are often motivated to learn by internal or intrinsic factors as opposed to external or extrinsic factors (Knowles, 1975). Additional reasons often cited include that adult learners desire to teach the newly acquired skill to others; they have specific job requirements; they have future aspirations; and they have a need to earn the course credit (Tough, 1979).

Many adult learners come from highly competitive backgrounds emphasizing winners and losers. Instructors need to discourage the impression that a lower grade given to one classmate results in a higher grade to another while encouraging the idea that the classroom environment is the perfect forum to practice team building skills. As a practical exercise, team members can also be required to assist one another in the completion of assignments.

Build Interest in Learning

And when you lack interest in the case the job will likely lack skill and diligence in the performance…—Lincoln

As previously discussed adult learners acquire formal education for diverse reasons. If the course materials address non-relevant motivation, the individual will lose interest and retention. For example, if the reason for taking the course is team-building practice and the course is strictly lecture, the learner is very likely to not complete the course due to lack of interest.

Constructivism is a context-based approach to adult learning based upon the theory that learners gain understanding when they act on new knowledge with their present knowledge and resolve discrepancies as they arise. Often referred to as discovery learning, the constructivist framework recommends the following approaches: the educator's goal is to create self-directed learners; learner curiosity should be encouraged; activities should be done both independently and collaboratively; information is retained when learners reach understanding on their own; and when learners are given the opportunity to discover knowledge for themselves, they learn how to learn (Cruikshank, Bainer, & Metcalf, 1995).

Using constructivist theory, when learners receive information that conflicts with present knowledge, they experience an internal sense of discomfort. Adults are motivated to alleviate this discomfort by modifying knowledge structures, thereby engaging in learning (Dixon, 1994).

To learn, information must be retained. Generally adults retain between five and nine pieces of information in short-term memory. Because short-term memory is immediately lost, retention occurs in long-term memory and is often related to repetition and contextual relevance (Miller, 1956).

"Teachable Moments" theory takes the concept of repetition leading to retention a step further. A developmental task, when learned, makes the achievement of succeeding tasks possible. When the timing is right, the ability to learn a specific task will be possible, and this "timing" creates the "teachable moment." Therefore, repetition is paramount so that when the learner's "moment" occurs, the knowledge can be assimilated and retained (Havighurst, 1953).

Dispelling Incorrect Beliefs

There is a vague popular belief that lawyers are necessarily dishonest. I say vague, because when we consider to what extent confidence and honors are reposed in and conferred upon lawyers by the people, it appears improbable that their impression of dishonesty is very distinct and vivid. Yet the impression is common, almost universal.—Lincoln

A "vague popular belief" exists that older adult learners are less capable of knowledge retention and the acquisition of new skills than younger adults. Scientific studies conclude that, in the general population, memory deterioration is minor until extreme old age. Memory problems occur when adults are forced into meaningless learning, pure memorization, or learning that involves only reassessment of old knowledge (Merriam & Caffarella, 1991). New information related to existing knowledge increases the likelihood of long-term memory retention regardless of age (Dixon, 1994).

If possible some flexibility concerning deadlines and due dates should be built into the class. Research shows that when the pace is controlled, middle-aged adults have the same ability to learn that they had in their youth. Young through middle-aged learners score high in self-confidence and goal focus while older learners are generally more responsible and detail oriented (Merriam & Cafarella, 1991).

All adults, regardless of age, learn best when they discover concepts, ideas, new skills, and useful knowledge through active participation and well-planned structured experiences. Older learners may also appear less capable due to lack of technical expertise. When encountering diversity, whether based on age, race, gender, or culture, the most important role-model skill for the educator is to show respect. Showing respect for learners benefits everyone and creates an atmosphere of tolerance and understanding. It recognizes that everyone learns at a different pace and everyone has something important to contribute.

Honestly Respect the Learner

Resolve to be honest at all events; and if in your own judgment you cannot be an honest lawyer, resolve to be honest without being a lawyer. Choose some other occupation, rather than one in the choosing of which you do, in advance, consent to be a knave.—Lincoln

It's an old adage, but nonetheless true: "Treat people the way you would want to be treated." Teach with enthusiasm; respect your learners as well as yourself; and be a role model worthy of emulation.

The curriculum must be inclusive to retain relevance for diverse learners. An honest examination of class materials often reveals a dominant-culture world view. Suggestions for creating an inclusive learning environment (Imel, 1995) include:

- Allow reasoned, respectful disagreement between learners as well as between learners and the educator.
- Value and integrate into class discussion the life experiences of adult learners, both as individuals and as members of cultural/social groups.
- Accommodate diversity in learning styles. If specific analytical skills are required, teach them within the course structure.
- Acknowledge and celebrate multiple perspectives due to ethnicity, age, gender, sexuality, class, religion, physical abilities, etc.

In conclusion, although diverse in their approaches, researchers generally agree that outstanding adult educators encourage a team mentality in environments where learners participate in active dialogue between equals; diversity is valued and accepted; life experience is acknowledged; and all perspectives are respected.

References

Beder, H. W., & Darkenwald, G. G. (1982). Differences between teaching adults and pre-adults: Some propositions and findings. *Adult Education, 32*(2), 142-155.

Brookfield, S. (1986). *Understanding and facilitating Adult learning* San Francisco, CA: Jossey-Bass Publishers.

Cranton, P. (1996). *Professional development as transformative learning.* San Francisco, CA: Jossey-Bass Publishers.

Cruikshank, D. R., Bainer, D. L., & Metcalf, K. (1995). *The act of teaching.* New York, NY: McGraw-Hill, Inc.

Dixon, N. M. (1994). *The organizational learning cycle: How we can learn collectively.* London, UK: McGraw-Hill, Inc.

Havighurst, R. (1953). *Human development and education.* New York, NY: David McKay Company.

Imel, S. (1995). Inclusive adult learning environments. *ERIC Clearinghouse, 162.* Retrieved from http://ericacve.org

Johnson, D. W., Johnson, R. T., & Smith, K. A. (1991). *Cooperative learning: Increasing college faculty instructional productivity. ASHE-ERIC Higher Education Report No. 4.* Washington, DC: The George Washington University, School of Education and Human Development.

Kirkpatrick, D. (1994). *Evaluating training programs: The four levels.* San Francisco, CA: Berrett-Koehler.

Knowles, M. S. (1975). *Self-directed learning: A guide for learners and teachers.* New York, NY: Association Press.

Merriam, S. B., & Caffarella, S. (1991). *Learning in adulthood.* San Francisco, CA: Jossey Bass.

Miller, G. A. (1956). The magical number seven, plus or minus two: Some limits on our capacity for processing information. *Psychological Review, 83*, 81-97.

Reinsmith, W. (1994). Two great professors: Formidable intellects with affection for students. *College Teaching, 42*(4).

Tice, E. T. (1997). Educating adults: A matter of balance. *Adult Learning, 9*(1).

Tough, A. M. (1979). *The adult's learning project: A fresh approach to theory and practice in adult learning.* Toronto: Ontario Institute for Studies in Education

Vella, J. (1994). *Learning to listen, learning to teach: The power of dialogue in educating adults.* San Francisco, CA: Jossey-Bass.

Wright, J., Miller, S., & Kosciuk, S. (1997). Does active learning cause credible differences in student competence? *Focus on Calculus, 13*.

Ziegahn, L. (2001). *Considering culture in the selection of teaching approaches for adults.* Columbus, OH: ERIC Clearinghouse on Adult Career and Vocational Education.

5

Successful Learning and Teaching Approaches: Self Reflection as a Bridge to Self-Directed and Lifelong Learning

Larissa Chuprina, PhD
Lana Zaher, MATESOL
City University of Seattle
School of Management

Abstract

With the advent of the global economy and global education and with the need to adapt to changing lifestyles and value systems, lifelong learning, including the skills of self-direction and self-reflection, have gained new importance with educators and employers. One of the major forces generating the need for life-long learning is the rapid change in all spheres of life. Self-directed learning is becoming a necessary skill to adapt to these changes. Educators and educational establishments are looking into inno-vative approaches to educating adults, paying close attention to non-traditional forms for learning and methods of delivery. In this way self-inquiry and self-evaluation are needed at the begin-ning, during, and after instruction. Educators can enhance lifelong learning among their students by facilitating the development of characteristics and skills, such as goal setting, taking responsibil-ity for learning, understanding selves as learners, reflection, and self-assessment. This chapter investigates successful approaches to self-direction in teaching and learning in English-language courses.

Introduction

As previous studies show, the ability to learn and adapt are related (Chuprina, 2001; 2003). Both learning and adaptation skills have become survival skills in the age of continuing change. Furthermore, the research in the area of Self-Directed Learning (SDL) suggests that self-awareness is a cornerstone of lifelong learning that should be encouraged and modeled in academia/ training (Chuprina, 2004; 2007). Another important advantage of SDL is its capacity to promote ongoing reflective thought and responsibility for learning (Caffarella, 1993).

Knowles (1975) provides a comprehensive definition of SDL: "Individuals take the initiative, with or without the help of others, in diagnosing their learning needs, formulating learning goals, identifying human and material resources for learning, choosing and implementing appropriate learning strategies, and evaluating learning outcomes" (p. 18). Garrison (1997) adds that SDL focuses on the external management of the learning process where the learner decides what to learn and how to approach the learning task. He offers a further clarification of SDL as "an approach where learners are motivated to assume personal responsibility and col-laborative control of the cognitive (self-monitoring) and contextual (self-management) processes in constructing and confirming meaningful and worthwhile learning outcomes" (p. 18).

It is also necessary to note that while self-teaching and self-direction imply a degree of independence or autonomy, the learning that occurs through self-teaching does not generally take place in isolation (Tough, 1966). In fact, SDL implies good communication and collaboration skills, and according to Brocket & Hiemstra (1991), "Those individuals who engage in self-teaching are highly likely to seek the assistance of others, such as close friends and relatives, subject-matter experts and fellow learners" (p. 41).

Behaviors and characteristics which support lifelong learning include taking risks, trying new things, self-reflection, listening, gathering information, and being open to new ideas and information (Kotter, 1996). These characteristics and learning skills do not come on their own and should be explicitly taught. Faculty should build into the curriculum encouragement for students to engage in the SDL process, self assessment, and self reflection opportunities.

Background

Guglielmino, Gray, Le Arvary, Asen, Goldstein, Fran Kamin, Nicoll, Patrick, Shellabarger, & Snowberger (2009) stated,

> Learners benefit greatly from a content base on which to build, but if we allow the learning of content to crowd out time for reflection on learning and exploration of individually-selected topics that create excitement about learning and build skills and attitudes that will support lifelong learning, we will do a disservice to our learners and our cultures. Our times require continuous lifelong learning (p. 26).

One of the compelling attributes of the SDL approach in formal, content-based, and structured academic environments is the opportunity for students to become conscientious learners through reflection on their process of learning. Bringing SDL into the curriculum of those institutions that are dedicated to developing lifelong learners has a potential for creating the balance between learning by the individual, the pressures of testing, and the penalties for not reaching the standards. Encouraging self-direction does not mean ignoring accountability; self-direction in learning exists along a continuum in each individual. More than that, each learning experience offers different levels of opportunity for self-direction (Guglielmino, et al., 2009) with personal and collective growth.

As practice shows, in traditional educational settings such skills as learning how to learn, how to solve problems, and how to use reflection and self-assessment through self-inquiry activities have not been part of the curricula; they are expected to be part of a student's existing tools. Reflection and assessment of one's own learning process are two of the most important skills for lifelong learning. Reflection Practice (RP) includes a proactive examination of one's goals and practices. It helps students construct their knowledge based on their previous experience and incorporate new ideas and concepts to reach the goals they set for themselves. Self-reflection also prompts the learner to think about the mode of learning that fits best in the given situation.

Through reflection on their learning process, students provide valuable information on their learning preferences, their strengths and weakness, and the goals they want to achieve. This informs the teacher as to what materials and methods of knowledge delivery to choose to address the variety in interests of the participants. Teachers become facilitators and advisors in the learning process and also provide resources to meet the students' learning needs.

It is self-reflection that integrates intellectual and emotional human development and provides meaning and purpose in learning and academic and professional pursuit. This connection allows people to maintain vigor in learning and keeps students motivated and responsible for their own learning.

Another way to approach the development of the characteristics and skills that contribute to lifelong learning is to include reflection in the learning process in SDL contracts to help students set their learning goals for the quarter, academic year, or career and life paths.

A misconception about SDL and self-reflection is that teachers and classmates should be excluded. In fact, Cunningham (2001) noted that reflective practice draws upon the input of other learners and is collective by nature, which creates a basis for partnerships in learning in the classroom. By creating an atmosphere of collaboration in class, teachers model how to relate to others in the class and in real-life situations. Language learning, for example, creates an atmosphere for social interaction within and beyond the classroom; therefore, it is an imperative for ELP instructors to use real-life situations and authentic materials for classroom reading and discussion. The process of working together and being involved in conversations and discussions in the class enhances students' social, reflective, and lifelong learning skills.

Practices, Examples, Issues

Self-assessment and self-directedness are embedded in the City University of Seattle (CityU) Academic Model. This Academic Model focuses on student learning, which is "carefully designed by faculty to encourage self-directed learning within an appropriately defined structure of expectations. Students are actively encouraged to define and take responsibility for their own contributions to the learning process with the understanding that their engagement is critical for substantive learning to take place" (City University of Seattle, Academic Model).

Selected ELP courses include graded and non-graded reflective assignments. At the beginning of the term of study, students are asked to reflect on their current knowledge and skills, set goals, and then assess their learning progress in the middle and at the end of the term as well as discuss what areas they would like to explore and improve further on their own after the end of the course. The self-assessment assignments are graded on completeness and depth of reflection to promote candid and non-defensive student reflection. Some of the reflective assignments include:

- Online discussion forums in which students are asked to reflect on their own skills at the beginning of the term of study and identify areas of strength and improvement. The students are asked to think about their initial knowledge and skills. At the end of the course, students participate in an end-of-course forum to reflect on their learning and to discuss it with their peers and the instructor. Online asynchronous forums are particularly beneficial in that they allow each student to get peer and instructor reinforcement, encouragement, and suggestions. Each student is required to post a reflection and respond to at least one of his or her peers. To keep the reflections and responses focused on course objectives, guidelines for reflections and peer responses are provided. Once the responses are posted, the instructor has the opportunity to provide feedback to each student.

- Worksheets with questions to promote depth of self-reflection.
- Initial assessments and diagnostics administered by the instructor. After completing these assessments, students are asked to reflect on how they did in addition to receiving feedback from the faculty.

The reflection assignments are designed according to the learning outcomes of the course. For example, in an academic and professional writing course, students are asked to think about the papers and the academic and professional writing tasks they completed in the past, the challenges they encountered, how they dealt with the challenges, and what they learned from the process. The students are also asked to discuss their strengths and the areas where they need improvement as writers. At the end of the quarter, students are asked to review their beginning-of-term reflections and goals and to assess their learning in the course. In reading classes the students are asked to think about their reading skills and challenges and set goals to improve their reading speed and comprehension. At the end of the term, students reflect on their growth and set future goals. In grammar, listening, and speaking classes, students complete similar reflective activities as relevant to the course content.

Having students complete reflection assignments at the beginning of the term allows faculty to tailor instruction. Most CityU courses include required assessments developed by the department but allow for some instructor-determined assignments. Faculty can use this opportunity to create assignments that address student learning needs and interests. Furthermore, faculty can adjust the required assessments and select topics for them based on students' initial self-assessments. For example, if one of the course curriculum requirements is to complete a case study, the instructor may select a topic relevant to student needs or interests.

The materials, textbooks, and additional resources are also selected to respond to student interests and learning needs. The texts and exercises in the textbooks selected for all the levels of English learners help students acquire skills they identified as lacking in addition to the skills required to complete the course. Integration of the required and desired knowledge and skills plays an effective role in maintaining interest and motivation among students.

ELP instructors also attempt to facilitate the development of learning skills and reflective practice on one's learning process in students along with language learning and focus on the content. Additional techniques available for teachers to invite students to participate in self-reflection and self-evaluation are as follows:

- In-class and on-line journaling with questions that help students reflect on their learning goals, learning needs, and the learning process; self-reflective writing brings in connectivity between the mind and emotions.
- Course learning outcomes included in syllabi underlining the importance of learning and study skills, which provide meaning and purpose in learning the course content.
- Rubrics for written assignments, oral presentations, and constructive participation, providing students with information on the requirements in each category, such as content knowledge, organization, quality of writing, research, ethical citations, presentation, and other components. This provides specific expectations for presentations, at the

same time allowing for creativity and self-expression in the students' assignments.

- Classroom Assessments Technique (CAT) forms, which are available on the Faculty Portal, contain specific questions leading students through the self-inquiry process in a certain subject (e.g., reading; listening and speaking; and grammar and writing) as well as give students room to respond to open questions and the opportunity to offer suggestions to teachers on the class organization, content delivery, and the teaching-learning process.
- Mid-term and end-of-course student evaluations, which allow instructors to gather information regarding whether each student is learning and allow students to reflect on their instruction based on their feedback. These student reflections help teachers make adjustments to their curriculum, lesson plans, and the choice of classroom materials to meet students' learning needs.

Due to the multi-level character of the majority of language classes, instructors use individualized approaches. The information shared by students through their self-inquiry and reflection helps ELP instructors maintain an environment conducive for learning.

Self-reflective practices can offer important input for teaching, learning, and planning. In their book *Self-Direction in Adult Learning: Perspectives on Theory, Research, and Practice,* Brocket & Hiemstra (1991) suggested the following steps to enhance self-direction in learning and learner responsibility through the self-reflection and planning process to achieve desirable learning outcomes:

1. identifying needs, objectives, and benefits from the learning activity;
2. identifying resources, specifying learning activities, and establishing criteria for successful accomplishments;
3. carrying out the learning activities, analyzing obtained information, and recording progress towards some personal changes;

4. evaluating the learning outcomes and how they can be used in a real-life situation/self-planning (1991, p. 106-107).

Instructors provide structure and find time throughout the course for reflective practice as they discuss the importance of goal setting, encourage students to set their personal goals, and make plans to achieve them. By doing this every week of the quarter, instructors ensure that self-evaluation skills and reflective practice become part of the learning process.

Students are also directed to think about their study habits and learning preferences by answering questions such as:

What time of the day do you learn the best?
Do you learn better by yourself or together with other students/friends?
How do you learn better? When you just listen or write it down?
Which specific language skills would you like to improve: listening, reading, speaking, or writing?

Hiemstra (2000) offered the following list of the educational changes that are taking place in the American society:

- **Continuing Education Unit (CEU)**—A unit for measuring participation in a variety of formal and informal learning activities (ten classroom hours of instruction equals one CEU). In some instances this unit replaces the college credit.
- **Learning modules**—Short credit or noncredit blocks of learning in which a person can participate independently at home, at work, or at community learning centers.
- **Credit for experience**—The granting of college credit for community service, life experiences, or occupational experiences.
- **Credit by testing**—The granting of a certain amount of credit, usually college credit, through an examination program. The College Proficiency Examination Program (CPEP) and the College-level Examination Programs (CLEP) are the most widely used systems.

- **Non-traditional college offerings**—The offering of mini-courses, internships, travel courses, intensive summer session courses, and weekend courses for college credit.
- **External degree—or the open-university or campus-without-walls approach**— this usually refers to the granting of a college degree based on a variety of learning experiences, formal courses, and/or assisted activities.
- **Online learning**—The use of computers, the Internet, and computer-mediated conversations permits study in the home, at work, or in neighborhood resource centers, sometimes combined with some type of tutorial service, to present learning opportunities on a variety of topics.
- **Learning contracts**—The mutual negotiation between an educational facilitator-expert and a learner on some specified learning activity or even a full course for credit.
- **The adult learning project**—A deliberate effort to learn something new, primarily through self-initiated effort and typically outside of any institutionalized cassette or CD-Rom instruction.
- **Voucher system for learning**—Each person is entitled to a certain number of years of education, but the education can be obtained any time that help is needed. Although not yet a reality in the United States, this form of learning takes place in various parts of the world.
- **Open entrance/open exit**—A person will be able to enter the school setting for a self-determined period of time and then exit, often with a plan for later reentry and study.
- **Facilitative self-training workshops**—Retreat-like settings in which individuals are helped by resource specialists to experience self-growth.

Such nontraditional activities, alternative learning modes, or innovative educational changes are based primarily on the assumption that lifelong learning is a natural circumstance within which autonomous, self-directed learners participate according to their needs and interests. More change can be expected and must happen if education is to meet a goal of truly helping people with a lifetime of challenge (Hiemstra, 2000).

The library is another resource which facilitates students in lifelong learning. Librarians at City University of Seattle actively help new students in their use of the library's resources and teach students how to conduct research. Instructors make a point of organizing tours to the library and help students find books for reading based on their level of English and their interests. This collaboration with the library plays a significant role in the development of the students' lifelong learning skills and lays a foundation for further success.

Implications for Training Faculty

Hiemstra (2000) suggests that those who work with students must learn to think of themselves more as educators instead of fairly narrow subject matter specialists. By facilitating student learning and helping them learn to use the many resources now available electronically, instructors promote attitudes of and commitment to lifelong learning in their students.

Faculty too might benefit from these approaches to learning and teaching. Faculty self-reflection on their teaching beliefs and practices can make more transparent the potential gaps in their approaches to teaching. Both students and faculty might benefit from such self-reflection.

As pointed out by Manz & Manz (1991), "Self-directed learning is in the heart of human resource effectiveness, yet it is perhaps the most overlooked form of learning" (p. 3). It is also truly related to higher education and professional training. The many applications and opportunities for future research and practice include:

- SDL skills for the new faculty orientation
- SDL approaches among faculty and staff
- SDL skills training for business managers
- SDL approaches and skills for teachers in training and in their first years of practice

To disseminate the practice, the following steps can be offered:

1. Organizing Train-the-trainer seminars and providing practical application handbooks.

2. Offering professional development workshops to interested faculty.
3. Starting study group(s) where experienced and novice teachers can exchange their perspectives on teaching and also share self-directed learning plans for professional growth.
4. Encouraging peer evaluations and mentor programs which include reflection on the teaching-learning process so that instructors can internalize the steps and skills for self-directed learning and teach these skills explicitly to their students.

One of the recent innovations is the use of e-portfolios for educators and students. E-portfolios allow one to maintain a portfolio as a lifelong project, collecting samples of work and assignments which demonstrate their level of expertise.

Future Research and Directions

The topics of self-reflection and lifelong learning in academia are very important and timely for both researchers and practitioners. Though the topics have been well researched within the last twenty-five years (IJSDL publications, n.d.), it would be interesting to research how faculty are engaged in reflective practices and in self-directed learning, whether for professional or personal development.

Since it has become clear that perspective on the meaning of self-direction in learning differs among cultures, it is essential for researchers and practitioners to understand the degree to which language reflects culture and vice versa and the degree to which language affects one's thinking (Boucouvalas, 2009; Ho & Crookall, 1995). For example, collaboration and interdependence are part of the self-directed approach in Asian cultures (Nah, 2000; Sinclair, 1997). Therefore, another interesting area of research is to study the phenomena of self-directed learning and self-reflection from a sociolinguistic approach. The knowledge of how students from different cultures and language backgrounds construct the meaning of self-directed learning in academia would help educators who work in the global environment understand the SDL application across cultures.

Another area of research interest includes self-reflection and self-assessment as part of SDL approaches and in computer-aided second-language learning, especially writing, where students have an opportunity to save their writing assignments together with teacher and peer feedback. It would be of value to explore the incorporation of self-assessment and reflection in ESL computer-assisted classes. A similar study on self-assessment and reflection in computer-aided ESL classes conducted in Sweden (Sullivan & Lindgren, 2002) showed that this method is not restricted to an L2 environment but can be equally effective in other learning situations.

Conclusion

Self-assessment and self-reflection practices conducted by students can provide a bridge between accountability-based assessment and formative assessments conducted by the faculty. Both student and teacher assessments are needed to give a clearer and bigger picture of the learning processes and the learning environment.

The practice of using learning reflections and self-evaluation techniques within the curriculum of language teaching is highly valuable for the academic setting and supports a shift from teacher-centered learning towards learner-centered approaches. Students who reflect on their learning and participate in self-evaluation to identify their areas of strength as well as their areas which need improvement tend to be more successful not only in academic programs but also in professional and personal life. This phenomenon can be explained by the fact that self-directed learning brings about intrinsic motivation for learning and feelings of competence. More than that, self-reflection connects the mind to what matters and integrates intellectual and emotional domains in human development.

Where teachers and advisors become facilitators and partici-pants in the knowledge transfer and learning process, students take charge of their learning. To facilitate self-directed learning skills and allow students to take responsibility for their learning, faculty have to know the principles of adult learning theories, including self-reflection and self-evaluation skills, and model these skills in their classes.

Guglielmino et al. (2009) state that in order to prepare lead-ers, workers, citizens, and specialists capable of working within the context of the globalization of the economy and education, it is imperative that individuals responsible for education and human resource development incorporate the development of self-directed lifelong learners as a primary aim of their programs.

Faculty need to become facilitators in the learning process, with attention given both to the content and the process of learn-ing within the curriculum and instruction. Since the development of self-directed learning skills is a lifelong pursuit for teachers and students, the best teachers are, first of all, self-directed learners. It is essential in an age of rapid change and global education to help learners engage in reflection on their learning and make feedback a part of the learning process.

References

Brocket, R. & Hiemstra, R. (1991). *Self-direction in adult learning: Perspectives on theory, research, and practice.* London and New York: Rutledge.

Boucouvalas, M. (2009*).* Concept of SELF in self-directed learning. *International Journal of Self-Directed Learning, 6* (1).

Caffarella, R. S. (1993). Facilitating self-directed learning as a staff development option. *Journal of Staff Development, 14*(2), 30-35.

Chuprina, L. & Durr, R. (2007). Self-directed learning readiness as predictor for cultural adaptability in expatriate managers.

International Journal of Self-Directed Learning Symposium Group, 3(1).

Chuprina, L. (2004). Facilitating expatriate managers in their cross-cultural adaptability. *Proceedings of Hawaii International Conference on Education* [CD-ROM]. Honolulu, HI.

Chuprina, L. (2003). Development of self-directed learning skills in students enrolled in ESL/adult education classes. *Proceedings. Midwest Research to Practice Conference in Adult Continuing and Community Education.* The Ohio State University, Columbus, OH.

Chuprina, L. (2001). *The relationship between self-directed learning readiness and cross cultural adaptability in U.S. expatriate managers.* Unpublished doctoral dissertation, The University of Tennessee.

City University of Seattle, Academic Model, para 2. Retrieved from http://www.cityu.edu/about/profile/academic_model.aspx

Cunningham, F. (2001). Reflective teaching practice in adult ESL settings. *National Center for ESL Literacy Education & Center for Applied Linguistics.* Retrieved from ERIC Digest: EDO-LE-01-01

Garrison, D. R. (1997). Self-directed learning: Toward a comprehensive model. *Adult Education Quarterly, 48* (1), 18-33.

Guglielmino, L., Gray, E., Le Arvary, K., Asen J., Goldstein, D., Fran Kamin, F., Nicoll, M. Patrick, N., Shellabarger, K., & Snowberger, D. (2009). Self-directed learners change our world: SDL as a force for innovation, discovery, and social change. *Journal of Self-Directed Learning, 6*(1).

Hiemstra, R. (2000) Lifelong learning: *An exploration of adult and continuing education within a setting of lifelong learning needs*. Retrieved from http://www-distance.syr.edu/lllch1. html

Ho, J., & Crookall, D. (1995). Breaking with Chinese cultural traditions: Learner autonomy in English language teaching. *System: An International Journal of Educational Technology and Applied Linguistics, 23*(2), 235-243.

IJSDL publications. (n.d.). Retrieved from www.sdl.global

Manz, C. & Manz, K. (1991). Strategies for facilitating self-directed learning. *Human Resources Quarterly, 2*(1), 3.

Nah, Y. (2000). Can a self-directed learner be independent, autonomous, and interdependent? Implications for practice. *Adult Learning, 18.*

Sinclair, B. (1997). Learner autonomy: The cross-cultural question. *IATEFL Newsletter, 139.*

Sullivan, K. & Lindgren, E. (2002). Self-assessment in autonomous computer-aided language writing. *ELT Journal, 56*(3), 258-256.

Tough, A. M. (1966). The assistance obtained by adult self-teachers. *Adult Education, 17.*Zsiga, Peter L., Liddell, Terry, & Muller, Kenneth. (2009). Self-directed learning among managers and executives of non-profit organizations. *Self-Directed Learning, 6*(1).

Self-Direction in Adult Learning: Best Practices

Gina Smith, EdD
Pete Anthony, EdD
City University of Seattle
School of Management

Abstract

An adaptive and flexible methodology that encompasses a blend of effective practices is necessary in self-directed learning. The characteristics of self-directed learners are identified, and innovative methods to promote learning for this category of highly-motivated adult learners are presented, even for those with barriers to overcome. Both theoretical views and practical applications are discussed.

Introduction

Adults become self-directed learners to fulfill a personal and intrinsic desire to gain knowledge. The reasons behind self-directed learning are varied and dimensional, but the key element is an individually-motivated desire to learn. However, no two learners approach self-directed learning in the same way (Brocket & Hiemstra, 1991), and this requires numerous methods and mechanisms to support individual lifelong learning. Alternative learning delivery, such as online or hybrid learning environments, can promote self-directed learning and offer innovative structures for those individuals driven to seek new knowledge. A number of varying theoretical insights help to explain the advantages and barriers associated with self-direction in adult learning.

Curriculum designers and university faculty can best take advantage of motivated adult learners by understanding the different issues related to their learning. Despite the wide range of differences among adult students, self-directed learners exhibit common characteristics. Penland (1979) described self-directed learners as ones who set their own pace by using their own style of learning within their own structures. Knowles (2002) points out that adult learners need to know what they are learning, why it is important, and how it will be useful. A number of opinions offer the best ways to administer and deliver education programs for self-directed adults, but they seem to share the same need to provide motivated learners with the knowledge and skills that they can apply directly and quickly in the pursuit of personal goals.

Employing the proper curriculum design and delivery methods is a key to meeting the needs of self-directed learners. Much focus has been paid to the way that instruction is delivered, as student-focused, activity-driven, authentic instruction has emerged to take the place of the traditional lecture-centric model (King, 1993). This shift has been driven by an emergent belief that real learning only happens when students have the ability to engage with material directly. "When students are engaged in actively processing information by reconstructing that information in such new and personally meaningful ways, they are far more likely to remember it and apply it in new situations" (King, 1993, p. 30).

Curricular Design in Support of Self-Directed Learning

The needs of the self-directed adult student are evolving. These learners prefer a flexible learning strategy that includes the ability to begin the educational process immediately versus waiting for a structured class to begin. Self-directed students enjoy learning and have a positive attitude toward the learning process; however, those who are self-directed need innovative educational structures. If accommodations related to their learning styles are provided, these learners may go further in their education and have fewer negative feelings about required traditional classes (Cross, 1981).

At the university level, an important aspect of authentic instruction is in the design of the curriculum. Opportunities for self-direction need to be built into course activities. Assessments should be structured in a consistent and cohesive manner that focuses on the needs of the learner. One method for ensuring that learner-centered content is part of both the program and its courses is to include it by incorporating all four stages of the Suskie (2004) Model. Learning goals, or program and course outcomes, can be established that allow students to take an active role in their own learning. Assessments that are authentic and learner-centered should be a central part of this process. Rubrics that are aligned with authentic instruction should seek evidence of learning relative to the outcomes. Lastly, results from program assessments can be applied to the continuous improvement of both the program and its courses to ensure that instructors are properly providing authentic, student-centered opportunities for self-directed learning, with the purpose of helping students achieve their learning goals. Inclusion of opportunities for self-direction in all parts of the design, delivery, and even the review process can be a valuable method of ensuring that self-direction opportunities remain at the forefront during the program and course development process.

Characteristics of the Self-Directed Learner

The actual mechanics of learner-centered curriculum design that accommodate self-direction can be difficult given the variability in learning styles. Having a better understanding of the specific characteristics of the self-directed learner is useful in the curriculum design process.

The relationship between teacher and learner should reflect mutual respect and both should view it as a facilitative partnership rather than a teacher-student relationship (Maehl, 2000). The experience of adult learners needs to be recognized by the teacher since self-concept has been formed by previous experiences (Maehl, 2000). Additionally the dimension of self-direction is perpetuated by societal conditions. Maehl (2000) states that rapid population growth is propelling adults to independently seek out new knowledge due to "the increasingly competitive and globally oriented economy, the increasing availability of learning resources due to technology, and the now permanent need to engage in learning" (p. 16).

Rubenson's Expectancy-Valence Model is applied to adult learning since it represents the way in which adults weigh their likely success in organized education in terms of expectations and preparedness (Cross, 1981). Adults considering an educational program must consider all factors related to going back to school, such as cost in time and money as opposed to income that may be earned upon the completion of the degree. The adult student must also consider time away from family. Each of these factors will impact the level of self-direction and motivation that an adult brings to the learning process.

Boshier's Congruency Model is similar to Rubenson's model since the motivation behind learning is based on the interaction between internal and external factors (Cross, 1981). Each of these is directly related to environmental factors. Boshier expands this theory by relating the variables not only to success but also to failure. If an individual has a negative self-image, he/she is more likely to drop out of an adult learning situation (Cross, 1981).

Self-direction holds many advantages in adult learning. Adults face opportunities to learn every day that represent self-direction due to contradictions and paradoxes. Merriam & Caffarella (1999) stated that dialectical thinking allows one to accept alternative truths or ways of thinking about instances that occur in everyday life (as cited by Kelsey, 2006). Alternative truths lead to wisdom. Merriam (2001) stated that wisdom is seen as the hallmark or seal of adult thinking. Kelsey (2006) stated that wisdom is the ability to problem-solve, listen, weigh advice, deal with different kinds of people, make sensible judgments, and learn from mistakes. Each of these characteristics is a potential advantage in self-direction. "Wisdom teaches us to respect all people, to celebrate their differences, to be guided by a single ethic-service about self. Moral authority is primary greatness" (Covey, 2004, p. 299).

Strategies to Enhance Self-Direction

Several strategies are available to enhance self-direction in organized education. Four such strategies are signals, reward systems, transformational leadership, and symbols. To engage learners and capitalize on their sense of self-direction, instructors need to build learning environments that can utilize or reinforce these strategies.

To better illustrate how each of these strategies can be used in organized education, it is best to view them in a relevant context; to this end each strategy will be considered in the context of learning about leadership with university-level graduate students.

- **Signals**. "Leaders build culture with the signals that their actions convey" (Marion, 2002, p. 240). Positive signals from leaders within an environment promote an effective culture. They can also send a signal of motivation to others instead of a signal of discouragement (Zaretsky, 2000). Signaling positive communication is also a strategy used to enhance adult interactions since "people work out their common understandings, the norms of behaviors, and their expectations by interacting and communicating with one another" (Marion, 2002, p. 240). Instructors can take advantage of the motivation and drive exhibited by self-directed learners by showing them how they can take their energy and turn it into positive leadership using communication signals that influence those around them in both their personal and professional lives.

- **Reward systems**. Organizations also shape culture through "…recognition, prestige and advancement. Such rewards reinforce appropriate cultural behavior" (Marion, 2002, p. 241). When faced with an opportunity to learn, it is human nature to want to know the payoff. The payoff with adult learning is gained knowledge and often an increase in pay or position. Harvey (1995) stated that leaders should personalize change through the rewards they give and the reassurance will have a positive affect on the recipient. This can be a strong advantage when educating self-directed leadership students who are likely to be strongly motivated by intrinsic rewards.

- **Transformation**. Another strategy to enhance self-direction is the ability to transform. Transformation can raise the culture of an organization to a more effective level of motivation and morality (Sergiovanni, 2004). Transformation is defined as the operation of change, whether the change is looked at through the need to learn in math, grammar, genetics, business applications, or any other subject. Transformation, then, converts one situation into another by insertion, deletion, or permutation (Merriam-Webster, 2005). A self-directed learner transforms his/her educational setting by redefining the structures that house learning. Then he or she has the ability to design new ways to think and react as a transformational leader. The final purpose comes in validating real-life situations by using transformational leadership skills. Vaill (1996) determined that the ways to learn are self-directed, creative, expressive, feeling, on-line, continual, and reflexive.

- **Symbols**. Symbolic leadership transforms a culture into an environment of enhanced self-direction since symbols may prompt the vision and communication of a goal (Dollarhide, 2003). Clear vision is crucial to an effective adult learning outcome since facilitators must consider and plan individualized outcomes for their learners (Maehl, 2000). Adult learners need symbols that reflect the flexible, yet clear vision of the learning process.

Innovative Structure

An adult learning program should facilitate access by providing an easy approach, a welcoming environment, supportive services, and adaptability to individual circumstances. The program should establish a friendly climate of learning for adults, both in a physical facility that is suitable and in a psychological environment that is warm, mutually respectful, trusting, supportive, and collaborative (Maehl, 2000, p. 78).

An innovative and effective structure incorporates these provisions to promote self-directed adult learning. "The program should involve learners in diagnosing their learning needs, setting learning goals, designing a plan of learning, managing the learning experience, and evaluating learning outcome" (Maehl, 2000, p. 78).

When self-directed learning is planned in a university program such as graduate-level leadership, a number of steps can be taken to ensure that motivated learners are able to take full advantage of the program's flexible structure. The following are innovative steps that can be taken to support self-directed learners:

- Program modularization—Design the program in a way that provides students with milestones that they can reach, as doing so will serve as a strong motivator to reach the next milestone. An example of such a modular design is to have a program core, followed by groups of courses that the students can take to earn certificates, all of which combine together to make up a degree. Self-directed students will be motivated by their completion of the core. which will propel them to move onto the first certificate and then each subsequent one until they have completed the program.

- Course modularization—Design the courses in modular sections to give motivated students accomplishments that they can point to as motivators for their next challenge. Few things are more motivating than progress (Amabile & Kramer, 2010) and both the programs and the courses can be set up to provide many progress checkpoints throughout.

- Online and hybrid delivery models—Self-directed learners appreciate flexibility (Brocket & Hiemstra, 1991) and courses that offer flexible schedules will allow them more control over their learning. Fully online models are often popular with such students while others appreciate a flexible mix of online and face-to-face instruction.

- Flexible scheduling—Completion time to degree can be an important factor for a self-directed learner. Thus, designing programs that allow learners more control over the program's pace can appeal to these learners' sense of motivation and personal achievement.

- Simulations—Using simulations to empower self-directed learning is an effective adult learning strategy. The students are placed in scenarios where they can make their own decisions and be evaluated on the results of their actions, often directly in the simulation. Simulations create a learning environment for students that allows them to utilize self-directed learning as they make their own decisions based on their actions and analyses of competition and resources.

- Team building—Adults work in teams in today's world, so effective team building is an essential adult learning strategy. Self-directed learners may have well-established patterns of self-reliance and may be less comfortable working with others as it requires them to relinquish control. Team assignments are an important way to help create an environment that respects the needs of self-directed learners while it provides opportunities for collaborative leadership.

- Challenging, flexible, and independent capstones—Self-directed learners want choices (Brocket and Hiemstra, 1991) and one area where choice can help motivate learners is in a program's capstone. Having multiple options available to students as they get ready to complete their program allows the self-directed learner to select the option that best suits his/her choices and goals.

Opportunities to Overcome Common Barriers

Common barriers associated with adult learning include presumptions, scheduling issues, and resistance related to change (Carp, Peterson, & Roelfs, 1974, as cited by Cross, 1981).

To overcome common barriers, the self-directed learning structure needs to recognize and respect individual experiences of the past, while incorporating a flexible and warm environment that moves toward the future (Maehl, 2000). "We must begin with the faith that all people have the capacity to develop and exercise their own intelligence in shaping their own future" (Dewey, as cited in Pai & Adler, 2001, p. 103).

"You can learn to walk only by taking baby steps" (Harvey, 1995, p. 23). Small, precise, and clearly defined steps that lead to a defined outcome also create a positive learning environment that reduces resistance. To motivate those with reluctance, the environment needs to provide a "clear payoff...provide them with a good enough reason to do so" (p. 11). After providing a clear reason for direction for learning, it is imperative that questions are asked to facilitate rather than teach. "Change is best facilitated with questions, not statements" (p. 14).

Andragogy is the way in which educators help adults learn (Conlan, Grabowski, & Smith, 2003). Andragogy is applied to develop positive attitudes toward learning. Knowles (2002) used several principles, or recognized abilities, to implement an effective adult learning design:

1. The ability to develop and be in touch with curiosities. Perhaps another way to describe this skill would be the ability to engage in divergent thinking.
2. The ability to perceive one's self-objectively and accept feedback about one's performance non-defensively.
3. The ability to diagnose one's learning needs in the light of models of competencies required for performing life roles.
4. The ability to formulate learning objectives in terms that describe performance outcomes. The ability to identify human, material, and experiential resources for accomplishing various kinds of learning objectives.
5. The ability to design strategies for making use of appropriate learning resources effectively.
6. The ability to carry out a learning plan systematically and sequentially. This skill is the beginning of the ability to engage in convergent thinking.
7. The ability to collect evidence of the accomplishment of learning objectives and have it validated through performance (Knowles, 2002, para. 5).

Knowles (2002) recognized the abilities needed to promote learning and assist reluctant learners to overcome common barriers. When applied learning plans are carried out effectively.

Adults have a desire to gain knowledge and are capable of doing so successfully through self-directed learning. Self-direction incorporates strategies that make adult learning more applicable and systematic. An adaptive and flexible methodology that encompasses a blend of effective practices is necessary in self-directed learning. The future of adult education will continue to change through these practices. "In building democracy we must begin with the faith that all people have the capacity to develop and exercise their own intelligence in shaping their own future" (Dewey, as cited in Pai & Adler, 2001, p. 103).

Future Research Directions

When considering the nature of self-directed learners, instructional designers need to broaden their sense of educational strategies, particularly in regard to online education. Variations to online discussion questions could be explored in an effort to enhance their effectiveness and the level of challenge they provide to self-directed learners. Other possible research could center on the effectiveness of student-designed course activities. One example might be to test if online students will be more challenged, motivated, and self-directed in their courses if they are allowed to develop their own case studies that are based either on the content knowledge learned in the class or real world scenarios pulled from their own experience. The need to determine the level of effectiveness of student-designed education, as indicated by performance on key metrics and outcomes, remains an area of research that would help inform instructors and curriculum designers about the best ways to engage self-directed learners.

Additional research into self-directed learning based on a qualitative phenomenological study might add insight into lived experiences from alumni. Efforts to gather graduates' perceptions about best practices regarding instructional design and delivery would be valuable in determining what they found motivating or constraining. This information might provide data for analysis of additional best practices for future facilitators to use in their respective classes.

Conclusion

The concept of adult learning theory must be addressed in the effort to design a rigorous program based on best practices for working with self-directed learners. Best practices for program design can employ lessons from the Expectancy-Valence Model, b) Boshier's Congruency Model, c) signals, d) reward systems, e) transformation, and f) symbols. These components drive the transformation of self-directed learning into a rigorous forum by which adult learners are supported as well as held to a standard of excellence.

The facilitation of a program for self-directed learners must also apply theoretical concepts to practical application leading to a collection of innovative practices that includes a) program modularization; b) course modularization; c) online and hybrid delivery models; d) flexible scheduling; e) simulations;

f) team-building exercises; and g) challenging, flexible, and independent capstones. By empowering students through the use of
these tools, programs can promote personal development as well
as collaboration among students and instructors that enhances a
self-directed learning environment.

References

Amabile, T. M., & Kramer, S. J. (2010, January - February). What really
motivates workers? *Harvard Business Review*. Retrieved
from http://hbr.org/2010/01/the-hbr-list-breakthrough-
ideas-for-2010/ar/1

Brocket, R. G., & Hiemstra, R. (1991). *Self-direction in adult learning: Perspectives on theory, research and practice*. New York:
Routledge.

Conlan, J., Grabowski, S., & Smith, K. (2003). *Current trends in adult
education*: *Emerging perspectives on learning, teaching, and
technology*. Retrieved from http://www.coe.uga.edu/epltt/
AdultEducation.htm

Covey, S. (2004). *The 8th habit*. NY: Free Press.

Cross, P. (1981). *Adults as learners increasing participation and facilitating learning*. San Francisco, CA: Jossey Bass.

Dollarhide, C. (2003, June). School counselors as program leaders: Applying leadership contexts to school counseling.
Professional School Counseling, 6(5), 304-308.

Harvey, T. (1995). *Checklist for change: A pragmatic approach to creating and controlling change*. Lancaster, PA: Technomic.

Kelsey, K. (2006). *Cognitive development in adulthood*. Retrieved
from file:///C:/Documents%20and%20Settings/Gina%20
Smith/Local%20Settings/Temporary%20Internet%20

Files/Content.IE5/09EV45E7/5123-7%5B1%5D. ppt#292,32,Dialectical Thinking

King, A.(1993). From sage on the stage to guide on the side. *College Teaching, 41*(1), 30-35.

Knowles, M. (2002). *Lifelong learning: A dream.* Retrieved from http://www.newhorizons.org/future/Creating_the_ Future/crfut_knowles.html

Maehl, W. (2000). *Lifelong learning at its best.* San Francisco, CA: Jossey-Bass.

Marion, R. (2002). *Leadership in education: Organizational theory for the practitioner.* Columbus: Merrill Prentice Hall.

Merriam, S. B. (2001). *Andragogy and self-directed learning: Pillars of adult learning theory.* Retrieved from http://www.fsu. edu/~elps/ae/download/ade5385/Merriam.pdf

Merriam, S.B. & Caffarella, R.S. (1999). *Learning in adulthood: a comprehensive guide.* San Francisco: Jossey-Bass Publishers.

Merriam-Webster's Collegiate Dictionary (2005). Retrieved from http://www.m-w.com

Pai, Y., & Adler, S. (2001). *Cultural foundations of education* (3rd ed.). Upper Saddle River: Merrill Prentice Hall.

Penland, P. (1979). Self-initiated learning. *Adult Education, 29,* 170-179.

Sergiovanni, T. (2004, May). Building a community of hope. *Educational leadership, 61*(8), 33-37.

Suskie, L. (2004). Assessing student learning: A common sense guide. San Francisco: Anker Publishing Company.

Vaill, P. (1996). *Learning as a Way of Being*. San Francisco: Jossey-Bass.

Zatetsky, E. (2000). Charisma or rationalization? Domesticity and psychoanalysis in the United States in the 1950s. *Critical Inquiry, 26*(2), 328.

7

The Six Thinking Hats: A Constructivist's Technique to Facilitate the Transfer and Application of Critical and Creative Thinking

Cheryl A. Szyarto, EdD
City University of Seattle
School of Management

Abstract

In business, education, and elsewhere, being constructive and creative is more than just desirable—it is essential. Individuals must be skillful communicators and astute problem solvers to succeed in a world marked by rapid growth and accelerating change. The problem in higher education is that students subjected to traditional institutional teaching methods develop learning patterns that are inadequate and leave them ill-prepared to navigate life's difficult and often unpredictable conditions under which people must exercise their will and judgment. The purpose of this chapter is to describe how de Bono's (1999) *Six Thinking Hats* can serve as a powerful instructional technique that college and university instructors can use in on-ground, online, or hybrid-model courses to engage students actively in critical and creative thinking via a constructivist approach.

Introduction

One of the foremost goals of education, including adult education, is to develop students' general thinking skills (Van Gelder, 2005). Critical thinking skills in particular are especially challenging to teach (Van Gelder, 2005), yet are vital to students' success in today's competitive workforce. In colleges and universities worldwide, students represent a wide variety of races, religions, cultures, and professional sectors. Instructors have the distinct duty of preparing a diverse body of individuals to be astute problem solvers and effective leaders on local and global levels.

The broad problem is that institutional learning, or learning within formal educational systems, is very often plagued by a traditional institutional learning philosophy, according to which instructors are the disseminators of information or knowledge, and the students are merely the passive recipients (Vaill, 1996). In other words traditional institutional learning can be disempowering for students because it is assumed to occur *offline*, in the confines of a classroom dominated by the beliefs, attitudes, and curriculum shared by an individual deemed to be the subject-matter expert (Vaill, 1996). The more specific problem is that students subjected to traditional institutional teaching methods develop learning patterns that are inadequate and leave them ill-prepared to navigate permanent *white water*, Vaill's (1996) metaphorical term for life's difficult and often unpredictable conditions under which people must exercise their will and judgment.

According to Vaill (1996) traditional institutional learning patterns are inadequate because "neither the philosophy nor the practice of institutional learning was designed for permanent white water—neither in formal educational systems themselves nor in the worlds that learners enter as 'graduates' of those educational systems" (p. 41). To prepare learners to succeed in a world of accelerating change, college and university teaching faculty have to explore instructional methods that empower students to become independent critical thinkers who make sound workplace decisions and clinical judgments, demonstrate effective leadership, achieve professional success, and participate wisely in a democratic society (Yang & Chou, 2007). Teaching about critical thinking is insufficient. For students to internalize critical thinking skills, apply them appropriately, and transfer them to settings outside of the classroom, they must engage in activities that require critical thinking (Van Gelder, 2005). Students are most likely to improve their critical thinking skills with deliberate practice (Van Gelder, 2005). Modeling such skills, while helpful, is insufficient. Instead, "[l]earning must be a way of being" (Vaill, 1996, p. 42), which to Vaill (1996) is "an authentic way of living and working, thinking and feeling, in the world of permanent white water" (p. 42).

It is essential to discuss the process of critical thinking. De Bono's (1999) *Six Thinking Hats* is a proven practice for engaging students in critical thinking, revolutionizes learning in the adult classroom, and promotes learning as a way of being (Vaill, 1996). Instructors implementing *The Six Thinking Hats* technique can effectively challenge students to free themselves of the habitual ways of thinking that often lack creativity and innovation, stifle learning, and inhibit problem solving. Based on the constructivist learning theory and the importance of critical and creative thought, *The Six Thinking Hats* is a technique teaching faculty can use in online, on-ground, or hybrid model classes to broaden students' perspectives, to assist them in developing successful strategies for addressing, interpreting, and applying the core issues presented in class, and to promote skill transference.

Critical Thinking

Critical thinking is a complex practice because it assumes a variety of definitions, consists of a myriad of elements, and often pairs with other types of thinking. Proficiency in critical thinking, or purposeful thinking (Facione, 1998), is "essential to lifelong learning and to dealing effectively with a world of accelerating change" (Celuch & Slama, 1999, p. 135). More is involved in critical thinking than just the possession of intellect (Bailin, Case, Coombs, & Daniels, 1999; Facione, 1998). Researchers hold different views as to how critical thinking skills develop. A comparison of the varied definitions of critical thinking is necessary to understand the complexity surrounding the development of learners' critical thinking practices.

Sound critical thinking involves the ability "...to take one's thinking apart systematically, to analyze each part, assess it for quality and then improve it" (Elder & Paul, 2002, p. 34). Critical thinking first involves a systematic analysis of one's own thought processes in a given scenario, including the formation of inferences and points of view, the existence of assumptions, and the understanding of information, inferences, concepts, and implications (Elder & Paul, 2002). According to Bailin, Case, Coombs, and Daniels (1999), "Having the intellectual resources necessary for critical thinking does not solely make one a critical thinker" (p. 294). Instead, the processes involved in becoming a skilled critical thinker and the employment of critical thought in today's world are complex.

Cognitive skills and affective dispositions are crucial to critical thinking (Facione, 1998; Harris, 1998). According to Facione (1998), cognitive skills, such as the ability to interpret, analyze, evaluate, infer, explain, and self-regulate, are just as important to critical thinking as are affective dispositions. The term "critical spirit" (Facione, 1998) reflects the components of Vaill's (1996) theory on learning as a way of being and suggests the importance of affective dispositions to critical thinking. In contrast to Facione's (1998) reports, Bailin et al. (1999) do not characterize critical thinkers as possessing skills and abilities; they reported, "Doing so encourages educators to think of the task of developing critical thinking as simply a matter of teaching students a set of new and discrete skills or abilities" (p. 290). Teaching critical thinking and merely sharing good examples of critical thinking with students is insufficient (Bailin et al., 1999; Vaill, 1996; Van Gelder, 2005). Instead, students must engage in authentic learning experiences and, through such experiences, pursue reflexive learning (Vaill, 1996), which is "a process of becoming a more conscious and reflective learner, more aware of one's own learning process and how it compares to the learning processes of others (Vaill, 1996, p. 47).

Like Vaill (1996), Kirby and Goodpaster (2002) looked deeply into the concept of thinking and learning. They considered it imperative to understand the extent to which sound critical thinking depends on a number of variables. Among such variables are an awareness of personal barriers, sensing, memory, language, feeling, cognitive organization, logic, scientific thinking, persuasive thinking, problem solving, evaluation, decisive action, and creativity.

Exploring how cognition, logic, and feeling/emotionality (three of the aforementioned variables) relate to one's ability to think critically is imperative to developing sound critical thinkers in today's classrooms. Is one element more crucial than another or are all elements equal components of sound critical thinking? Are cognition, logic, and emotionality interdependent?

Cognition, Logic, and Emotionality

Cognition, as defined in Merriam-Webster's Pocket Dictionary (1995), is "the act or process of knowing" (p. 64). Developing one's cognition appears to influence one's ability to think critically. For example, improved cognitive skills will enable the learner to deal more effectively with the unpleasant state of cognitive dissonance (Kirby & Goodpaster, 2002). Kirby and Goodpaster (2002) explained, "When we find ourselves in a state of cognitive dissonance we will often try to change our thoughts or our behaviors to...reduce tension" (p. 38). However, avoiding instances of cognitive disharmony is unnecessary. Instead, effectively managing cognitive disharmony is ideal. Cognitive discord prompts further questioning and self-regulation since changing one's thoughts otherwise does not reflect Facione's (1998) idea of sound critical thinking.

In light of Kirby and Goodpaster's (2002) findings, the need to develop cognitively is apparent; doing so will fuel the ability to adjust schemata so that the learner does not negatively "shape, restrict, and stereotype…perceptions and thinking" (Kirby & Goodpaster, 2002, p. 44). An understanding of logic is equally important to the need for cognitive development. Physiologically, one's life is dependent on the function of the heart. If "thinking logically and identifying reasoning fallacies in one's own and in others' thinking is the heart of critical thinking" (Kirby & Goodpaster, 2002, p. 141), then the existence of critical thinking is dependent on the existence of logical reasoning.

Building on this idea, Facione (1998) argued that the ability to identify, interpret, analyze, evaluate, and explain the strengths and limitations of an argument involves a thorough understanding of logic. Elder and Paul (1999) stated, "A habit of consciously working to seek the logic of things is one of the most powerful ideas for the improvement of thinking. It helps generate a lifelong habit of seeking clarity, accuracy, precision, depth, breadth, and significance in our thought" (para. 36). If Elder and Paul's (1999) contention holds true, then an individual's commitment to understanding logic reflects an individual's commitment to lifelong learning.

Just as logic relates to critical thinking, so too does emotionality. How, though, do they relate? Emotions influence one's thinking. In support of this notion, Jarrett (1993) explained that emotions "move us to act or to have a disposition to act" (para. 27). Clearly, Jarrett established a cause and effect relationship between emotions and thinking. Schwarz, as cited by Mandel (2003), indicated that an individual's "emotions—positive or negative—…may systematically bias judgment and decision making in a number of ways" (p. 139-140). An individual's emotionality does influence the ability to think critically.

Critical thinking assumes a variety of definitions. The underlying concept, though, is that critical thinking is purposeful thinking (Facione, 1998, p. 3) comprised of specific elements (Elder, & Paul, 2002; Facione, 1998) and dependent on outside variables and other forms of thinking (Kirby, & Goodpaster, 2002; Vaill, 1996). Factors influencing cognitive thinking include cognition (Elder, & Paul, 2002), logic (Elder, & Paul, 1999; Facione, 1998; Kirby, & Goodpaster, 2002), and emotionality (Jarrett, 1993; Schwarz as cited by Mandell, 2003). Ideas conflict on how to develop and refine students' sound critical thinking practices. However, experts assert that participation in alternate modes of learning fosters critical thought (Harris, 1998; Vaill, 1996), while traditional institutional learning methods do not (Vaill, 1996).

Creative Thinking

Creative thinking is an evolving construct (Norton, 1994), which involves developing something new—an idea, process, practice, etc.—using the skills of "flexibility, originality, fluency, imagery, associative thinking, attribute listing, metaphorical thinking, and forced relationships" (Edgar, Faulkner, Franklin, Knobloch, & Morgan, 2008, p. 46). A creative thinker engages in four thought processes: fluency, flexibility, originality, and elaboration (Edgar et al., 2008). A fluent thinker is one who generates a plethora of ideas, while a flexible thinker is able to shift viewpoints easily to examine ideas from varied perspectives (Edgar et al., 2008). Originality involves the conception of new ideas or solutions while elaboration involves the ability to expand upon existing ideas (Edgar et al., 2008). Creative thinkers are curious, nonjudgmental, open-minded, persistent, imaginative, and willing to face challenges (Edgar et al., 2008).

Educators are responsible for helping learners develop their creative abilities. However, student creativity is stifled by the traditional structure of the present-day educational system (Edgar et al., 2008). Innovative teaching strategies are essential if instructors want to succeed at challenging students to free themselves of the habitual ways of thinking that often lack innovation, suppress learning, and inhibit problem solving.

Relationship to Critical Thinking

Supporting Vaill (1996) as well as Kirby and Goodpaster's (2002) insight into critical thinking, Harris (1998) agreed that more is involved in becoming a critical thinker than just perfecting the skills of analysis that are addressed through formal education. He concurred that creative thinking is crucial to successful problem solving and is, therefore, vital to critical thinking. Harris (1998) and Vaill (1996) shared another viewpoint: "Creativity has been suppressed by education" (Harris, 1998, para. 27). Harris (1998) went on to state, "In practice, both kinds of thinking operate together much of the time and are not really independent of each other" (para. 2). If Harris was accurate in asserting that creative and critical thinking are interdependent, then educational institutions relying solely upon traditional teaching methods are suppressing learners' creative thinking and are consequently stifling the development and application of learners' critical thinking practices.

Teaching and learning cannot be limited to preparation courses and formal degree programs (Vaill, 1996). Vaill (1996) explained, "By inadvertently creating meaningless learning experiences, institutional learning exacerbates white water problems and leaves the learner unsure of how he or she is ever going to live effectively in the chaotic organizations of the present and future" (p.43). Educators must integrate the art of critical and creative thinking into student-centered, hands-on, contextual learning experiences representative of practical, real-world circumstances. Through constructivist teaching and learning practices, the aforementioned experiences prepare collaborative learners to apply and transfer such thinking in a world of accelerating change and increased workforce demands.

Constructivism

Defined as a lasting change in behavior, human learning is an intricate phenomenon that researchers have explored in varied contexts and through a number of theoretical perspectives (Schunk, 2004). Relevant to the development of *The Six Thinking*

Hats technique, constructivism is a learning theory founded on the premise that learning should be an active process for students whereby they use their past knowledge to develop, or construct, new ideas or concepts (Brandon & All, 2010). Classified as a social cognitive learning theory, constructivism stresses the notion that human learning occurs in a social environment (Schunk, 2004). Proponents of constructivism stress the importance of observational learning and emphasize the relationship between personal, behavioral, and environmental factors (Schunk, 2004).

Constructivism contrasts significantly with more traditional institutional learning approaches through which instructors rely on textbooks and lectures to impart knowledge to students, the passive recipients of such information. In a constructivist's classroom, students are at the center of all learning experiences while the instructor becomes the facilitator or mediator "who needs to create meaningful zones of proximal development and cognitive bridges through social interactions" (Brandon & All, 2010, p. 90). Students in the constructivist classroom are engaged actively in student-centered learning experiences during which students are responsible for creating their own knowledge, making decisions, solving problems, and sharing diverse perspectives in a collaborative environment (Brandon & All, 2010). *The Six Thinking Hats* (de Bono, 1999) is a powerful instructional technique college and university instructors can use in on-ground, online, or hybrid-model courses to engage students actively in critical and creative thinking via a constructivist approach.

The Six Thinking Hats Technique

Using *The Six Thinking Hats* technique can broaden students' perspectives and assist them in developing successful strategies for interpreting course content while meaningfully applying the core skills within a given curriculum. Instructors implementing *The Six Thinking Hats* technique effectively will challenge students to free themselves of the habitual ways of thinking that often lack creativity, impede learning, and hinder problem solving. The technique is one that instructors can use to promote students' transfer and application of critical and creative thinking skills to today's competitive workplaces, where collaboration, sound decision-making, innovation, and reflexive learning are essential to their achievement. *The Six Thinking Hats* unleashes the full thinking potential of students and the teams on which they serve (The de Bono Group, LLC, n.d.b). By employing *The Six Thinking Hats* technique, all learners fulfill valuable roles and are equal contributors to the thought process (The de Bono Group, LLC, n.d.b).

Each of the six figurative hats (white, red, yellow, black, green, and blue) represents a different purpose or style of thinking: objective thinking, informed intuition, positive and constructive assessment, negative assessment, creativity and innovation, and process control (de Bono, 1999). By figuratively wearing and switching hats during the critical thinking process, students can become more focused and mindfully involved (The de Bono Group, LLC, n.d.b) as they explore problems from various points of view. Ideally students will make better, more informed decisions (de Bono, 1999). Prior to exploring the application of the technique, a brief description of each of the six hats is necessary to best understand its function.

The white hat. Simply put, the white hat calls for an examination of information, either that which is known or needed (The de Bono Group, LLC, n.d.b). When wearing the white hat, the student is exploring only facts (The de Bono Group, LLC, n.d.b). Just as a computer can provide facts and figures objectively, the student wearing a white hat retrieves or identifies facts in a neutral manner and remains objective when presenting factual information (Gross, 1998).

The red hat. The red hat symbolizes emotion or feelings and intuition (The de Bono Group, LLC, n.d.b). Unlike when wearing the white hat, students wearing the red hat can share/express their emotions and their feelings and opinions, which may include their likes and dislikes (The de Bono Group, LLC, n.d.b). By wearing a red hat during any thought process, the learner validates emotions as relevant to the overall thinking process (Gross, 1998). According to Gross (1998), when learners wear red hats, they do not need to justify feelings or seek logic to ground them. To think critically learners must be aware of emotions that may influence their overall thought processes.

The yellow hat. Signifying sunshine and brightness, the yellow hat represents optimism (Gross, 1998). When wearing a yellow hat, the learner's task is to conduct a positive and constructive assessment of the given circumstances. Gross (1998) explained, "Effectiveness is the aim of yellow hat constructive thinking" (para. 6), from which "concrete proposals and suggestions result" (para. 6). Yellow hat thinkers explore the value and benefit of any situation (The de Bono Group, LLC, n.d.b).

The black hat. Focused on negative assessment, the black hat represents the devil's advocate (The de Bono Group, LLC, n.d.b). When wearing the black hat, students are responsible for forming judgments (The de Bono Group, LLC, n.d.b). In other words black hat wearers have to identify dangers and difficulties as they examine the ways in which things could go awry (The de Bono Group, LLC, n.d.b). The de Bono Group, LLC (n.d.b) cautions that the black hat is the most powerful and possibly the most useful hat yet can be detrimental if overused. Gross (1998) added, "Black hat thinking should not be used to cover negative feelings, which should make use of the red hat. In the case of new ideas, the yellow hat should always be used before the black hat" (para. 7).

The green hat. The green hat signifies creativity and innovation (Gross, 1998). When wearing a green hat, the learner generates new ideas and fresh perspectives (Gross, 1998). Green hat thinkers explore possibilities and alternatives to existing concepts (The de Bono Group, LLC, n.d.b). They purposefully express new and perhaps divergent perceptions of a given circumstance (The de Bono Group, LLC, n.d.b).

The blue hat. The blue hat thinker is akin to a facilitator. The learner wearing a blue hat manages the thinking process and is responsible for ensuring each participating thinker follows the roles and guidelines involved with *The Six Thinking Hats* technique (The de Bono Group, LLC, n.d.b).

Practical Application

The Six Thinking Hats technique emphasizes a parallel thinking process and is best employed in learning environments where team productivity, communication, problem solving, and both critical and creative thinking are necessary (The de Bono Group, LLC, n.d.b). University instructors can employ *The Six Thinking Hats* technique in large whole-group forums and in smaller team forums. The technique can be very effective and have the greatest instructional impact when instructors first provide students with a practical, problem-based learning (PBL) experience and then challenge teams of students to apply course content and approach the problem collaboratively, with each team member fulfilling the role of one of the six thinking hats. Members on smaller teams can wear multiple hats, provided each team has all colored thinking hats represented. Teams can convene and debrief, thereby ensuring triple-loop learning for all involved parties. The value of discussion questions, case study explorations, and PBL experiences increases with the use of *The Six Thinking Hats* technique because students are challenged to recognize and understand the full complexity of course content and its application to the real world.

Requisite knowledge for successful application. To utilize *The Six Thinking Hats* technique effectively, instructors need to model the use of the technique for students and then offer guided practice in either whole group or team settings. Thereafter, instructors need to monitor students' independent application of the technique and be prepared to facilitate the use of the technique by proposing leading questions as necessary. Careful advance planning of problem-based learning experiences related to course content is essential.

Benefits. Students who are able to use the technique learn how to examine problems, decisions, and opportunities in a systematic manner (The de Bono Group, LLC, n.d.b). Learning team meetings can be more productive and shorter as a result (The de Bono Group, LLC, n.d.b). Conflict is reduced in learning team and whole-group settings where the participants utilize *The Six Thinking Hats* technique (The de Bono Group, LLC, n.d.b). Learning team and whole-group meetings become more results oriented, thereby motivating learner participation (The de Bono Group, LLC, n.d.b).

Limitations and assumptions. The use of *The Six Thinking Hats* technique has its limitations, and its value is based on a number of basic assumptions. The technique's effectiveness is limited by student attendance and the quality of student participation. The related assumption is that students will be intrinsically motivated, present for, and committed to the collaborative teaming process and the role(s) they serve within it. The length of a course may also serve as a limitation. The related assumption is that the length of any given course will afford instructors the time needed to model the technique and provide students with adequate guided and independent practice in the context of the curriculum.

Relevance to Higher Education

The Six Thinking Hats technique has been utilized in higher education with great success. Colleges and universities nation-wide have reported noteworthy advancements in course deliv-ery following the use of *The Six Thinking Hats* technique in their instructional programming. Instructional leaders from varied degree programs, specifically those in business management, are beginning to institute the use of *The Six Thinking Hats* technique as a key component of the curriculum.

For example, instructors teaching courses offered at Luther College in Decorah, Iowa, have incorporated *The Six Thinking Hats* since the late 1990s (de Bono Consulting, n.d.). By 2003, Luther College offered courses in which *The Six Thinking Hats* was part of their core curricula (de Bono Consulting, n.d.). Additional courses offered at Luther College incorporating the technique were offered in 2004 and then again in 2005, signifying the success of the technique's application. According to Dr. Schweizer, professor of Management, Economics, and Business Development at Luther College, instructors who use specific techniques to prompt crea-tivity, such as *The Six Thinking Hats*, position students "to be ready, willing, and able to learn continually after leaving school" (de Bono Consulting, n.d., para. 5).

Instructors in the Department of Educational Psychology at Texas A&M have also incorporated *The Six Thinking Hats* technique into their instructional programming with great success. Dr. Juntune, professor of graduate-level courses in gifted education and undergraduate courses in creativity and child development at Texas A&M, uses de Bono's (1999) techniques (including *The Six Thinking Hats*) because she feels the skills gained through their application can be utilized universally across all fields of study at the university level, "including engineering, education, psychology, agriculture, business, and architecture" (de Bono Consulting, n.d., para. 8). Juntune (n.d.) also believes that students gaining experience with *The Six Thinking Hats* technique will experience advantages in the job market because such training will add value to their resumes (de Bono Consulting, n.d.).

In addition Joy Rupp, the executive director of Human Resources Development at Rose State College in Oklahoma "has established an initiative to include critical thinking, via *The Six Thinking Hats*, in every syllabus and workshop" (de Bono Consulting, n.d., para. 11). According to Rupp (n.d.) the use of *The Six Thinking Hats* technique has significantly strengthened communication and has resulted in improved decision making, fewer instances of miscommunication, and more efficient problem solving (de Bono Consulting, n.d.). According to Rupp (n.d.) *The Six Thinking Hats* technique "at Rose State College is as needed as the walls that support the buildings. Without the walls the ceiling would crash down. Thinking of going back to our old ways without de Bono Thinking Systems would feel like the ceiling falling in on us" (para. 14).

Future Research Directions

Instructors, administrators, or independent researchers seeking opportunities for qualitative study may wish to explore how certain demographics, such as age, cultural diversity, workplace experience, and educational background influence a student's receptiveness to *The Six Thinking Hats* technique. Quantitative researchers may wish to examine what correlation, if any, exists between the use of *The Six Thinking Hats* technique and students' mastery level(s) of course content on varied assessments. The mixed-methods researcher may wish to pursue both avenues of suggested research.

Conclusion

Past and present, Western culture depends on the use of critical thinking (de Bono Group, LLC, n.d.a). In business, education, and elsewhere, being constructive and creative is more than just desirable—it is essential. Individuals must be skillful communicators and astute problem solvers to succeed in a world marked by rapid growth and accelerating change. By engaging in parallel or constructive thinking whereby each thinker safely and freely shares thoughts in parallel with the thoughts of others (The de Bono Group, LLC, n.d.a), individuals increase their productivity and maximize opportunities for learning. *The Six Thinking Hats* technique is a powerful proven practice for promoting and enhancing students' use of critical and creative thinking practices. The technique is one that instructors of online, on-ground, and hybrid-model classes can use to maximize learning and collaboration via a constructivist approach.

References

Bailin, S., Case, R., Coombs, J., & Daniels, L. (1999). Conceptualizing critical thinking. *J. Curriculum Studies, 31*(3), 285-302.

Brandon, A. F., & All, A. C. (2010). Constructivism theory analysis and application to curricula. *Nursing Education Perspectives, 31*(2), 89-92.

Celuch, K., & Slama, M. (1999). Teaching critical thinking skills for the 21st century: An advertising principles case study. *Journal of Education for Business, 74*(3), 134.

de Bono, E. (1999). *Six thinking hats.* Boston, MA: Little, Brown and Company.

de Bono Consulting. (n.d.). *Innovation in higher education with the Edward de Bono thinking systems.* Retrieved from http://www.debonoconsulting.com/Innovation-in-Higher-Education-With-the-Edward-de-Bono-Thinking-Systems.asp

Edgar, D. W., Faulkner, P., Franklin, E., Knobloch, N. A., & Morgan, A. C. (2008). Creative thinking: Opening up a world of thought. *Techniques: Connecting Education & Careers, 83*(4), 46-49.

Elder, L., & Paul, R. (2002). Critical thinking: Distinguishing between inferences and assumptions. *Journal of Developmental Education, 25*(3), 34.

Facione, P. (1998). *Critical thinking: What it is and why it counts.* Retrieved from http://www.calpress.com/pdf_files/what&why.pdf

Gross, R. (1998, Summer). Peak performance: The six thinking hats. *Armed Forces Controller, 43*(3), 38-39.

Harris, R. (1998). *Introduction to creative thinking.* Retrieved from *VirtualSalt* at http://www.virtualsalt.com/crebook1.htm

Jarrett, J. L. (1993). The place of art in the education of feeling. *Arts Education Policy Review, 95*(2), paras. 1-40.

Kirby, G. R., & Goodpaster, J. R. (2002). *Thinking* (3rd ed.) Upper Saddle River, NJ: Prentice Hall.

Mandel, D. R. (2003). Counterfactuals, emotions, and context. *Cognition and Emotion, 17*(1), 139.

Merriam-Webster's pocket dictionary. (1995). Springfield, MA: Merriam-Webster.

Norton, J. L. (1994). Creative thinking and the reflective practitioner. *Journal of Instructional Psychology, 21*(2), 139-147.

Schunk, D. H. (2004). *Learning theories: An educational perspective (4th ed.).* Columbus: Pearson.

The de Bono Group, LLC. (n.d.a). *Parallel thinking.* Retrieved from http://www.debonogroup.com/parallel_thinking.htm

The de Bono Group, LLC. (n.d.b). *Six thinking hats.* Retrieved from http://www.debonogroup.com/six_thinking_hats.php

Vaill, P. (1996). *Learning as a way of being: Strategies for survival in a world of permanent white water.* San Francisco, CA: Jossey-Bass.

Van Gelder, T. (2005). Teaching critical thinking. *College Teaching, 53*(1), 41-46.

Yang, Y. C., & Chou, H. (2008). Beyond critical thinking skills: Investigating the relationship between critical thinking skills and dispositions through different online instructional strategies. *British Journal of Educational Technology, 39*(4), 666-684.

Teaching Project Management Effectively: The Direct Path from Class to Work

Jennifer Diamond, MA, PMP, RMP
City University of Seattle
School of Management

Abstract

Many adult learners approach higher education as a career strategy to increase applied skills as well as achieve a recognizable credential. Through clear and early disclosure of a carefully designed course path that includes individual and team objectives, assignments, and expectations, the instructor can fulfill the obligation to create a learning environment in which students prepare for the workplace. Maintaining awareness of the students' needs for an efficient, effective and workplace-complementary learning environment also contributes to how the instructor operates in either the online or face-to-face classroom. Students of project management particularly require coursework that demonstrates, as well as defines, the discipline and pathway to work.

Introduction

Teaching working professionals begins with several key assumptions:

- Instructors collaborate in the learning process with students.
- Students invest in applied learning with the intent to use new knowledge in the workplace either immediately or in the near future.
- Instructors deliver information in an engaging and absorbable manner, relating the content and learning experience to how the knowledge will be applied.
- Students apply adult decision making to their dedication of time and attention to class participation.

These assumptions establish the paradigm whereby the instructor supports the self-directed learning journey of the student. The requirements of the course experience mimic requirements for information exchange and performance management in the workplace, including clear expectations, effective and efficient communication of information with frequent checks for understanding, a fast path from learning to doing, and expectations of accountability.

Even more than other management-related disciplines, project management coursework requires a specific balancing between theoretical concepts and actual practice and between individual and team activities. Managing projects is not an individual activity; instead, group results define project success. Practice of project management concepts therefore requires team application, both online and in the classroom. Each project management student also requires individual support and opportunities for enhancing his or her skills as a project participant and as a leader.

Understanding the Expectations of the Workplace

The assumptions under which instructors operate now must acknowledge students as peer adults. "…The vast majority of college and university students are "non-traditional"—largely working adults struggling to balance jobs, families, and education" (Stokes, 2008, p. 1). These students are engaging in the shared objectives of the class and are collaborating with the instructor to create the learning environment. The needs adult students have in their educational environment mirror the needs employees have in their professional environments, including the ability to work collaboratively.

The processes and behaviors in a well-performing working environment can be characterized by the presence of feedback mechanisms; active engagement with workers to manage performance; and accountability for the effectiveness of how performance is managed and achieved.

> In effective organizations, managers and employees have been practicing good performance management naturally all their lives, executing each key component process well. Goals are set and work is planned routinely. Progress toward those goals is measured and employees get feedback. High standards are set, but care is also taken to develop the skills needed to reach them. Formal and informal rewards are used to recognize the behavior and results that accomplish the mission. All five component processes working together and supporting each other achieve natural, effective performance management" (U.S. Office of Performance Management, 2011, para. 7-8).

Setting goals and communicating expectations contribute to employee performance by providing clarity and direction. Individual goal setting in the form of the job description is the professional equivalent of a course syllabus, providing the educational path to performance success. "At its most basic level, preparing job descriptions can help an organization clarify what it really wants to accomplish and how it wants to go about it. At the same time, employees understand what is expected of them" (Marino, 2005, para. 7). The role of the job description is not limited to just performance standards, just as the course plan is not just about class assignments. Job descriptions "can be extremely useful in delegating work and documenting assignments, helping to clarify missions, establishing performance requirements, counseling people on career and advancement opportunities… suggesting ways to enrich the work experience" (Marino, 2005, para. 2). Similarly, students expect instructor-provided course tools to include details and context about the learning environment to be effective and to stimulate learning.

Workplace goal setting does not stop with the individual and neither can the classroom experience. The nature of work, as a team activity, must also be taken into account. According to Peter Senge (1990), "…Almost all important decisions are now made in teams, either directly or through the need for teams to translate individual decision into action" (p. 236). The trend toward teamwork also extends to how organizations are structuring themselves around that work. "Organizations are becoming more and more project-based. Flat, flexible organizational structures are becoming the norm, replacing the hierarchical, bureaucratic structures of the past" (Flannes & Levin, 2005, p. 9). Because workplace expectations now often require the skills and ability to participate effectively on teams to execute project objectives, course design and the management of the learning environment should also include group-based learning and practice.

Creating a learning environment for working professional students that reflects the combined team and individual performance expectations in the workplace requires a holistic understanding of what is needed to create that environment. Comparing Billington's (1996) seven key characteristics of highly effective adult learning programs and Lewis' (2007) five conditions in which project participants can control their own work, reveals alignment between the learning and work environments on the basis of the three characteristics of effective performance management: a feedback system; a participative and engaging environment; and ownership and accountability for the outcome.

Characteristics of Highly Effective Adult Learning Programs (Billington, 1996):	For a team member to have self-control, five conditions must exist (Lewis, 2007):
• Students feel safe, supported, recognized for uniqueness, abilities and life achievements. • Experimentation, creativity and intellectual freedom are valued. • Faculty members respect students as peer adults. • Self-directed learning and student accountability for defining and meeting learning needs are part of the learning program. • The program maintains "optimal pacing" to stimulate and challenge. • Active interaction and practice support theory. • Feedback mechanisms allow collaboration between students and faculty to make ongoing adjustments.	• The team member has a clear definition of the work and its purpose on the project. • The team member has a plan for how the work will be done. • The team member has the required skills and has been given the required resources to be successful. • The team member receives timely feedback to measure and adjust performance. • The team member has enough authority to take action to correct deviations from the work plan.

The commonalities of feedback, engagement, and accountability are the basis of aligning the classroom with the workplace. For the project management students in particular, the classroom needs to reflect workplace expectations of being a performing team member and a performing leader as well. "As organizations become flatter, the project manager's interactions with internal and external stakeholders increase, calling for an enhanced ability to apply people skills to a greater variety of people and personalities" (Flannes & Levin, 2005, p. 9). An additional workplace requirement for a project manager to serve as a leader requires that this also be met in the learning environment by preparing a student to serve in that role.

For project management students, the three core workplace environment characteristics are joined by a fourth, a focus on adaptable leadership. These form the foundation upon which the instructor teaches the techniques and practices of the project management discipline.

> The project manager's two major functions are to integrate all elements of the project system and provide leadership to the project team. His or her effectiveness will depend on conceptual, human, and negotiating skills as well as, to a lesser extent, on technical skills (Goodwin, 1993, para. 1).

Teaching the connection between adaptable leadership and specific project management skills, processes and practices is an important aspect to enable students to fully practice as a project manager. The Project Management Institute (2004), as a recognized source of standards for the project management discipline, articulates the need for managers to be able to analyze a situation and respond with project management tools and techniques in a way that meets the unique needs of that situation.

> The increasing acceptance of project management indicates that the application of appropriate knowledge, processes, skills, tools, and techniques can have a significant impact on project success… "Good practice" means there is general agreement that the application of these skills, tools, and techniques can enhance the chances of success over a wide range of projects. Good practice does not mean the knowledge described should always be applied uniformly to all projects; the organization and/or project

management team is responsible for determining what is appropriate for any given project (p. 3).

Aligning the Classroom with the Workplace

For project management students, the four central learning environment requirements—presence of feedback mechanisms, active engagement, accountability for results, and opportunity for adaptable leadership and practice—are similar to the expectations of other working professionals. Workplace learning is aimed at efficient skill augmentation, measuring the knowledge employees gain against the time and cost the company invests. This is the same analysis adult learners apply to their own education, measuring career value against the cost in time and tuition.

For instructors to be able to collaborate with project management students to create the learning environment they need, one additional workplace element needs to be applied, this time for the instructor. The management concept of "servant leadership," with its focus on service-oriented leading versus power-oriented leading, provides the construct for how to teach for value in this adaptive and responsive environment.

The seven key practices of servant leadership are self-awareness, listening, changing the pyramid, developing colleagues, coaching, not controlling, unleashing the energy and intelligence of others, and foresight (Keith, 2010, para. 6). Self-awareness and listening refers to the instructor's investment in feedback and engagement with students, including bringing a personal connection to the class and the content, adapting as needed to enhance the student experience, and adjusting to student expectations of the class. Changing the pyramid and developing colleagues remind an instructor to view students with respect as peer adults and developing professionals, maintaining the parallel with the workplace, and remaining mindful of the exchange of value for time and cost.

Coaching, instead of controlling, and unleashing the energy and intelligence of others, points to how the instructor designs courses to take the four required project management learning environment elements into account. In particular, creating a learning environment fostering adaptable leadership and application of project management techniques requires creativity to replicate the challenges of a workplace equivalent while fostering team and individual learning.

Instructors serving as collaborators with their project management students focus on how to meet the four core requirements of effective feedback, active engagement, accountability for results, and the opportunity to practice adaptive leadership and application of project management skills and techniques. The instructor puts this into practice, starting with course preparation and clear communication between students and the instructor, moving on to assessing and supporting learning of course material and then on to putting learning into action.

Setting the Stage with Open Communication

Beginning with the course materials, the instructor prepares the course plan, including learning objectives, reading and assignment schedules, grading rubrics, and applicable course policies and instructor expectations. Just as the workplace experience begins with goal setting through job descriptions and performance expectations, in class the instructor begins by giving the roadmap for the course. Opening feedback loops early, the instructor also solicits student input from the class, allowing the opportunity to refine both expectations of students and course details.

Clear communication in both language and form is a requirement in the working world and a core element of effective feedback. Course tools prepared in a way that meets workplace standards for clarity also reduce barriers to student learning and achievement, increasing the effectiveness of the course itself. Communication style drives learning efficiency as well and can provide clear feedback and contribute to effective engagement. The manner in which instructors use language to communicate with students can either enhance the learning process or slow it down. Heavy on experience and light on theoretical narrative, example-driven lectures and discussions create immediacy and enhance absorption. Using an approachable narrative style also communicates respect for students.

For project management students particularly, clarity in explaining concepts and examples demonstrates as well as instructs. Project management as a discipline requires that project managers teach team members how to participate on the projects they manage as part of the fourth workplace requirement to adapt leadership and project management technique.

The project management requirement to have the opportunity to practice adapting leadership drives more than just the way to present lectures. It drives how to design the course schedule. As expectations are set, course reading about theory needs to happen early so that application can follow. Team forming also needs to happen early so that the team can begin to function in advance of the due dates of team assignments. Setting those expectations at the outset of the class meets objectives of preparation and clear disclosure. This is also the time to confirm learning expectations from students and to meet them, if possible.

The course schedule in Table 1 is an example of communicating class expectations and displays a distillation of reading expectations, team and individual assignments, course schedules, and a grading schedule. Students appreciate a customized schedule, reducing confusion about deadlines, the simplest of barriers to course success and engagement.

All assignments are due Sunday night no later than midnight PST of each week.

Session	Dates (Bold is due date)	Text reading timing	Assignments (In addition to weekly participation)	Individual Assignment Points	Team Assignment Points	Participation Points	Total
Week 1	1/10-1/16	Part 1 Schein Part 1 DeLuca				1	1
Week 2	1/17-1/23	Part 2 Schein				3	3
Week 3	1/24-**1/30**	Part 2 DeLuca	Individual-The importance of org culture to project management	10		2	12
Week 4	1/31-**2/6**	Finish DeLuca	Team-Project Summary and Stakeholder Map		10	2	12
Week 5	2/7-2/13	Finish Schein				3	3
Week 6	2/14-2/20					3	3
Week 7	2/21-**2/27**		Individual-Political Savvy for Project Managers	20		2	22
Week 8	2/28-3/6					2	2
Week 9	3/7-**3/13**		Team-Definition of PM Approach to Stakeholders		20	2	22
Week 10	3/14-**3/20**		Final Course Distillation	20			20
				50	30	20	100

Table 1: Example of customized course schedule

Working in Teams

The core of projects is team work, and the core of teaching project management is teaching in teams. In the classroom environment, forming into learning teams as an early exercise establishes group expectations and relationships. Team members learn from each other and immediately experience team dynamics.

The instructor has a key role in facilitating team work. He or she needs to define assignments at the start of a class with an emphasis on clarity, but the job includes making sure teams can form around their project as an anchor for the rest of the class material, meeting requirements for feedback mechanisms, active engagement, and opportunity to adapt leadership. For the seminar or in-class environment, periodic team work, interspersed with lecture/discussion, allows the teams to apply each discussion topic on the spot. These intervals include working with each team individually to confirm understanding and to monitor the team dynamic as it develops. Each member of the team is studying to be the project manager, but in the classroom, leadership needs to be shared so that it can be part of the lesson for all students. Helping with guidelines on how to rotate leadership, close monitoring of how the team works, and providing for frequent delivery of results are ways that the instructor supports effective team behaviors.

The team assignments themselves encompass self-determination, creativity, fair distribution of work, and written and verbal communication, aligning with the objectives of the working environment. Teams should choose their own case for the course assignments, either a published fictional case or an actual project from a team member's workplace. The assignments might include creation of project management artifacts, preparation of written reports, and presentations. Such work has enough content to require each team member to contribute fully, sharing in accountability for results, and enough scope and range to require creative adaptation of course content to the team's chosen project.

As a strategy to support team effectiveness, the instructor should conform grading to the performance measurement standards in the work environment. Setting clear expectations includes the distribution of grade points between team work and individual work and team grading that earns team members the same grade with appropriate exceptions. This also reinforces the intent to match workplace measures of shared accountability.

Online or virtual teams are a reality in the workplace and are also an appropriate structure for online project management courses. The use of electronic team workspaces and collaboration tools contributes to making online teaming in class an effective learning environment. The instructor observes interaction in online team rooms and can give feedback as needed.

Evaluation and Feedback

In the workplace clear expectations and collaboration are part of project management, and team products are meant to be shared. In the project management classroom, students can learn from each other by reviewing assignments posted to a common online forum. Individual and team analyses or papers make excellent learning tools, as each student can see how his or her work compares to efforts of other students. Writing quality, analytical maturity, and overall level of work appear to rise once students can see what their fellow students are producing. While students can be initially resistant to this approach, they quickly see that the work of fellow students can foster great discussion and growth.

The instructor can support the feeling of student safety in the classroom by grading assignments and giving feedback privately. The varying quality of student work visible in open team spaces is self-evident. The instructor can provide general announcements about that quality, offering suggestions or tips and techniques about the subject matter, but actual grades and specific feedback to each student are private. Once again, this aligns with the workplace, where work products and team performance feedback are reviewed publicly but individual performance feedback is usually discussed privately.

Conclusion

Working adult students use their education as a career tool to advance their skills and abilities in the workplace. Adult students come to the classroom to learn the methods of their discipline in a safe environment that reflects what they experience in their jobs, including the core workplace requirements of feedback mechanisms, active engagement, and accountability for results. Project management students also have the additional requirement of a learning environment that supports their practice of adapting leadership and application of their project management discipline in preparation for the demands of their workplaces.

Instructors who follow the guidelines of servant leadership teach with clarity and responsiveness to frame the class and then focus on empowering self-directed learning and adaptation through team and individual work. The collaboration between instructor and students is based on respect, an understanding of the demands of the working world, and a willingness to engage in an exchange of ideas to add value to the learning.

References

Billington, D. (1996). *Seven characteristics of highly effective adult learning programs.* Retrieved from http://education.jhu.edu/newhorizons/lifelonglearning/workplace/articles/characteristics/

Flannes, S. W., & Levin, G. (2005). *Essential people skills for project managers.* Vienna, VA: Management Concepts, Inc.

Goodwin, R. S. C. (1993, July/August). Skills required of effective project managers. *Journal of Management in Engineering, 9*(3), 217-226.

Keith, K. (2010). *The key practices of servant leaders.* Retrieved from http://www.greenleaf.org/whatissl/TheCharacteristicsOfServant-Leaders.pdf

Lewis, J. P. (2007). *Mastering project management: Applying advanced concepts to systems thinking, control & evaluation, resource allocation.* New York, NY: McGraw-Hill.

Marino, M. (2005, February). Understanding the importance of job descriptions: How to put them in writing. *Public Relations Tactics, 12*(2), 26. Retrieved from http://proquest.umi.com. proxy.cityu.edu/pqdweb?index=34&did=800061771&Src hMode=3&sid=1&Fmt=3&VInst=PROD&VType=PQD&RQT =309&VName=PQD&TS=13020717

Project Management Institute (2008). *A guide to the project man-agement body of knowledge* (4th ed.). Newtown, PA: Project Management Institute.

Senge, P. (1990). *The fifth discipline: The art and practice of the learn-ing organization.* New York, NY: Currency Doubleday.

Stokes, P. J. (2008, May 14). *Hidden in plain sight: Adult learners forge a new tradition in higher education.* Retrieved from http:// www2.ed.gov/about/bdscomm/list/hiedfuture/reports/ stokes.pdf

U.S. Office of Personnel Management (2011). *Performance man-agement overview.* Retrieved from http://www.opm.gov/ perform/overview.asp.

Inspiring Action for Sustainable Business: A Five-Phase Approach

Kurt Kirstein, EdD
Jennifer Diamond, MA
City University of Seattle
School of Management

Abstract

Given the serious nature of environmental and social problems that currently face the world, it is imperative that business programs offered by higher education institutions provide a balanced approach to educating future business leaders. Part of a successful approach to business education will involve inspiring a sense of urgency among students regarding the needs of many aspects of society. This chapter will describe a sustainable business course intended to teach students the importance of leading businesses that balance economic, environmental, and social concerns. Presented in five phases, a detailed description of the structure of the course is provided. The concluding sections of the chapter contain an analysis of what was learned from the course design process along with a discussion of sustainability education issues that need addressing in the future.

Introduction

Traditional business education has focused, nearly exclusively, on economic factors where students are taught strategies to maximize profits. However, decades of experience have shown that a singular focus on economic factors produces business leaders who carry these perspectives into the community and run organizations that frequently maximize profits at the expense of the environment and society. A new approach to business education is needed to ensure that students understand that running a successful business involves more than the short term economic factors that often define an organization. Increasingly consumers are paying attention to the environmental impacts of companies and are using this information in purchasing decisions. This is becoming an important driver in business strategy.

Changes in the way business is conducted cannot come quickly enough. The world is in need of a new approach to organizational leadership. Both business and academia can be at the forefront of these changes with intentional action. Business must choose strategies founded in social and environmental responsibility while higher education institutions must prepare the drivers of these strategies.

This chapter will introduce a course on Environmental and Corporate Responsibility that was designed and delivered at City University of Seattle in 2010. First, the need for the course will be reviewed, followed by a description of its five phases addressing specific outcomes that the course designers intended. The chapter will conclude with an analysis of the extent to which the course was successful in accomplishing its goals.

Background

Only recently has sustainability—or its commonly accepted synonym, sustainable development—entered mainstream consciousness in the United States (Bardaglio & Putman, 2009). While experts focus on the dangers of carbon emissions and the many possible bleak outcomes that await us if emissions go on unchecked, sustainable development entails much more than carbon. Several of the frameworks currently in vogue regarding sustainability include the Global Reporting Initiative (GRI), the Natural Step (TNS), and the Triple Bottom Line (TBL). All three point out that sustainable practices involve the use and disposal of the earth's resources; the impacts that we are having on air, water, and the planet's ability to regenerate itself; and the social aspects of our actions including fair labor, community impacts, and economic well-being.

While many look to business as the agent of change in regard to sustainable development, academic institutions are also well suited to take on such challenges (Rappaprot & Creighton, 2007). Universities around the US are adopting the message of sustainable development in two key ways. First, many have undergone significant efforts to reduce carbon footprints, such as eliminating waste sent to landfills, limiting resource utilization, and even planning new campus buildings that meet acceptable green building standards. Second, a number of institutions around the country now offer academic programs aimed at educating future business leaders about the need to run their organizations in a sustainable manner. The hope is that a sufficient number of graduates will get the message and will begin to help American companies change course in their future business strategies.

An urgent need for a change in course seems apparent. All plausible projections indicate that civilization is on the cusp of exceeding the planet's ability to support it (Flannery, 2009; Senge, Smith, Kruschwitz, Laur, & Schley, 2008). In late 2007 Rajendra Pachauri, director of the Intergovernmental Panel on Climate Change, said, "What we do in the next two to three years will determine our future. This is the defining moment" (Pachauri, as cited in Friedman, 2009, p. 43). Dumaine (2008) cited research from the

Pentagon that described famine, widespread rioting, and even war to be expected as nations fight to defend or expand their dwindling supplies of food, water, and energy. Despite its wealth and military power, the US will not be shielded from the impacts of these events.

Yet while a pressing need exists to address issues related to sustainable development, too few academic institutions are answering the call, and those that do are often providing only rudimentary coverage of these topics. Academic business programs that have traditionally focused solely on the economic aspects of business are slow to change (Weybrecht, 2010). This is further complicated by the fact that nearly 45 percent of the courses in business programs are taught by adjunct faculty who do not have the connection to campus-wide sustainability initiatives that their fulltime, resident counterparts do (Kirk & Spector, 2009). Many part-time faculty members tend to be practitioners hired to bring field-related expertise to their courses. Their relationship to their universities rarely extends beyond the requirements of their courses. Hence, campus-wide sustainability initiatives have little impact on what they teach. Therefore, even in institutions where sustainability is a priority, a significant number of business courses may not address it.

Student Motivation to Learn About Sustainability

In 2009 a poll conducted by the Pew Research Center ranked the issues that Americans cited as the highest priorities for that year. At the bottom of the list of twenty concerns was climate change; nineteen other issues ranked above it, including terrorism, energy, deficit reduction, and even moral decline. Gertner (2009) points to research to suggest that environmental issues and climate change, indicated as pressing by many experts, are viewed by many Americans as distant problems both in time and space. Many Americans believe that these are issues happening elsewhere and that they can be dealt with in the future. Even when confronted with direct evidence, as in rural Alaska where evidence of climate change is present, the issue remains a distant concern.

Goleman (2009) points out that our current way of life has removed and desensitized us to many of the traditional threats to our survival. For the most part, we are safe from the dangers posed by the environment. We rarely worry about freezing, starving, or being consumed by a predator. The downside of this is that we are lulled into a false sense of security and our separation from the environment has allowed us to make short-term decisions that collectively have catastrophic long-term impacts. Due to the long-term nature of the threats related to environmental and social problems and our perception that they pose no real, direct danger to us, we feel safe in ignoring them.

Additionally, most business schools provide a nearly exclusive focus on the financial, economic, logistical, and strategic factors associated with a traditional business education. Most students expect this type of traditional focus in their business programs as, in many cases, the primary motivation for attending business school is to earn a degree that will teach them how to enhance their economic well-being. Given these factors, how can academic institutions work to expand the perspectives of their students in regard to sustainability? How can they get them to see the need to focus as much of their energy on social justice and environmental protection as they traditionally have on economic factors? Is there a way to link the environmental and social aspects of sustainability to economic drivers to ensure students can see a clear business case for all three?

Delivering Sustainability Education

In 2008 the School of Management at City University of Seattle set out to incorporate sustainable business into its MBA program. To accomplish this task, four sustainability courses were added to a program core allowing students to specialize in Sustainable Business. Students could also earn a graduate certificate in Sustainable Business. The goals of the program were to introduce students to the problems that require a sustainable approach and then provide them with a set of tools to prepare them for the unprecedented challenges they would likely face as future business leaders.

The first version of the program fell short, as it focused too much on specific management behaviors. It failed to make the case for the importance of sustainability, and students could not see the urgency; there was not enough of a push to get students to shift away from the economic paradigm. In 2010 a small but significant change was made to the program. The first sustainability course was replaced with a new course that did a better job presenting a sense of urgency for social and environmental issues. It was based on a number of intended student outcomes. In this course students were to:

- Evaluate the various environmental problems including pollution, waste management, and global warming along with the drivers that are causing these problems as they relate to business.
- Assess the systems, both locally and internationally, that have caused significant environmental problems. Describe the role of companies and individuals in contributing to these problems.
- Explain the consequences of a failure to address environmental problems on both a local and global level.
- Explain the concept of sustainability as it applies to business, society, and the environment.
- Demonstrate how environmental problems have an impact on social justice.
- Analyze arguments concerning what the role of business should be in addressing environmental concerns.

These outcomes were to be achieved through five distinct course stages, each of which is described in the sections to follow.

Stage 1: Creating a Sense of Urgency

For students to view the future of business in a new way, they needed to be made aware of the severity of the problems that the world currently faces while understanding the extent to which those problems could impact them, their families, and their communities in a much more immediate sense. They also needed to know the full scope of problems that were contributing to environmental decline and social injustice. Additionally, while knowledge regarding climate change seems to be increasing in the business community, it is only a small part of the challenges that will require a new business paradigm. There was also an urgent need for students to understand issues concerning pollution, disease, resource utilization, biodiversity destruction, and the extent to which problems such as these were contributing to the decline in the quality of life for an increasing number of the world's population. All of these topics were of significant interest to the instructional designers at City University as they created the first phase of the new sustainability course.

Myriad resources are available to present the large number of social and environmental problems that are an outgrowth of our traditional approach to business. The instructional designer's choice of *The Necessary Revolution* (2008) by Senge, Smith, Kruschwitz, Laur, and Schley was made largely based on the first four chapters, which present a comprehensive review of a number of environmental and social problems as well as the actions and mindsets that created them. To further establish a sense of urgency, the students were asked to select an environmental problem and conduct an in-depth analysis to ensure that they understood the complexity of the systems that created and sustained these issues. The goal of this assignment was to solidify students' understanding of at least one serious environmental problem, and by sharing what they had learned, they were given the ability to expand the perspectives of each other on a number of sustainability-related fronts. From the syllabus the requirements of the assignment were as follows:

> Students should select a problem and conduct a high-level review of books, articles, or the Internet to identify the way in which the problem results from the actions of corporations or specific industry practices. The successful paper will use concise and clear writing, with tables and graphics

as appropriate; describe a corporate practice that damages the environment; describe the type of damage (i.e., damage to forests, communities, etc.); describe the degree of damage; discuss potential consequences if the problem is not addressed; and offer alternative sustainable business practices to replace the current damaging practice.

The activities in this first stage helped set a baseline of understanding regarding the types of problems that warranted urgent action on the part of current and future business leaders. They also underscored the need for a different direction in business and presented preliminary information regarding the value of a sustainable approach in organizational leadership. Another goal of this phase was to raise concern on the part of the students as they began to get a clearer picture of the state of the world and the ways in which businesses were contributing to these conditions.

Stage 2: A Need for Action

The next stage built upon the first; it was intended to demonstrate the likely outcomes of current environmental and social problems if the world fails to act in a decisive way. To this end students were asked to select one current environmental problem and conduct an analysis of what was likely to happen should no action be taken to resolve the given problem. The list of environmental problems found in Senge et al. (2008) provided a good starting point; however, students were welcome to select a problem from another source. The assignment asked students to examine topics such as coastal erosion, water pollution, or agricultural decline over a span of twenty to one hundred years. They were then asked to seek supporting secondary research regarding their selected problem and to cite sources as they produced an impacts paper that provided an assessment of the likely conditions that would result from a failure to act. From the syllabus the text of this assignment included the following requirements:

Researchers are calling for swift and decisive action to avoid many of the worst potential impacts of environmental issues. Many have predicted severe impacts to coast lines, water supplies and agriculture, just to name a few. The problem is that the general public is largely shielded from any discussions of the potential impacts of environmental problems as these subjects are not popular discussion topics in the media. Yet, understanding the likely impact of inactivity is a key in motivating people to take action.

Through this assessment, students will select an environmental problem and find and summarize scholarly sources that project what might happen in 20, 50, or 100 years if no action is taken to rectify the chosen problem. Students should be specific in their projections and should cite their sources. The question to be answered here is: "Based on current research, what is the world likely to look like if we do nothing to solve a selected environmental problem?"

To supplement this investigation, students read Flannery's (2009) *Now or Never*, which underscores the need for action and highlights the dangers associated with inactivity. Flannery also provides some specific measures that societies can take in crafting responses to climate change. He concludes his book with a number of perspectives provided by well-known individuals from the fields of environmentalism, business, and ethics.

This stage of the course was intended to ensure that students had a fuller understanding of the seriousness of the problems they were likely to face as future business leaders. Flannery's arguments also provide an element of hope, allowing students to realize their ability to have a real impact on these problems. This also served as a transition into the next stage of the course.

Stage 3: Establishing a Position

As business students gained knowledge about environmental and social issues, the hope was that they would be inspired to act. Yet such action was likely to meet resistance in a number of different forms, such as disinterest or outright opposition. It was important to help students establish a position on these issues and to do so in a way that was genuine and natural. Once students established positions, it would be helpful to show them how to strengthen their views and stand firm in the face of potential opposition.

To this end students were asked to identify an argument put forward by someone in favor of or opposed to environmental action and to conduct a critical analysis of that argument to assess its validity. Students were asked to analyze the argument and the supporting evidence as part of an effort to determine the extent to which the argument was based in fact or opinion. The goal was to help students strengthen their skills at identifying the many methods that are used to obscure the issues related to sustainability and to counter those methods when making a case in favor of sustainable action. The text of the assignment was as follows:

> Much of the reason for the lack of response to environmental issues can be attributed to "experts" who argue that these problems don't really exist. The most common argument has been that global warming is a myth or that it is a naturally occurring process. Corporations and governments have cited such arguments to support their decisions to take no action in response to environmental problems even though the vast majority of the scientific community holds a different position.

> Knowing how to analyze the various arguments can be a key in understanding and analyzing them. It is important for students to be able to dissect an argument, analyze its validity, check its sources, and then offer an informed response in support of or against the position of the argument's authors. This exercise will allow students the chance to identify a book, article, or broadcast where an argument is made for or against the need for action to resolve environmental issues. The student is to deconstruct that argument and analyze its components for validity and critical

support. Then the student should show why the argument is or is not valid and offer a response to the authors of the argument.

At the same time that students were conducting their analyses of arguments, they were reading McDonough and Braungart's (2002) *Cradle to Cradle*. This was in contrast to the content from the two previous books that discussed the dire threats posed by environmental and social problems. It was time to turn students' attention to possible solutions. McDonough and Braungart's work presented new ways of thinking that was solutions-focused without drilling too deep into specifics. The goal was to begin to get students to think about solutions that they could be a part of as future business leaders. This transitioned into the final book of the course, discussed below, that presented a number of solutions that companies around the world were taking as part of a new sustainable business paradigm.

Stage 4: Link to Social Justice

In its first three stages, the focus of the course was primarily to address environmental concerns. However, it has been noted in the literature that environmental concerns often lead to social problems that impact a society's quality of life (Rappaport & Creighton, 2007; Weybrecht, 2010). Additionally, it has been noted around the world that the environmental actions of rich countries have a disproportionate impact on poorer nations. These issues needed to be addressed to give students a fuller understanding of the social side of sustainability. Thus, an effort was made during the design of the course to directly link environmental problems with social concerns and to present those links within the framework of corporate social responsibility.

Not only was it important for students to understand social issues at a macro level, but they needed to understand how the decisions they might make as business leaders were likely to impact the communities and stakeholders that they interacted with. This was to offset any possible sense of removal. Once the students knew that their actions led to potentially negative impacts, they could then take a different approach in the leadership of their organizations. They were encouraged to be responsible business managers by having a fuller understanding of those who would be impacted by their actions. The description of the assignment included the following requirements:

> Many experts have pointed to the relationship between environmental problems and social injustices that often result directly from the decision and actions of polluters. A specific example would be a corporation that pollutes a river rendering it toxic to downstream residents who may depend on it for drinking water and irrigation. Many other examples have been cited, some of which have global implications.

> Students are to survey the literature to find such connections, analyze them and their impacts, and provide a 5-8 page summary in which they include arguments, provided by researchers and scholars, which show that social injustice can directly result from the creation and/or neglect of environmental problems. Areas of focus might include agriculture, access to clean water, fishing rights, coastal preservation, or food distribution networks. The goal of this assignment is to see the real impacts of environmental problems in human terms so it will be important to note the links between the environment and the conditions of those that depend on the environment.

As students were analyzing the ties between environmental problems and social impacts, they were also reading Dumaine's (2008) *The Plot to Save the Planet*, which begins with the same warnings as many other books on climate change but spends a majority of its effort presenting cases of companies around the world that are taking real action to address environmental problems. This was to show students that, despite the concerns that are impacting many different parts of the world, large, powerful organizations are recognizing the need for action. These organizations are embracing new operational methods that account for pressing environmental and social needs. The goal in including Dumaine's book was to show students that action can be taken not only on an individual basis but among large institutions as well.

Stage 5: A Call to Action

The final phase of the course was a call to action issued to students, giving them the opportunity to respond to environmental or social problems that they have identified in their own communities or organizations. It was an opportunity for them to take what they had learned from the books and assignments in the first four phases of the course and put it to use in an applied real-world fashion. The description of the assignment included the following requirements:

Corporate responsibility is demonstrated through actions and solutions. Understanding problems and their impacts, from environmental to social, is part of the work. Enacting the solution and shifting the trends is the rest.

Students are to identify a problem area with which they are familiar, in the workplace, industry or community, and provide a summary of that problem and its implications across the areas discussed by the course materials. Statements of implications need to be supported by literature corroborating either the student's specific conclusions or describing similar situations and related impacts.

Students will then identify an action approach including initiating steps that can be followed by participants in the workplace, industry or community. The action approach proposed needs to be supported by literature providing examples of this approach applied elsewhere along with the results. The goal of this assignment is to personalize the need to take action to improve environmental problems and identify ways to act on corporate social and environmental responsibility.

This assignment was the student's final project as they completed the course. For many it concluded the process of building a foundation in sustainable business that they could carry forward into further study of these topics.

As stated earlier the overall purpose of this course was to increase awareness of the fact that business is more than the traditional disciplines associated with academic business programs. The hope was that students would recognize the impacts of the environmental and social problems currently facing the world and would be compelled to take action with a newfound appreciation of the urgency of these issues. Not only did the course deliver what the designers hoped it would, but the work of the students exceeded all expectations.

Results

This course was offered for the first time in the fall of 2010 as the opening course for the sustainable business series offered to MBA and certificate students. It was offered in an online format through the university's Blackboard learning management system. As the course ran, it became clear through a number of indictors that it was going to be a success.

The first of these success indicators was the quality of the discussions occurring in the discussion boards. Students were actively engaged in contributing important content in their posts. A second indicator of success was the quality of the work that students were submitting through their assignments. They were engaged and willing to provide the type of effort necessary to generate high quality work. This level of quality was seen on a number of the assignments. As the course finished, students had the chance to submit evaluations which provided an additional indicator of success, showing positive remarks both in regard to the course and the instructor.

A major key to the success of this course was the instructor, who made sure students understood the significance of the course's content. Having an interest in sustainability, the instructor was able to contribute important suggestions and content both to the syllabus and to the Blackboard shell. Through these activities the instructor became an important part of the design team and created the final assignment to address the need to ask students to take action. Even more evident and important was the instructor's commitment to her students along with her understanding of the challenges they faced as they worked through topics that were likely to require them to change their fundamental approach to business. In a course that challenges students to this extent, a skilled instructor can make a substantial difference. In this particular case, the course evaluations underscored the success of the instructor with one student even referring to her as "inspiring."

Future Direction in Sustainability Education

Teaching business students about sustainability is challenging; some don't care, while many are simply focused on the traditional economic aspects of business. Still, a large portion of students have not had the opportunity to learn about sustainable business practices. Despite the urgency of problems that the world currently faces, the majority of businesses and universities continue to operate under a traditional business paradigm; they have yet to see the sustainability light. To do so requires overcoming two key challenges that have often plagued efforts to teach sustainable business in traditional programs.

The first challenge is the fact that most sustainable content in traditional business programs is contained within a single course or a group of courses. This approach falls short for students who either don't get enough exposure to these concepts or who choose not to take those particular courses. A different approach to business program design is needed. Given the importance of sustainability to the future of business, it should be fully integrated throughout the entire business curriculum. Moving forward, issues of sustainability are going to impact accounting, marketing, leadership, operation, logistics, etc., and it should be included as part of all of these courses.

The second challenge comes from the fact that sustainability has traditionally been viewed as the antithesis of successful business. It has often been regarded as something for business to contend with or find a way to avoid. Many have seen it as a costly burden that impacts potential profits and creates unnecessary expenses. However, as Hitchcock and Willard (2009) point out, there is a clear business case for sustainability. These practices can save money, generate profits from new business ventures, and can position a company as socially responsible, which is becoming an increasing part of the criteria that consumers are using to choose products. There are real financial and economic benefits to attending to the environment and society as a whole. This presents an opportunity to integrate what has previously been seen as two competing forces into a singular approach to business that shows students an integrated way to respect all parts of the triple bottom line.

Conclusion

A key to educating future business leaders in regards to sustainability issues is to first establish a sense of urgency relative to the problems that we face. Once that urgency is established, students can begin to shift their focus toward solutions and new business paradigms that respect the economic, environmental, and social aspects that are a part of business now and will continue to be into the future. According to Pies, Beckmann, and Hielsher (2010), the role of business in society is to contribute to the solution of complex social problems. Thus, business education should teach management competencies to enable future managers to meet these societal demands. Academic institutions have a responsibility to prepare their students for all of the challenges they will face in the future. The traditional approach to business education simply no longer fits. It's time for a new model that is better matched to the needs of today's global community.

The experts are saying that our world is in trouble. We need to take immediate action to protect our air, water, land, and the many biospheres on which we depend from further degradation at the hands of businesses operating around the world. Given that the urgency of these problems is likely to increase in severity throughout this century, it is of paramount importance that academic programs fully prepare future business managers with the skills to lead their organizations with a balanced approach. Even when they are aware of the need to do so, academic and business leaders often cannot break from the traditional economic focus. The irony is that by focusing only on economic aspects and failing to respect those related to the environment and society, business and higher education are placing all three in jeopardy.

References

Bardaglio, P., & Putman, A. (2009). *Boldly sustainable: Hope and opportunity for higher education in the age of climate change.* Washington, DC: National Association of College and University Business Officers.

Dumaine, B. (2008). *The plot to save the planet: How visionary entrepreneurs and corporate titans are creating real solutions to global warming.* New York, NY: Three Rivers Press.

Flannery, T. (2009). *Now or never: Why we must act now to end climate change and create a sustainable future.* New York, NY: Atlantic Monthly Press.

Friedman, T. L. (2008). *Hot, flat and crowded: Why we need a green revolution and how it can renew America.* New York, NY: Farrar, Straus and Giroux.

Gertner, J. (2009, April). Why isn't the brain green? *The New York Times.* Retrieved November 6, 2010, from https://www.nytimes.com/2009/04/19/magazind/19Science-t.html?_r=1&pagewanted=print

Goleman, D. (2009). *Ecological intelligence: How knowing the hidden impacts of what we buy can change everything.* New York, NY: Broadway Books.

Hitchcock, D., & Willard, M. (2009). *The business guide to sustainability: Practical strategies and tools for organizations* (2nd ed.). Washington, D.C.: Earthscan.

Kirk, F. R., & Spector, C. A. (2009). A comparison of the achievement of students taught by full-time versus adjunct faculty in business courses. *Academy of Education Leadership Journal, 13*(2), 73-81.

McDonough, W., & Braungart, M. (2002). *Cradle to cradle: Rethinking the way we make things.* New York, NY: North Point Press.

Pies, I., Beckmann, M., & Hielscher, S. (2010). Value creation, global competencies, and global corporate citizenship: An ordonomic approach to business ethics in the age of globalization. *International Journal of Business Ethics, 94,* 265-278.

Rappaport, A., & Creighton, S. H. (2007). *Degrees that matter: Climate change and the university.* Cambridge, MA: MIT Press.

Senge, P., Smith, B., Kurschwitz, N., Laur, J., & Schley, S. (2008). *The necessary revolution: How individuals and organizations are working together to create a sustainable world.* New York, NY: Doubleday.

Weybrecht, G. (2010). *The sustainable MBA: The manager's guide to green business.* West Sussex, England: John Wiley & Sons.

Service Learning

George Kelley, MBA, MA, MS
City University of Seattle
School of Management

Abstract

Service Learning is an academic model providing students and faculty hands-on experiences and an opportunity to develop in-depth knowledge and skills through projects aimed at identifying and meeting real community needs. President Barack Obama has made Service Learning a major priority of his administration's education reform initiatives for all student levels including higher education. Students are challenged and empowered to identify community needs, plan projects to address them, and implement their projects benefitting both the community and the service providers (students, faculty, and institution). Service Learning combines service with a learning experience and can be implemented in a variety of subject areas if the projects align with and serve desired learning outcomes. The challenges and achievements of Service Learning and its implementation are discussed, along with suggestions for further research.

Introduction

Service Learning provides students the opportunity to combine, utilize, and apply skills and concepts developed in the classroom along with acquired personal and professional knowledge in real-world projects. This method is considered a form of experiential learning and is often described by professionals and students as a "hands-on," practical form of learning (Watkins & Braun, 2009).

While Service Learning is a form of experiential learning, it is much more than a mere hands-on or practical approach; it substantially enriches the learning process by providing faculty and students the opportunity to serve communities, especially at-risk social and economic constituencies or those who lack sufficient personal, business, management, or leadership resources needed to achieve their desired outcomes and aspirations. Generally the local communities serve as primary service targets and subjects; however, global communities are also increasingly being served when resources afford the opportunity.

Bringle and Hatcher (1995) advanced what has become a commonly accepted definition of Service Learning, asserting it as a "course-based, credit-bearing, educational experience," where "students (a) participate in an organized service activity that meets identified community needs and (b) reflect on the service activity in such a way as to gain further understanding of course content, a broader appreciation of the discipline, and an enhanced sense of civic responsibility" (p. 112). This definition has gained popular acceptance because it effectively conveys the model's conceptualization by clearly connecting its two primary outcomes, service and learning, in a significant collaboration (Butin, 2010).

Many scholars have bifurcated Service Learning into two different segments, one that accentuates and emphasizes service and the other learning. They have perceived them as exclusive rather than linked in a distinctive and meaningful way. Service was viewed as a means in itself, the primary objective being to serve rather than as a means or method of learning (Butin, 2010). Volunteer activity and community service comprised the service component of the model, while internships, practica, and field-based education (such as student teaching) served the learning aspect of the model (Butin, 2010). Further segmentation, including the notion of Service Learning as either "academic," "community-based," or "field-based," provided opportunity for additional differentiation.

While such distinctions might be useful, they can also limit and constrain the use of Service Learning programs. Advocates have been articulating broader, more comprehensive and consistent definitions of the construct to provide opportunities for a wider reach. Sigmon (1979) argued for adoption of the "Four Rs": respect (for all parties to the process and situations involved); reciprocity (mutual cooperation and collaboration); relevance (to the course, learning, and impact to communities); and reflection (research, self-engagement, self-inquiry, and self-development) (Butin, 2010).

The Four Rs make no distinction as to discipline or segment, instead serving as a common architecture applicable to all such approaches to learning. So the only question begged when applying the Four Rs is whether the course, activity, or program supports or empowers them. If the method does not, then it should be revised; and if it cannot, then it should be discarded.

Butin (2010) has identified four distinctive Service Learning classifications or perspectives: (1) Technical Perspective, (2) Cultural Perspective, (3) Political Perspective and (4) Anti-foundational Perspective (Butin, 2010). Butin's (2010) perspective serves as a platform for common understanding and dialogue and argues that Service Learning is multi-faceted and fosters multi-disciplinary synthesis. The Technical Perspective Butin defines addresses the legitimacy of Service Learning as an innovative education reform initiative, with particular emphasis on implementation and the linkage between the practice and student outcomes, particularly personal, social, and cognitive (Butin, 2010). The Cultural Perspective focuses on how social learning contributes to and affects social networks, social meaning and identity, democratic renewal, and civic engagement (Butin, 2010). The Political Perspective identifies interactions with and potential impact on equity, power, access, consensus, and conflict. The Anti-foundational Perspective examines the relationship between

Service Learning and truth, assumptions, convention, context, and success and failure.

Service Learning has been at the forefront of a national conversation over the past twenty years on how educational institutions can and should foster better community and global citizenship among students (Watkins & Braun, 2009). Policymakers, academics, and community leaders have identified Service Learning as a means for doing just that, by moving students and education from the classroom into communities (Watkins & Braun, 2009). As a result Service Learning continues to gain momentum as more institutions consider its adoption into programs and courses. But after a decade of solid growth, it is far from being institutionalized in higher education (Butin, 2010). The academic community, argues Butin (2010), has not yet adopted Service Learning. Clearly more research and persuasion is needed to establish its efficacy.

Employing Service Learning

Service Learning is usually employed in internships, practica, student leadership organizations, and in courses where interacting or collaborating with external constituencies and groups are both possible and mandated. It is not limited by a disciplinary focus. Service Learning is multi-disciplinary and is easily applied across academic disciplines (Butin, 2010). A 2004 annual membership survey by Campus Compact reflects the following distribution of utilization of Service Learning by academic departments: Education (69 percent), Sociology (54 percent), English (55 percent), Psychology (55 percent), Business (46 percent), Communication (46 percent) and Health (45 percent).

At City University of Seattle, Service Learning is used in the education, business, and psychology departments, primarily in internships and practica where they are designed to provide students with opportunities to apply classroom concepts and skills to real-world problems in local organizations under the supervision of faculty and an organizational mentor or coach. While most internships provide experiential learning opportunities (particularly in business), they do not offer the "service" component required in Service Learning. They generally do not serve at-risk social and economic constituencies or those who lack sufficient personal, business, management, or leadership resources needed to achieve desired outcomes and aspirations. Notable exceptions are student teaching and select internships and practica supported by the education and psychology departments.

While internships and practica do not necessarily—by design or structure—support Service Learning, an extra-curricular program known as Students in Free Enterprise (SIFE) does. Service Learning is the primary pedagogy used in SIFE. At City University of Seattle, SIFE is both an extracurricular student activity/organization and a credit-bearing, experiential course.

SIFE is a non-profit global organization launched by Sam Walton in the late 1970s. SIFE's mission and purpose is to "Develop tomorrow's leaders to create a sustainable world through the positive power of business" (sife.org). SIFE teams comprise some 42,000 students at more than 1,500 universities in 40 different countries who interact with more than 100 national and local corporate and organizational sponsors (sife.org). SIFE team members (students) at City University of Seattle can earn up to six graduate or five undergraduate elective credits for their participation in the program. They may also petition to substitute SIFE credits for course equivalency in the marketing, project management, leadership, or sustainability emphasis areas that are part of the Master of Business Administration (MBA) Program. The SIFE team at CityU has among the highest representation of globally diverse membership of any SIFE team in the United States. The 2009–2010 team was represented by students from nineteen different countries, including the United States.

SIFE members work on projects and serve on teams addressing real local and global community, business, social, economic, and cultural problems or issues. Most of the constituencies served are at-risk social and economic groups or those lacking sufficient personal, business, management, or leadership resources needed to achieve desired outcomes and goals. Such opportunities are not usually possible or available in the majority of traditional academic courses. SIFE members combine knowledge derived from their academic coursework, their personal and career experience, and their membership in SIFE, enabling them to both serve others and learn. Learning occurs at the conceptual as well as the practical level. SIFE members are able to test classroom models and theories and develop and hone critical organizational and life skills, including:

- Leadership
- Management
- Team Process
- Communication
- Relationship Building
- Presentation
- Project Management
- Multi-Cultural Awareness and Acceptance
- Professional Networking
- Analysis
- Critical Thinking
- Finance
- Marketing and Media Management
- Sustainability
- Self-Reflection
- Self-Awareness
- Resource Development

A recent SIFE project that was conducted by CityU students, the Women's Empowerment Initiative, provides an excellent understanding of how SIFE applies the service learning model. The project involved identifying an at-risk constituency and conducting a needs assessment. The needs assessment that was conducted identified gaps that existed in current public service levels due to local resource constraints. The proposed project to address those needs met SIFE and Service Learning model criteria. SIFE criteria require projects that address community economic, social, or environmental issues and create positive impact for project participants (sife.org). Service learning criteria require a formal academic component and community-based learning. Analysis was then performed to determine if the SIFE team had sufficient resources to address the service gap and also address the needs. The analysis led to the development of a project proposal identifying specific constituency issues, including employability, academic performance, career direction, parenting assistance, psychological health as a result of lower socio-economic demographics, limited access to educational resources, low self-esteem, family dysfunction, criminality, single-parent family structure, and teen parenting. A curriculum was developed to be delivered through workshops, seminars, and one-to-one teaching. Specific at-risk communities were identified, venues for delivery determined, implementation dates selected, costs assessed, benefits established, and metrics created. Finally, it was determined that a critical success factor for acceptance and implementation of the project proposal was leveraging resources through existing university partnerships.

The next step involved discussions with university partners, including a local National Football League (NFL) franchise to determine if collaboration was possible and if the resources that the project needed could be shared or provided. The discussions proved fruitful and a collaborative partnership was established. SIFE project team members then brought the NFL franchise together with other local community advocacy groups to implement the project. The resources provided by partners included curriculum development assistance, mentoring, coaching, venues for delivery, resources needed for delivery, and promotion of the project.

The Women's Empowerment Initiative provided SIFE team members with the opportunity to apply course concepts and knowledge from marketing, project management, human resources management, communication, leadership, international management, information technology, and operations courses. Course concepts and skills applied included problem solving, needs assessment, multi-cultural team process, multi-cultural communication, development and delivery of PowerPoint presentations, research, teaching, planning, budgeting, resourcing, marketing, networking, conflict resolution, mentoring, coaching, negotiation, and public relations.

Implementation

Implementation of Service Learning projects should also include an analysis of the impact on participants. In the case of the SIFE initiative, all project stakeholders were positively impacted. SIFE project team members developed and honed critical management, leadership, and life skills. Their socially responsible service to subjects who were economically and culturally challenged prompted self-reflection and self-awareness, heightened their awareness of the importance of community and citizenship, and enhanced their confidence and self-esteem. Additionally, they were able to see a clear linkage between the classroom and real-world application while they were experiencing significant personal and professional growth.

The at-risk subject group was also positively impacted. In addition to the content presented in the workshops, seminars, and one-on-one meetings, subjects were able to form mentoring and coaching relationships with team members; build interpersonal skills, including social interactions with presenters and other participants; develop appreciation of citizenship, community, and service by recognizing and understanding the service provided to them by project team members and stakeholders; and build confidence and enhance self-esteem by successfully completing the program. Additionally, many subjects identified team members as "role models," enabling them to develop a greater sense of possibility for future career and life success.

Project stakeholders including faculty, advisors, partners, and the university were also positively impacted. Faculty were able to connect classroom and academic program competencies and concepts to project activities, including planning, research, project management, content development, presentation, budgeting, team process, and communication. Additionally, faculty forged community relationships, enhancing the brand equity of the institution and creating opportunities for sustainable partnerships. Finally, faculty demonstrated socially responsible service to others, providing an example of citizenship and institutional commitment to stakeholder communities. Advisors, partners, and the university were able to contribute to the advocacy and support of needy, at-risk communities; exhibit socially responsible service to others; demonstrate individual and organizational citizenship; and increase brand awareness and equity.

Another major benefit of Service Learning is its capacity to have a positive impact on international students. Most international students have not been exposed to Service Learning curriculum or projects in their native countries. It is an entirely new experience for them. Service Learning projects provide them with an opportunity to have a rich multi-cultural experience. It takes them out of the classroom and provides them with a glimpse of American culture generally not available through most academic programs or courses. It involves them in socially responsible community projects, some with at-risk communities (like the Women's Empowerment Initiative) that enfranchise understanding and assimilation of America's version of core social-cultural values, such as compassion, empathy, cultural sensitivity, social justice, patriotism, and equity. It also instills appreciation of, and a desire for, community service, volunteering, and charitable giving. As a result of this process, international students who have participated in Service Learning projects return to their native countries inspired and motivated to apply American values and understanding they have developed here in meaningful projects at home.

A recent SIFE project illustrates how students' values and perspectives can be strengthened and refined through their participation in SIFE. Three SIFE members from Indonesia developed a project aimed at educating elementary school students about the Three Rs of environmental stewardship: reuse, reduce, recycle. They chose this project after researching pollution in their home country. They discovered that Indonesia was considered to be the fourth largest polluter in the world and that there were virtually no education programs to teach the importance of environmental awareness in Indonesian schools, particularly at the elementary level. They believed educating young students was key to developing a sustainable environmental program for their country. They developed a curriculum and piloted it at a local elementary school. After successfully piloting it in the United States, they partnered with a local school district in their hometown in Indonesia and began to teach the program there. They reported back that the program had been very well received and was changing student behavior. The school where they introduced it is practicing recycling for the very first time and many of the students reported that their families were also recycling.

Broader integration and application of Service Learning into courses and academic programs rests on increasing awareness of the academic legitimacy, practical student learning outcomes, and social benefits of Service Learning. Over the last twenty years a significant body of research and discussion has emerged advocating for the efficacy of Service Learning as an academic pedagogy. The works of Butin (2010), Pringle and Hatcher (1995), Astin (1998, 1999), Cuban and Anderson (2007), Furco (1996, 2002), Bell (1971, 20002007), Boyle-Baise (1999, 2007), Ellison and Eatman (2008), and Colby (2003, 2007), among many others have contributed to a broader understanding of Service Learning, its definition, structure, limits, constraints, and efficacy.

Perhaps the most compelling argument for the broader integration of Service Learning is the "engaged university" movement (Ellison & Eatman, 2008) advocating public engagement and civic renewal (Butin, 2010). If public and private education is commissioned to serve the broader goals of democracy, and in particular the cultivation of community, social responsibility, and citizenship, then it is clear that Service Learning should hold a salient position in pedagogy (Ramaley, 2000). When this linkage becomes pervasive, academic institutions, administrators, faculty, and policy-making bodies will more fully adopt the engaged university concept and integrate Service Learning into courses and programs, recognizing its contribution to the student, community, and institution.

Summary and Recommendations

Service Learning can be implemented in numerous projects and assignments and in an array of courses and programs. Education, sociology, English, psychology, business, communication, and health programs at CityU currently use Service Learning in courses with outcomes and competencies, such as team process, project management, interpersonal communication, conflict resolution, marketing, research, critical thinking, relationship building, self-awareness, self-reflection, leadership, accounting, presentation, teaching, sustainability, resourcing, and public relations. Others will also find Service Learning an excellent method for connecting students to assignments and few methods are better suited to cultivate social responsibility, service to others, community, civic renewal and citizenship than Service Learning.

A recent accounting course project provides an excellent example of Service Learning. MBA students in an accounting course were assigned a class project involving the preparation of tax returns. The assignment required student teams to identify local residents who did not speak English fluently and assist them with tax preparation. Project planning, including identification of the culture targeted and documentation of the process used for locating candidates for the assignment, was required. One team chose local Spanish-speaking residents as their target. Members of the team were either Americans who spoke Spanish fluently or were international students from Spanish-speaking countries. The team decided to videotape its sessions to document the process. They also submitted completed returns to faculty for quality-control inspection, assuring that the returns were completed accurately. The assignment enabled students to apply classroom concepts in a real-world setting and provided them with the opportunity to serve others. Feedback from both the subjects and students indicated a high level of satisfaction with the project; in fact, subjects asked if this process could be sustained and if they could refer others in the future.

This example is one among many that could be chronicled. Integration of Service Learning may be constrained by resources; however, in most cases it seems that awareness, enterprise, innovation, and commitment to student learning are the primary constraints.

Service Learning will enjoy broader integration when administrators, faculty members, policy-makers, and others familiarize themselves with the theoretical constructs of Service Learning, its practical applications, the best practices of current and former practitioners, and its mandate. Additionally, organizations like

SIFE that have developed expertise in its application and practice can be consulted to serve as models for development and implementation.

It appears that the major constraints and limitations for broader integration of Service Learning are awareness of its mandate, constructs, practical applications, and the best practices of current and former practitioners. These are all limitations that can be assuaged. Specific courses and learning outcomes may not be a good fit for Service Learning, although most academic disciplines do report successful employment of the concept and strategies. Faculty time and supervision as well as resources required for successful coaching, mentoring, supervision, monitoring, and project implementation might also constrain acceptance and implementation. Faculty will clearly spend more time managing Service Learning projects than other assignments. Legal and risk assurance/mitigation factors may need addressing.

Opportunities for Future Research

Service Learning is a relatively new practice in higher education and has seldom been employed in adult learning; however, it is a practice or method gaining popularity and credence. As a presidential candidate, Barack Obama advocated for Service Learning as a means to promote citizenship and as a strategy for higher levels of student retention and productivity (Schweber, 2009). Since becoming president, the Obama administration has proposed bold initiatives that would make Service Learning an integral component of secondary and higher education and that position it to have a transformative impact on students, schools, and communities. Given this mandate and the growing acceptance of Service Learning as pedagogy, outstanding opportunities exist for integration of this approach and future research into this practice.

Research assessing the sustainability and efficacy of projects should be undertaken to determine the positive impact of Service Learning on students, faculty, community members, and participating institutions. Studies assessing the impact and relationship between Service Learning and career advancement, continuing education, and community service could serve to further demonstrate the efficacy of this model on student outcomes.

References

Bringle R. and J. Hatcher. (1995). A service learning curriculum for faculty. *The Michigan Journal of Community Service Learning, 2,* 112-22.

Butin, D. (2010). *Service Learning In Theory and Practice.* New York: Palgrave Macmillan.

Course Instructor Guide. Service-Learning Pedagogy Resource. Retrieved from www.unc.edu/apples/faculty/2009%20 Faculty%20Guide.doc

Ellison J, & Eatman, T.K. (2008). *Scholarship in public: Knowledge creation and tenure policy in the engaged university.* Retrieved from: www.imaginingamerica.org/IApdfs/TTI_REPORT%20 FINAL%205.2.08.pdf.

Kaye, C. B. (2010). *The complete guide to service learning: Proven, practical ways to engage students civic responsibility, academic curriculum and social action.* Minneapolis, MN: Free Spirit Publishing.

Ramaley, J. A. (2003). *Renewing the civic mission of the American university. The John Dewey lecture.* University of Michigan. Retrieved from danm.ucsc.edu/~dustin/library/Ramaley_ Dewey_Lecture.doc

Schweber, H. (2009,March 24*). Obama's Biggest Program of All - Service Learning.* The Huffington Post. Retrieved from http://www.huffingtonpost.com/howard-schweber/ obamas-biggest-program-of_b_178729.html

Sife.org. (n.d.). Retrieved from http://www.sife.org/AboutSIFE/
Pages/AboutSife.aspx

Sigmon, R. (1979). Service learning: Three principles. *ACTION 8*(1),
9-11.

Watkins, M., & Braun, L. (2005). *Service-Learning: From Classroom to
Community to Career*. Indianapolis: JIST Life.

Reflective-Heuristic Practice, Crisis Management, the PMNB, and Simulation: An Integrated Methodology

Robert A. Brownlow, EdD
City University of Seattle
School of Management

Abstract

Effective Project Management (PM) training is a delicate balance between the scholarship of academe and the scholarship of application. Reflective-heuristic practice, crisis management (CM), and the rigor of a Project Management Notebook (PMNB) can be combined with guided simulation to facilitate students becoming effective practitioners in the use of Project Management. The chapter briefly explores reflective practice, crisis management, and the PMNB as tools for achieving that end. A ten-week simulation that has proven effective in teaching students how to project the application in problem solving efforts is described.

Introduction

Merriam and Caffarella (1999) have emphasized the role of experience in learning, especially when linked to reflective thought and action. Their views echo Mezirow (1991) in terms of thinking about what you are doing as you are doing it (e.g., being fully in the moment with congruent thought, action, and projecting forward the consequences of an action). Experience and public reflection make learning a socially interactive process (Jarvis, 2006). This emphasizes the power of collaborative learning through work teams (Davis, 2002) and how collaboration transforms the classroom into a practitioner learning community (Joyce, Weil, & Calhoun, 2004). The process works best when delivery mechanisms are compatible with desired learning outcomes (Mager, 1997).

Guided simulation can be an effective tool for creating a collaborative learning community manifesting purpose and responsibility, especially when it becomes a heuristic process that shapes meaning and gives perspective to solve problems abductively. While not all graduate education involves reflective heuristics, reflective heuristics, as manifested in critical pedagogy that utilize dialogic and dialectic methods, should be the cardinal objective of graduate training (Wink, 2011). While there are many approaches, there are no shortcuts.

Background

Reflective practice, as posed by Mezirow (1991) and Merriam and Caffarella (1999), creates intentionally acting practitioners who critically assess the premises underlying construction of the meaning of an experience and the meaning of that meaning. It is a hypothetical-deductive model stressing posing a problem based on presenting evidence and then developing and testing a hypothesis derived from critiquing the problem and the consequences of taking a specific action based on the content of the problem. It includes the process by which it is unfolding and the premises surrounding its diagnosis and the resolution of the course of action. Thus, heuristic reflection represents experimental-experiential problem solving through ongoing assessment of environmental feedback to improve performance by projecting forward the consequences of a chosen action.

Reflection projects forward the consequences of a proposed response and how that response should be adjusted as circumstances change. Applied to such disciplines as Project Management (PM), reflection rethinks how a project team coherently and intentionally applies protocols as it moves through the project's life cycle. Ideally this leads to double-loop learning wherein students traverse from neophytes to practitioners, with reflection the bridge between the two stages (Argyris, 1993).

Premise reflection promotes mindfulness in our actions and their results based on how a problem is posed. Mindfulness combines proposition analysis with creative insight to shape the meaning of an event and formulate a response to it (e.g., properly recognizing a crisis-inducing trigger and implementing an appropriate response). The challenge is that an action may be distorted by unwarranted presuppositions based on prior learning. Premise reflection re-assesses the adequacy of prior learning and opens it to contradiction. It involves a dialectic mindset that sometimes transforms our belief system.

A project team is a community held together by feelings of belonging, attachment, shared expectations of accountability, inclusion, availability to one another, and personal and professional respect. Project team reflection creates and nurtures an "emergent we" wherein experiences are enriched because they occur with, and are shared with, others based on nurturing relationships bonded by roles, accountability, and authority.

The evolution of the emergent we project team is a decidedly reflective heuristic process, especially when confronted with difficult problems.

Heuristic Reflection

The process begins when a project team is assigned a problem that it is expected to resolve. Resolution requires forming integrated critical thinking-based judgments about the problem's content, the unfolding process within its context, and the premise(s) underlying its elemental components and environmental circumstance. The conclusions resulting from this process are translated into actions whose consequences are thought forward to assess resolution effectiveness and to prevent reoccurrence of the same or similar problems in the future.

Pedagogically, heuristic reflection creates deep learning of the subject matter (e.g., project risk management) and its relationship to what is already known so it may lead to intentional action that mitigates adverse events and prevents their recurrence.

Risk management is a Project Management Body of Knowledge (PMBOK) component that especially lends itself to heuristic reflection and taking intentional action. Understanding crisis management and recovery is critical to becoming an effective, reflective PM practitioner.

Crisis management may be framed as a six phase process (Brownlow, 2006). The dotted clockwise rotation encircling Phases I–III represents tightly coupled punctuated actions intended to mitigate adverse events (Spender & Grinyer, 1995; Spender & Grinyer, 1996). Phases IV through VI are composed of reflective-heuristic actions indicative of double-loop learning. The dashed rotation encircling Phases IV–VI represents loose coupling of adaptive change initiatives implemented over time (Hsieh, 1992; Spender & Grinyer, 1995; Spender & Grinyer, 1996). The counter-clockwise rotation represents undoing the loss of collaborative relationships among and between project stakeholders that may have exacerbated Phases I through III. The critical component in successfully moving from Phases IV through VI is creating and nurturing a coalition of the willing (Kotter, 1995).

The area of intersection represents the potential for moving into the reconciliation and renewal process. Phases IV–VI emphasizes the differences between technical work and technical change and adaptive work and adaptive change as defined by Heifetz and Linsky (2002).

Phase I: Coming of the Forerunners:

Forerunners, sometimes called prodromals or triggers, are early warnings of project crisis. The typically complex, nonlinear dynamics of triggers can cloak detection (Barton, 2001). If stakeholders collaborate to identify and mitigate forerunners, they resolve project issues instead of suffering project crisis (Fink, 2002).

Phase II: Acuteness in the Now:

Phase II is the acute, rapid, chaotic expansion of events harming the project and fragmenting its network of collaborative relationships (Barton, 2001; Fink, 2002; Guinivan, 2004; Jederberg, 2005).

Phase III: Technical Resolution:

Technical resolution resolves pressing issues and returns to normal project operations while preparing to manage any immediate aftermath (e.g., recovering cost and schedule performance).

Phase IV: Post Mortem:

Post mortem is a rigorous assessment of what went well, what didn't, and why. It identifies weaknesses and/or threats that caused the crisis and how they may be mitigated to prevent recurrence, thus creating double-loop learning. An effective post mortem lays the foundation for moving forward.

Phase V: Reconciliation: Precursor to Renewal:

Reconciliation reassembles the fragmented stakeholder's collaborative network. There are five interdependent components. The first promotes dialogue to understand the meaning and meta-meaning of events impacting the project's performance and its stakeholder network. It involves asking and answering challenging, reflective questions to facilitate moving forward together (Baldwin, 2004; Boyes-Watson, 2005; Stone, Patton, & Heen, 1999).

Secondly, the nobility of each stakeholder's work is affirmed by acknowledging potential career injuries associated with a specific project role (such as reporting "bad news" to powerful stakeholders or having been given "bad" data to work with).

Phase V's third component is reestablishing any trust undone by the crisis. This is accomplished by recommitting to an inclusive project stakeholder community to prevent project silos and "hunkering down" (Feldman, 2004; Hurst, 2002; Putnam, 2000). Trust correlates with how stakeholders commit to their work and to each other through relational coordination (Gittell, 2003).

Reconciliation's fourth element is rebuilding shared vision based on valuing the project's outcomes. Shared vision is converted into results through engagement.

The final phase of reconciliation re-bonds the project's charter to the stakeholders' working-together network by nurturing extended community through proper conduct and relational coordination (Cohn & Friedman, 2002; Field, 2003; Gittell, 2001; Gittell, 2003; Hodson, 2001; Hodson, 2005; Reeves, 2004; Wheatley, 2003). The adverse rhetoric of crisis communication is replaced with reconciliation-promoting language. Wheatley (2003) and Palmer (2000) discuss faith in tomorrow, coming together, and the power of vocation to facilitate community and reconciliation.

Phase VI: Renewal: Full Recovery:

Renewal completes the process. Hurst (2002) defines renewal as that which replaces what was lost or forgotten. Achieving post-crisis project renewal requires adaptive strategies that balance changes in the project's external environment with improved relational coordination in its internal environment.

The first strategy nurtures sustainable relationships that transcend the hunkering down that sometimes accompanies crisis. Relational coordination sustains relationships and enables moving forward (Akdere, 2005; Cullen, Johnson, & Sakano, 2000; Gittell, 2003; Hurst, 2002; Ulmer & Sellnow, 2002; Weymes, 2003). Darling and Russ (2000) argue that congruence of purpose (e.g., commitment to the project's mission), shared values, collaboration, and responsive learning promote sustainable relationships.

The second renewal strategy links change initiatives to facilitate adaptive change in network relationships and work processes (Heifetz & Linsky, 2002; Hsieh, 1992). The third strategy reinforces adaptive changes necessary for double-loop learning. This places the work and responsibility of renewal where it belongs—on the project stakeholders.

The fourth strategy is to maintain engagement to enhance collaborative learning and ensure leadership accountability (Barr, Stimpert, & Huff, 1992; Darling & Russ, 2000; Gittell, 2003; Hodson, 2001; Lund, 2004). Collaboration relies on an integrated project social structure that harvests the power of functional diversity (e.g., how various functional roles within the project create the synergy of working together).

The Project Management Notebook (PMNB)

As a tool of good project management, a project's history is maintained in an audit-ready project management notebook that represents the project's infrastructure and contains all project decisions and criteria by which those decisions were made. The PMNB also shapes the project's culture (i.e., the values and norms that govern behavior among and between project team members and the team's social and relationship capital network) that, in turn, influence the willingness to collaborate, take prudent risks, deal with crisis, or engage in reflective practice. The project's infrastructure and culture are also influenced by events arising from its immediate external environment and how those events are responded to (Schein, 2004).

A PMNB can take many forms and vary in complexity, contingent on the oversight philosophy of the organization approving and overseeing projects.

Description of Basic PMNB Elements

- Project Mission

  What the project will accomplish (the problem to be solved).

- Scope

  Project size and boundaries.

- Project Execution Strategy

  How the mission will be accomplished; the schedule mileposts that must be met to accomplish the mission by its completion date; how scope is divided into individual work packages.

- Resource Requirements

  Defines what is needed to achieve the mission and when and where it will be deployed. It includes costs, schedules, labor, and equipment.

- Risk Planning

  A SWOT: An audit of the strengths, weaknesses, opportunities, and threats the project may encounter within its operating environment. Strengths and weakness are internal to the project; opportunities and threats are external to the project. Once this is complete, a Risk Breakdown Structure (RBS) that includes the probability of the risk (i.e., W/T) occurring, its trigger event, the impact of its occurrence, and mitigation plan should the risk occur, along with the cost of the mitigation plan.

- Formal Project Charter

  Formally launches the project and is signed by the authorizing authority.

- Management Oversight   Includes phased decision gates wherein movement to the next phase of the project is authorized. Oversight leads to project controls that track cost and schedule performance, scope creep, and role, authority and accountabilities (RAAs) tracking.
- Communication Plan   The overall plan for communicating project status, who communicates it, when it is communicated, and how it is communicated.

An Example Simulation

Moving through a project's life cycle, and responding to the vagaries in such movement, requires technical and adaptive work and technical and adaptive change as framed by Heifetz and Linsky (2002). It also requires ongoing reflective practice that fosters intentionality of action. To emphasize use of reflective heuristic practice and integrating its results into a PMNB, a simulated project, fraught with challenges, is deployed in a way that deliberately induces crisis. The simulation is as follows:

Week One

Students receive the following project information:

Exotic Motor Cars (EMC) designs, assembles, and markets exotic automobiles. EMC is known for rigorous quality, indefatigable reliability, hyper-responsive customer support, and brand exclusivity.

Workers are fiercely proud of their skills, products and relational coordination philosophy. Nowhere is this more evident than its fit-check facility in Central City, where motors are subjected to painstaking specification checks, test runs, dynamic-balance tuning, and other complex routines before being shipped to either North Prairie (forty miles north) where sedans, shooting brakes, and SUVs are assembled or to Mountain View (fifty-eight miles south) where coupes and roadsters are assembled. Once at the appropriate site, motors are queued for installation in the appropriate vehicle. Motors and vehicles are highly customized, based on customer specifications and option selections, and must be an exact match in regard to engineering physics and performance specifications.

EMC technicians are the best in the industry and loyal to the EMC brand despite occasional acrimony with management. Central City technicians have developed long-standing personal friendships that include off-work family activities. There are active employee resource groups and a highly engaged diversity council. Central City has a fifty-year-history and many employees have over thirty years of service.

Using Lean+ and Six Sigma methods, employees reduced fit-run check cycle time from two weeks to eight hours. Management promised no layoffs as a direct result of Lean+ and Six Sigma. However, due to a downturn in the market for exotic automobiles and increasing costs, management has decided to close Central City and move the fit-run check process to car-side point of use. There will be a 35 percent reduction in the workforce and significant savings due to the high cost of maintaining the aging Central City site. Remaining employees will be reassigned to North Prairie or Mountain View based on the collective bargaining agreement. Due to a possible sale of the site, the project has a hard schedule constraint of ten months. The move will break up many long-standing friendships and force remaining employees to commute long distances over heavily congested freeways. The union has filed a claim of unfair labor practice. EMC has argued that the Management Rights article of the Bargaining Agreement allows plant closings and employee reassignments.

Although EMC is emphasizing the positive aspects of the move, including a "generous" severance and retraining package, employees are grieving the change and see management as having gone back on its commitment to not lay anyone off as a result of process improvements.

Action:

Students begin developing the project plan, in the form of a PMNB, for a shutdown and move from Central City. The plan should focus on SWOT, RBS, people and communication, but also have all other PMNB elements covered in the PMBOK. Weekly status reports are required.

Particular importance is placed on documenting the assumptions made in the construction of the plan based on work content and the process by which content will be accomplished. This includes the premises underlying why the project is being planned the way it is.

Week Two

Rapier Racing, EMC's motor supplier, has quietly submitted a proposal to perform the fit-run-check function at its factory in Stuttgart, Germany, and then ship installation-ready motors directly to assembly line point of use in North Prairie and Mountain View. Due to the complexity of matching customized motors with uniquely optioned automobiles, Rapier estimates it will be twelve months before motors start arriving at North Prairie and Mountain View. If implemented the proposal would eliminate an additional 15 percent of the Central City workforce and save twenty-seven million dollars in direct labor cost.

Action:

Have students adjust the project plan to include Rapier's proposal, paying particular attention to cost, scope, risk, schedule impact, and potential mitigation strategies. The project communication manager is reminded that an activity report is due no later than two days before the next class.

Week Three

Word leaks that Rapier Racing has proposed shipping installation-ready motors directly to assembly line point of use. The union's Bargaining Unit alleges that outsourcing is another violation of the bargaining agreement, while management continues to argue that it retains such rights under the Management Rights article of the contract. Another ULP is filed.

Unbeknownst to management, Central City's labor-friendly mayor, who is up for reelection and concerned about the loss of tax revenue associated with EMC's move, uses back-channel means to inform the union that he will permit peaceful demonstrations against the plant move. Several days later the union orchestrates mass demonstrations. One hour before and after each shift employees picket the plant's main entrance and plan to do so indefinitely. Even though the pickets are informational, delivery drivers refuse to cross the picket line, thus disrupting motor delivery, which then disrupts the fit-run-check process, which then disrupts shipping motors to their destinations, which then slows assembly line production. For two minutes of every break period, workers chant, "You lie! You lie!" Employees start wearing tee shirts with the words "You lie!" stenciled on them and orchestrate rolling sickouts. EMC files an Unfair Labor Practice suit against the Bargaining Unit.

Customers begin complaining about delays in delivery of their expensive automobiles and threaten to cancel orders based on the negative press and perceived mistreatment of EMC workers. To worsen the community relations' issues, the producers of a planned James Bond film refuse to place an exclusive EMC roadster in the film.

Both the union and management retain legal council to supplement their legal staff. Meanwhile, it is discovered that much of the sensitive computing and tooling equipment used in the fit-check process fell out of calibration certification when it was moved. All shipped equipment must be re-certified and three hundred sets have been moved to date. Due to the sophistication of the equipment and the calibration process, it will take thirty days per unit to recalibrate.

Action:

Have students assess the cost and schedule impact of calibration recertification. Students must also consider how Employee Relations, Organizational Effectiveness, Human Resources, and other stakeholders will mitigate growing anger and fear among employees.

Inform students that another project status report is due and it must include Cost Performance Index (CPI) and Schedule Performance Index (SPI), as well as mitigation costs.

Have students discuss the assumptions they made in developing and modifying the plan to date and how the content and process of their project work is changing and what, if anything, should be done to deal with the evolving circumstances.

Week Four

Senior management and other stakeholders pressure for immediate resolution. Local media publishes human interest stories detailing how EMC's actions are displacing loyal, long-term employees, who will find it very difficult to find new jobs in the depressed labor market. Local, labor-friendly politicians hold public meetings. A prominent United States senator calls for investigative hearings on the relationship between EMC and Rapier Racing. Communication is politicized as the union and EMC battle for credibility. EMC leaders worsen matters by inadvertently giving contradictory direction.

The Bargaining Unit presents a plan for saving EMC more money than the shutdown and outsourcing will save. Management argues that the plan's statistics are distorted to gain public sympathy.

Due to the Bargaining Agreement, workers know who will be laid off and when. Long-standing friendships unravel. Fights break out.

In an unrelated event, an EMC transporter carrying forty motors and forty sets of diagnostic equipment to North Prairie is involved in a catastrophic three-fatality accident that erupts in flames. All motors and equipment are lost. There is now a shortage of installation-ready motors because EMC carries very little safety stock due to its "just-in-time" inventory philosophy.

Action:

Have students adjust all aspects of their project plan impacted by this latest round of events. This should include, but not be limited to, communication strategy (including media relations), RBS, litigation, transportation, schedule, parts shortages, and government relations. If students have not identified these factors in their RBS, they are instructed to do so. CPI and SPI are again reported, as are all mitigating actions to date and an assessment of their effectiveness. Have students prepare for a press conference to mitigate the collateral damage from adverse public relations fallout.

Students are again taken through a reflective practice exercise to identify what assumptions they have been making and how those assumptions were incorporated into adjustments to the project plan. This will also include ongoing assessment of lessons learned that are documented in the PMNB.

Week Five

Work to rule, rolling sickouts, and other concerted strategies have nearly halted work at Central City. Employees who can retire (and many can, due to their high years of service), retire, thus creating a critical skill shortage.

The press conference becomes a public relations disaster when a project spokesman provides inaccurate information which is immediately challenged by the media and union leaders. Things are made worse when an EMC executive speaks to the importance of being sensitive to all stakeholders' needs, especially those owning stock in the company. The story makes national news when the union president makes incendiary comments that further inflame the rank and file.

Action:

Students must again adjust all aspects of their project plan impacted by events to date. They must also prepare a communication plan for informing the workforce that EMC will outsource the fit-check process and how any negative impact will be mitigated. The union stages a public rally against EMC. EMC files another Unfair Labor Charges suit against the union.

Week Six

An explosion rocks Central City site and the subsequent fire destroys a major work-staging area. Sabotage is alleged, but an investigation is inconclusive, suggesting that a faulty transformer may have caused the blast. The fire's rapid spread is attributed to toxic chemicals that may have been improperly stored or used as an accelerant. All work at Central City site is terminated. The union denies any involvement and calls off all corporate campaign activity, since closing the site is now moot.

Federal agencies become involved in investigating the explosion and fire. There are rumors of calling a grand jury who will subpoena the PMNB. The Environmental Protection Agency is granted a court-ordered cleanup of Central City site once EMC vacates. The potential buyer withdraws its offer due to all the bad press and acrimony surrounding the planned move. To repair its public image, EMC offers to gift the site, bordered by a river, for a park to Central City and take a tax write-off.

Action:

Students close out the project, using proper PM protocols, and prepare an ISO-style audit. Although every component in the PMBOK will be covered, risk management, people strategy, and communication planning will be subjected to intense scrutiny by multiple investigative groups. A cost assessment for mitigation efforts is also requested.

Week Seven

Management requests a comprehensive "lessons learned" report for the entire project, plus assurance that the PMNB will be "bulletproof."

Action:

Based on reflective heuristic practices, students prepare a thorough assessment of the project. Special emphasis is placed on how presenting issues were discerned and evaluated based on presupposition. A key question to be addressed is what should have remained within the scope of the project and what should have been commissioned as a separate project. Also subject to inquiry will be why decisions were made the way they were and by what criteria they were made.

Week Eight

The EMC Board of Directors directs the project team to develop a plan to heal damaged stakeholder relationships (e.g., the union, employees, Central City leadership). The plan will either be an addendum to the original project plan or be commissioned as a separate project. The plan will be assessed based on hard measures that include relational coordination effectiveness. The plan must include all Phase V elements and be developed using reflective heuristic processes.

Action:

Have students develop a reconciliation plan to heal the relationship with Central City employees, the Bargaining Unit, the local community, and other stakeholders. The plan should include all project elements and be approached as an addendum to the original plan and then assessed in terms of an amended RBS. The plan should include all the elements of Phase V crisis management elements and use ongoing lessons learned as the basis for continued reflective process.

Week Nine

The EMC Board of Directors directs the project team to develop a renewal plan to increase EMC's organizational effectiveness and restore its lost vitality. The plan will include all project elements and be approached as an addendum to the original plan or commissioned as a continuation of Phase V CM. The plan must include all Phase VI elements.

Action:

Have students present their plan for Phase VI, being sure that they utilize reflective heuristic process.

Week Ten

A debrief of the exercise is held that includes how the project navigated through its life cycle and how it managed crisis, especially forerunner detection and the use of reflective-heuristic processes to create intentionality in action.

Clearly this is a complex project that includes multiple and powerful stakeholders, cost and schedule issues, risks, communication, and scope creep. Crucial questions abound. Does the Rapier proposal fall within the original project boundaries, or is it a case of scope creep? How do the accident and the loss of motors and equipment fit into the project, if at all? Would working closely with the Bargaining Unit, using trust and relational coordination, have prevented or minimized the union's adverse reaction? How does a project manager and her team resist political pressure to technically resolve the problem rather than taking adaptive, double-loop actions that prevent reoccurrence?

Other reflective questions surround development of the SWOT and RBS—how much should have been foreseen? What forerunners should have been heeded? What thought processes influenced decisions and were the consequences of decisions thought forward?

Future Research Directions

This integrative approach offers numerous opportunities for future research. For example, what systemic factors in the project's infrastructure, as defined by the PMNB, influence the SWOT and

RBS process and how can aspiring PMs best be taught these factors? How do content, process, and premise reflection influence development and nurturance of extended stakeholder networks that manifest relational coordination, and how can students best be taught these processes?

Another area worthy of exploration is how premise and content reflection influence forerunner detection, and how simulation exercises can facilitate such detection. A further area for research is exploring how PMNB construction promotes relational coordination, especially in times of crisis, and how findings can create new models of PM reflective heuristic practice for both students and practitioners. Still further, how can reflective-heuristic practice be applied to recovering and renewing stakeholder relationships that have been harmed by project crisis, and how can students best be taught to do that in a real way.

Finally, it is worthwhile to explore how this pedagogic strategy can be applied to developing organizational and educational leaders (Brownlow, 2006) and training of HR practitioners, especially in the fields of labor and employee relations.

Conclusions

Integrating reflective-heuristic practice, Crisis Management, and the PMNB with simulation as a primary learning tool promotes exploration of the content, process, and premises underlying how projects are managed. Students learn to find their way by applying reflective-heuristic practice to achieve a project's mission and document the rationale for decisions and subsequent action.

Having students develop reconciliation and renewal plans emphasizes the importance of maintaining relational coordination throughout the project's life cycle, especially if the project derails.

All of this is predicated on the seminal importance of "forward thinking" the results of decisions and actions. It is also predicated on the belief that the essence of PM work is people and results (Gray & Larson, 2008). These should be cardinal lessons learned, not only in the classroom but in practitioner life as well.

References

Akdere, M. (2005). Social capital theory and implications for human resources development. *Singapore Management Review, 27*(2), 1-25.

Argyris, C. (1993). *Knowledge for action: A guide to overcoming barriers to organizational change.* San Francisco, CA: Jossey Bass.

Baldwin, M. (2004). Where learning begins. *Reflections, 5*(5), 7-11.

Barr, P. S., Stimpert, J. L., & Huff, A. S. (1992). Cognitive change, strategic action, and organizational renewal. *Strategic Management Journal, 13*(5), 15-37.

Barton, L. (2001). *Crises in organizations II.* Phoenix, AZ: South-Western College Publishing, Thompson Learning.

Boyes-Watson, C. (2005). Community is not a place but a relationship: Lessons for organizational development. *Public Organization Review, 5*(4), 359-374.

Brownlow, R. (2006, May). *Finding way: Post-teachers' strike relationship recovery and school district renewal.* Paper presented at the annual Seattle University Leadership Conference, Seattle, WA.

Cohn, G., & Friedman, H. H. (2002). Improving employer-employee relationships: Biblical and Talmudic perspective on human resource management. *Management Decision, 40*(10), 955-962.

Cullen, J. B., Johnson, J. L., & Sakano, T. (2000). Success through commitment and trust: The soft side of strategic alliance management. *Journal of World Business, 35*(3), 223-242.

Darling, J., & Russ, D. (2000). Relationship capital. *Executive Excellence, 17*(5), 14.

Davis, J. (2002). *At the mercy of sadistic cats and megalomaniacal dogs: Dilbert as a reflection of and vehicle for organizational cynicism.* (ERIC Document Reproduction Service No. ED 465 972).

Feldman, M. S. (2004). Resources in emerging structures and processes of change. *Organization Science: A Journal of the Institute of Management Sciences, 15*(3), 295-310.

Field, J. (2003). *Social capital.* London, UK: Routledge.

Fink, S. (2002). *Crisis management: Planning for the inevitable.* Lincoln, NE: Universe, Inc.

Gittell, J. H. (2001). Investing in relationships. *Harvard Business Review, 79*(6), 28-30.

Gittell, J. H. (2003). *The Southwest Airlines way: Using the power of relationships to achieve high performance.* New York: McGraw-Hill.

Gray, C. F., & Larson, E. W. (2008). *Project management: The managerial process* (4th ed.). New York, NY: McGraw-Hill.

Guinivan, J. (2004). PR and public issues: The new age of activism. *Public Relations Tactics, 11*(6), 6-8.

Heifetz, R. A., & Linsky, M. (2002). *Leadership on the line: Staying alive through the dangers of leading.* Boston, MA: Harvard Business School Press.

Hodson, R. (2001). *Dignity at work.* New York, NY: Cambridge University Press.

Hodson, R. (2005). Management behavior as social capital: A systematic analysis of organizational ethnographies. *British Journal of Industrial Relations, 43*(1), 41-66.

Hsieh, T. (1992). The road to renewal. *McKinsey Quarterly, 3,* 28-37.

Hurst, D. K. (2002). *Crises & renewal: Meeting the challenge of organizational change.* Boston, MA: Harvard Business School Press.

Jarvis, P. (2006). *Towards a comprehensive theory of human learning: Lifelong learning and the learning society.* New York, NY: Routledge.

Jederberg, W. W. (2005). Issues with the integration of technical information in planning for and responding to nontraditional disasters. *Journal of Toxicology & Environmental Health: Part A, 68*(11/12), 877-899.

Joyce, J., Weil, M., & Calhoun, E. (2004). *Models of Teaching* (7th ed.). New York, NY: Pearson.

Kotter, J. P. (1995, March). Leading change: Why transformation efforts fail. *Harvard Business Review,* 59-66.

Lund, H. L. (2004). Strategies for sustainable business and the handling of workers' interests: Integrated management systems and worker participation. *Economic & Industrial Democracy, 25*(1), 41-74.

Mager, R. (1997). *Making instruction work: A step-by-step guide to designing and developing instruction that works.* Atlanta, GA: CEP Press.

Merriam, S. B., & Caffarella, R. S. (1999). *Learning in adulthood: A comprehensive guide.* San Francisco, CA: Jossey-Bass.

Mezirow, J. (1991). *Making meaning through reflection: Transformative dimensions of adult learning.* San Francisco, CA: Jossey Bass.

Palmer, P. J. (2000). *Let your life speak: Listening to the voice of vocation*. San Francisco, CA: Jossey-Bass.

Putman, R. D. (2000). *Bowling alone: The collapse and revival of American community*. New York, NY: Simon & Shuster.

Reeves, R. (2004). Friendship is the invisible thread running through society. *New Statesman, 133*(4684), 29-32.

Schein, E. H. (2004). *Organizational culture and leadership* (3rd ed.). San Francisco, CA: John Wiley and Sons.

Spender, J. C., & Grinyer, P. H. (1995). Organizational renewal: Top management's role in a loosely coupled system. *Human Relations, 48*(8), 909-927.

Spender, J. C., & Grinyer, P. H. (1996). Organizational renewal. *International Studies of Management & Organization, 26*(1), 17-41.

Ulmer, R., & Sellnow, T. (2002). Crisis management and the discourse of renewal: Understanding the potential for positive outcomes of crisis. *Public Relations Review, 28*(4), 361-366.

Weymes, E. (2003). Relationships not leadership sustain successful organizations. *Journal of Change Management, 3*(4), 319-332.

Wheatley, M. J. (2003). *Turning to one another*. San Francisco, CA: Berrett-Koehler Publishers, Inc.

Wink, J. (2011). *Critical pedagogy: Notes from the real world* (4th ed.). San Francisco, CA: Pearson.

Academic Writing: A Self-Assessment Strategy for Cadence, Fluency, and Vocabulary Choice

Judith Gray, PhD
City University of Seattle
Gordon Albright School of Education

Abstract

Entering graduate students typically demonstrate a wide range of academic writing competencies. The purpose of the instructional practice described in this chapter is to close the writing literacy gaps and raise the standard of graduate writing overall. The practice is designed to specifically address three significant traits of writing—cadence, sentence fluency, and vocabulary choice—by introducing several activities that will generate self-assessment and self-improvement of student writing. Students perform these exercises on samples of their own writing. As a result of the critiquing and revising inherent in the process, student writing dramatically improves. Ideally instructors would introduce the strategy early in the program or course of study to establish high writing expectations and a shared language and process for writing improvement.

Introduction

Adult students exhibit a wide range of formal writing abilities as a direct result of earlier writing instruction, availability of writing opportunities, and personal levels of competence. Often evidence of their writing strengths and weaknesses becomes apparent during the writing samples they are required to produce as part of a university's application process. Although composed under pressure at the time, the writing samples are clear windows through which faculty can ascertain what is lacking in terms of formal academic style and engaging content. In almost all cases, further attention and action are necessary to elevate candidates' writing to recognized scholarly standards.

Review of Literature

The literature on adult academic writing is mostly confined to the ends of the higher education spectrum. At one end are the research studies of undergraduate and community college writing improvement strategies while at the other end is a narrow band of writing advice and experiential strategies for doctoral candidates preparing their dissertations. What is well-recognized is that adult writing is a skill, a habit, and a process as well as a product. In colleges and universities, strong writing skills are expected and more frequently demanded of students by instructors who are frequently published writers themselves. Aitchison (2009) recognizes that nowadays, academic writing is moving from an emphasis on writing as a "discrete skill" to the idea that writing does not happen in a vacuum. The act of writing, Aitchison claims, is a "complex, context-specific social and cultural practice" (p. 906). As such she approaches writing from an "academic literacies" perspective, cogently arguing that writing is not an isolated competency but occurs in the broader context of the academic environment including "speaking, reading, critiquing and writing" (p. 906). Furthermore, Aitchison maintains that academic writing is best learned and taught side by side with the subject content and knowledge, rather than "bolted on as a separate activity" (p. 906). This notion that writing skills should not be considered in isolation from one another nor from the subject matter is also supported by British researchers Elander, Harrington, Norton, Robinson, and Reddy (2006), who claim that core writing criteria, such as use of language and sentence structure, are abilities that are not only "intertwined with subject knowledge" but "are needed *in order* to understand and produce knowledge" (p. 84).

Self-assessment approaches to writing improvement have been endorsed by teachers and scholars for some time. Peden and Carroll, researchers from the University of Wisconsin, endorse the American Psychological Association guidelines for psychology majors, which suggest that self-assessment assignments meet important personal, academic, and institutional goals by encouraging students to "assume responsibility for their education, become reflective learners, and also help instructors, departments, and institutions achieve their assessment goals" (American Psychological Association, 2007; Peden & Carroll, 2008, p. 313). Peden and Carroll conducted a quantitative text analysis of student's language in self-assessment and concluded that self-assessment assignments elicit different ways of writing. In particular they found that self-assessments "activate cognitive processes" and also produce more reflective thinking (p. 316). Self-assessment plays a complementary role in developing academic literacies with a particular emphasis on academic writing.

Practice

An instructional practice that has been employed and that has proven particularly effective in raising adult writing self-awareness and self-improvement is the coordinated deconstruction of three significant aspects of all writing criteria: cadence, sentence fluency, and vocabulary choice. These aspects are integrated to comprise the driving mechanism of the instructional strategy. Cadence is defined as the rhythmic arrangement and flow of sentences, including length and variety. Fluency is defined as the seamless internal structure of sentences, and vocabulary choices are just that—the selection of appropriate and precise language. This deconstruction process is described in the following sequence:

1. Cadence: Sentence structure quantification
2. Fluency: Conjunction identification
3. Vocabulary: Word choice analysis

This instructional practice was used in a Master of Education class as an example of its application. Prior to the implementation of the instructional practice, these graduate students retrieved copies of their individual initial interview essays. These essays were created at the time of the admission interview process. Following the standard formal interview, applicants spent an hour or longer writing a summary of the article "Parent Involvement" (Comer, 2007). The precise instructions to applicants were, "Please read this article and summarize the content in 2–3 pages. There is no time limit."

During the first quarter of their master's program, the participants enrolled in the course Fundamentals of Teacher Research and were introduced to scholarly writing, American Psychological Association (APA) style and formatting, and the avenues of graduate research open to them. Part of the first class meeting was devoted to the Six-Traits Writing Rubric (Northwest Regional Education Laboratory, 2000) and in particular the traits of sentence fluency and word choice. Although initially inspired by the Six-Traits Writing Rubric developed by North West Regional Education Lab (NWREL) in Oregon, the practice of scrutinizing adult writing to enhance its effectiveness in the areas of cadence, fluency, and vocabulary was tested at Antioch University by the author in 2008 and implemented at City University of Seattle in 2009 in both the Assessment and

Teacher Research courses. A description of the writing self-assessment activities and exercises which make up the instructional practice follows:

Cadence: Sentence Structure Quantification

Students were first instructed to read their application interview essays, number each sentence in order, count the words in each sentence, and record the numbers on a T-chart. See Figure 1.

Figure 1. *Sentence Word Count T-Chart*

	Sentence #	Word Count
Sample	1	12

Sentence #	Word Count
1	
2	
3	
↓	
n	

Next, each student prepared a sheet of graph paper with the sentence numbers on the horizontal axis, the word counts on the vertical axis, his or her last name, and graph labels. See Figure 2.

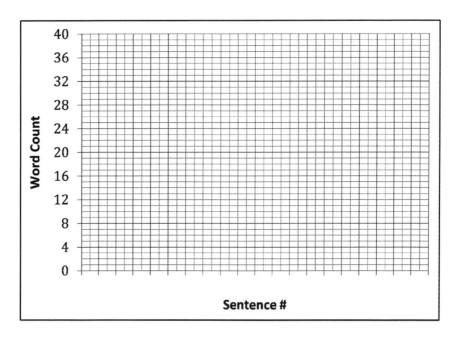

Figure 2. *Blank Cadence Graph*

Students then proceeded to plot the coordinates (x,y) from the T-chart correctly and link points to form a line graph. The subsequent graph was a visual representation of the cadence of their writing rhythms. The next steps were to self-analyze the graph by asking themselves the following questions:

1. What do I notice?
2. What is the value of this exercise?
3. What are my next steps?

Further critiquing and analysis were achieved by posting all student graphs on the wall followed by a group discussion focused on comparison, contrast and commendations feedback. This discussion was facilitated by the instructor. See Figure 3.

Figure 3. *Sample Cadence Graph*

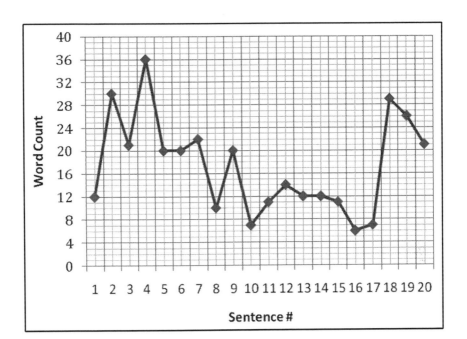

Sentence Fluency: Identifying First Words and Conjunctions

This instructional exercise required students to return to their essays and identify the first words of each sentence, the first three words and any conjunctions (connecting words e.g., because, although, and, if .... then). This data was entered on a Sentence Fluency Chart. See Figure 4.

Figure 4. *Sentence Fluency Chart*

#	First Word	First 3 words	Conjunction
Sample	**The**	**The day was**	**although**
#	**First Word**	**First 3 words**	**Conjunction**
1			
2			
3			
4			
↓			
n			

When the chart was fully completed, students carefully scanned their charts for interest, variety, and flow, thereby self-assessing their strengths and also those areas that needed attention and greater scholarliness. When this screening and critiquing had been accomplished, students turned to a partner to share findings and to reflect. See Figure 5.

Figure 5. *Sample Word Choice And Sentence Fluency Chart*

#	First 3 Words	Word Count	Bright Word(s)	Repeated Word(s)	Conjunction
1	**The** article "Educational	14	leadership	the	or, for
2	**It** talks about	19	benefits community involved	the	as, and
3	**Parent** involvement is	17	involve- ment par- ticipating present limited		but

4	**This** includes parent	20	includes social	the, parent	and
↓					
n					

Vocabulary: Word Choice Coding and Analysis

The students selected one page of their essays and assembled the following supplies: highlighter, red pen, and black pen or pencil. The purpose of this coding activity was to clearly and visually distinguish between *new* words, *dead* words, *bright* words, and words that were r*epetitive*. New words are the ones that the writer has never or rarely used in prior writing; dead words are words that are dull, imprecise, or clichés, e.g., get, stuff, thing, and nice, plus phrases such as "you know;" bright words are dynamic, high impact, or especially scholarly; and repeated words are those used more than once on the page. After choosing the page they wished to code, students conducted four vocabulary parses employing the following coding system:

new words   Circle in red
dead words   X out in black or draw line through
bright words   Highlight
repeated words   Underline in black

See Figure 6.

Figure 6. *Sample "Word Choice" Coded Page*

The article, "Educational Leadership," is about the SDP or School Development Program for change. It talks about the benefits of the students, as well as staff and community when the parents are involved. Parent involvement is not limited to just a parent being present in their students' life, but participating. This includes parent teacher conferences, the parent helping the student learn, getting involved in social events, performances and much more.   Parents and teachers working together is beneficial to not only the school, but the student by providing a school climate that involves "developmental pathways-physical, social-interactive, psycho-emotional, ethical, linguistic, and cognitive." (pg 2)

Having parents, teachers, students and staff working together is beneficial to the students, school, teachers, and in turn the community, under the SDP theory.

Key
blue = new words
red = dead words
words = bright words
_ = repeated words

Once this activity was completed, students recorded their own responses to the following prompts:

1. What do I notice?
2. What is the value of this activity?
3. What are my next steps?

Students then revised and re-submitted a second draft for consideration. See figure 7.

Figure 7. *Sample Second draft*

The article, "The Rewards of Parent Participation" (Comer, 2007) describes a School Development Program (SDP) that was implemented in the Oakland School district in 2005 to increase parent involvement. The author enumerates several benefits enjoyed by students, as well as staff and the community due to increased parent participation.

Parent involvement is not solely limited to parents being present in their student's home life, but also includes being engaged in the academics and activities of the school. For example, parent teacher conferences, tutoring, social events, and much more.

When parents and teachers work together everyone advances- students, teachers, and parents - because a school climate has been created that understands and respects the core connection to families. Parental involvement in Comer's School Development Program "not only improves teaching and learning; it can also transform families' lives (p. 40). By far the greatest benefit of the SDP is the greater awareness and support of the larger school community.

Comer, J. (2005). The rewards of parent participation. *Educational Leadership*, *62*(6), 38-42.

The entire instructional practice concluded with an opportunity to debrief the process using such questions as "What was effective?" "What was lacking?" "What needs to be adjusted?" "What do you now aspire to?"

Impact and Application

The positive impact of this strategy has been most apparent in the students' Teacher Research products. Students perceived remarkable improvements in their own writing and have been anxious to try the strategy in their future classrooms with beginning writers. These adult students also have acquired a common language with which to constructively critique their own writing and the writing of others.

This writing self-assessment strategy can be readily used by college and university instructors and also by classroom teachers and writer groups. The exercises and steps are user-friendly and lend themselves to tangible results, constructive analysis, and valuable feedback. Ideally the self-assessment process will enable adult learners to proceed productively and independently at their own pace, thus freeing up writing and research instructors to nimbly and more effectively address individual writing needs. In practical terms instructors would introduce the strategy early in the program or course to establish high writing expectations. Faculty interested in applying this strategy would need to collect original samples of student writing and make copies for the in-class exercises. It is further recommended that teaching faculty either observe a writing class where the strategy is being employed or attend a workshop to learn the effective use of the strategy and the nuances of its various exercises.

Opportunities for Further Research

Graduate student applicant writing samples strongly suggest that many entering students do not possess the necessary academic writing strengths to advance in their graduate studies and professional careers. It behooves institutions of higher education therefore to deliberately design and provide adult learners with an authentic writing program or process based on sound research. Therefore, recommendations for further research include

1. An in-depth review and critical analysis of initial interview writing samples using a validated writing rubric to develop a matrix or scale on which to place students.
2. An action research design study to compare students' writing before and after a Six-Traits Writing intervention, such as the one described in this chapter.
3. A qualitative study that monitors and analyzes student "writing logs" over time to determine cycles or patterns that surface as writing strengths materialize.

Adult academic writing rarely escapes the need for revision or improvement—whether it be the small details or the larger fluency issues. As academic writing and research instructors, it is our responsibility to keep our students' potential in our sights and actively facilitate its full realization.

References

Aitchison, C. (2009). Writing groups for doctoral educa-tion. *Studies in Higher Education, 34*(8), 905-916. doi: 10.1080/03075070902785580

American Psychological Association (2007). *APA guidelines for the undergraduate psychology major.* Washington, DC: American Psychological Association.

Comer, J. (2005). The rewards of parent participation. *Educational Leadership, 62*(6), 38–42.

Elander, J., Harrington, K., Norton, L., Robinson, H., & Reddy, P. (2006). Complex skills and academic writing: A review of evidence about the types of learning required to meet core assessment criteria. *Assessment & Evaluation in Higher Education, 31*(1), 71-90.

Northwest Regional Education Laboratory (2000). *The history of the 6 + 1 traits of writing.* Portland, OR: NWREL.

Peden, B., & Carroll, D. (2008). Ways of writing: Linguistic analysis of self-assessment and traditional assignments. *Teaching of Psychology, 35,* 313-318. Doi:10.1080/00986280802374419

Re-wiring Student Perceptions of What a Student Is

Nathan Kositsky, MS
City University of Seattle
School of Management

Abstract

At times it is necessary to reframe instructors' thinking about what a student is. Within this process of reframing, instructors can find a new identity for themselves in both the in-class and online environments. Techniques for turning control of content over to the students are discussed, including using the students as classroom lecturers. The principle employed in this approach is that if a person learns content well enough to teach it, then real learning has taken place.

Introduction

"A micromanager is the equivalent of a coach who cannot let his players play. He is a source of stress in a game where there's enough stress already" (Arzola, 2000, p. 44). Present teaching leans toward micromanagement by accident and then validates it through practice. The student appears in the classroom to encounter a syllabus, reading material, prepared lectures, already-built PowerPoint presentations, schedules, assignments, rubrics, and grading criteria. In fact, the student receives everything to be successful except the most important things – his or her own ingenuity and ownership. In a desire to be fully prepared in classrooms as well as be validated as institutions, universities have become micromanagers, forcing students into the role of customer service reps to their instructors. Students spend their time finding out what needs to be done, how to do it, when to submit it, and then deliver it to get good grades and, with repetition, a degree. This can be neither satisfying to the student nor the teacher, nor in larger part to society.

One alternative approach begins by substituting the instructor, professor, or lecturer as the guiding force in the classroom (Gordon & Anderson, 1981) and replacing that person with the students in the class. In other words make the students the classroom lecturer, one student after another, individually and in teams, delivering the content.

In this approach the students are placed in charge of presenting the lectures each week. They must know the material well enough to communicate it. In the very first class, the re-wiring of student perceptions of what a student is begins to transfer from "a passive order-follower" delivering what is expected into "a creative, independent thinker" seeing beyond an assignment to the underlying reasons why the assignment was called for and delivering on those underlying reasons through multiple communications channels.

The instructor may or may not resurface as the most knowledgeable and resourceful person in the room. If the instructor does not resurface, then it is possible that a greater learning has been achieved than was originally planned. An even better outcome is if the instructor keeps pace with the level of discovery in the environment. In such a case, learning has spread in all directions, both to students and faculty members. In any event the fact that the instructor remains the giver of grades holds an element of control in good stead. It's just a different type of control.

The predominant views of the topic can be found in a review of the works of Milton H. Erickson (Gordon & Meyers-Anderson, 1981; Festinger, 1957; Maslow, 1946; Reeve, 2009). Erickson is the most instructive. In his discussion of Pygmalion, Erickson warns that "intentionally or unconsciously we imbue the world around us with our own ideas about the way the world is, or should be" (Erickson, as cited in Gordon & Meyers-Anderson, 1981, p. 12). Instructors communicate their views of content and students learn to feed those views back so as to be considered a reflection of the instructor, which students have learned the instructor considers beautiful. That is a limiting experience for both instructor and student. Instructors must learn not to sculpt their ideals of beauty into their students, then like Pygmalion breathe life into them and marry them. The best way for instructors to learn this is to get out of the way. If students don't have a preconceived notion of what they are to look like, then they may discover and display their own natural beauty. Another thing that is learned from Erickson is the concept of ownership. Who owns the therapy? If the patient owns the therapy, then the therapy will be followed. If the students own the classroom, then they will expect the best from each other because it is *their* classroom.

Maslow (1946) and Reeve (2009) add a voice by instructing in the difference between the self-esteem need level and the self-actualization need level. Self-actualization is about others; self-esteem is about oneself. Self-esteem must be attained to be discarded, and it must be discarded lest the person live a life forever in the mirror, unable to truly embrace diversity of thought in others. The Hindus instruct that pride is the heaviest burden of them all. Yet instructors arrive at a position of teaching through achievement of self-esteem, and the Catch-22 is this self-esteem must be thrown away for effective teaching to begin. Teaching is about others, after all, and the instructor learns by being taught and, in being taught, nourished. Therefore, the instructor, in giving over control to student, becomes self-actualized, and that is also the gift the instructor grants students in the paradigm of students as lecturers.

Festinger (1957) warns that cognitive dissonance can create burnout. Cognitive dissonance asserts that the brain causes discomfort when a person holds to a belief contrary to fact. To reduce this discomfort, the person uses defense mechanisms to hide the truth. The instructor, in pain from listening too many years to his or her own voice and pet phrases, inadvertently can brutalize students with a lack of enthusiasm. The cure is to let students teach with their first-time enthusiasm.

Instructors may find that treating the classroom environment as a real work environment develops improved student habits and performance. Rather than merely grade an assignment, students are invited to redo less-than-adequate efforts, and consider the original submission as practice. They also have the benefit of instructor feedback from the first effort. If you don't get it right in the workplace, you must do it over. Soon you learn to do it right the first time.

The background can therefore be summarized as follows: Don't look upon beauty as a reflection of yourself. Allow for diversity in content and opinion. Give others the chance to be brilliant in order to delight in their own achievements. Avoid burnout by sharing the load. Treat the classroom as a real workplace.

Practices, Examples, Issues

The first class is critical. The second class is its validation. Therefore, do not expect students to believe change is really happening. However, the review of the syllabus will never be more attentively focused on when students know they will be responsible for content delivery. During student and instructor introductions, the question is raised as follows:

Instructor: "What are you here for?"

Student: "I'm here to learn."

Instructor: "So am I. Let's see if we can make that happen for both of us."

Teams are chosen after the standard introductions. Each team is responsible for one part of the content to be presented during Week Two. They vie for content responsibility on a first-come-first-serve basis. Thus, the first lesson is achieved: Respond quickly and be proactive. Now that students know what part of the Week Two lecture they are responsible for, they are told something like, "If you don't like the assignment, change it to your liking, but keep the intent of knowledge pure to the goals of the week." This is meant to confuse and free at the same time. It is likely that students will stick to the straight and narrow on the first assignment because they don't know the instructor's reactions. But at least the students know that the instructor has no preconceived notion of the presentation they will deliver. The students also know that they must discover the intent of the learning for the week.

The second part of the first class is critical to the success of the approach. The students are told something like, "Be creative. Make your points by filming a movie and posting it on YouTube or another social media site; link it to your PowerPoint, and we'll watch it that way; or use Facebook and Twitter to deliver your content and we'll go online and you can deliver your assignment like that. You can have handouts and signs and banners and skits. You can record your presentation. Take over the class in any way you want. It's your class, but it's mine too, so keep me interested. We're in this together. Show dexterity and knowledge." Instructors will find a buzz in the classroom as team members start talking to each other. Student will turn to each other and begin organizing content and setting up outside class meetings. Here is the first lesson for the instructor: Let the buzz continue for a while.

Another interaction may be as follows:

Student: "I am not creative."
Instructor: "For me, creativity is weighing the facts. There is a huge analytical component to creativity."
Student: "Maybe I *am* creative."

That kind of re-wiring is Erickson at work. If an instructor wants a student to understand something, what will that instructor *do* to help that student understand? That understanding is what is called being creative. This re-wiring goes on throughout the first couple of classes until every student becomes a cheerleader of the content presented. Instructors will discover learning scenarios that they would never have thought of on their own.

The second class is where the instructor establishes valid credentials and the students assert their claim to the success of the course. Several scenarios unfold:

1. The brilliant, comprehensive, inspiring, class-involving, interactive presentation/lecture
2. The conservative, incomplete presentation/lecture, or
3. The unprepared presentation/lecture

There are other variations on these themes, but in each the instructor's response is plenary. It is here that the instructor establishes that his or her job is not being turned over to the students, but rather it is how the instructor *is* doing his or her job. In the case of a brilliant presentation or lecture, the instructor can exclaim, "That's even better than the way I would have done it!" There is always a question and answer period following the presentation or lecture, and non-presenting students (the audience) are informed that this counts toward participation points, and since everyone was responsible for reading the week's material, specific questions based on knowledge are anticipated, including questions from the instructor, who is part of the class (audience) and who has the knowledge to confirm and/or expand upon the content details.

In the case of an unprepared lecture, it must be addressed directly with compassion. An interaction may be as follows:

> Instructor: "Yes, this is what can happen when you get together late in the week…if you got together at all. So, what could be done better here? Would you like another chance at it next week?"

It is a natural outgrowth to discuss how the presentation or lecture could be improved. The instructor should also have a presentation ready—in the hip pocket, so to speak—and deliver in whole or in part as an example. The instructor can ask how the students could expand on the same topic in the redo, perhaps this time matching the content to something they are *really* interested in. One example of how an instructor can align student interest with content is, "If you love music, show how a band might approach this topic."

Then the instructor can ask, "Would you like another shot at it next week? You can do it however you want to approach it, and remember, you'll still have the Week Three one to do as well." Instructors will find that students want to redo the inadequate effort. This sort of real-world experience offers students an opportunity to rework assignments, but from a different angle, relieving the instructor of the *redundo absurdum* of having to see the same thing twice.

For Week Four through the rest of the course, brilliance then becomes the common occurrence. Classroom management techniques afford a student this opportunity particularly when a classroom session is reframed as a ceremony. What is learned from indigenous people is that ceremony begins with an intention. Many instructors, lecturers, and professors don't do enough preparation or do too much preparation or walk in with the same old preparation. They don't take a sacred breath at the entry to the classroom to consider the intention. Sometimes an idea can change when a student comes up with something better than the original intention. This happens in microcosm. A student says something or presents something that hints like a symptom at an intention, and the instructor must be sensitive to hear it and see it, embrace it, and expand upon it. The classroom, after all, is no big ship; it can turn on a dime and must. *Staying the course* may look like strength from the outside, but it is really the limiting perspective of arrogance hiding ignorance.

Each course attracts students of unique makeup. The instructor can uncover this unique makeup with an exercise. Each student can construct a shield, and on that shield the student is asked to draw who he or she is, and what he or she cares about. The second class is filled with these shields. Each student presents his or her shield, explaining the significance of each symbol. These shields can be put up on the screen or placed around the classroom, a reminder of intention, upbringing, and experience. The third class has *team* shields. Students bring their individual shields to a team meeting and construct a team shield. The team shield is brought to class and is used as a team logo on presentations. The shields act as vessels to convey personal meanings that otherwise may have gone undiscovered.

These techniques or therapeutic patterns have a combined goal to move students from a classroom mentality to a career mentality. In the shifting process from order taker to creative thinker, it is common to establish the reality that "This can move you toward promotions in your careers."

Real-World Interaction:

Instructor: "There are only two rules. Show up on time and be prepared."

Student: "Why do we have those rules?"

Instructor: "They are to keep me sane."

Student: "Are there any more rules?"

Instructor: "Everything else is fair game. Show up on time and be prepared. If you do that, you will be thought of well and become successful. You can be as creative as you want. In fact, you are encouraged to be creative."

With this interaction, students suddenly understand that it really is *their* course. It's *their* classroom. It's *their* content, and they can't wait to present and show what they're made of.

On a macro level, it's all about managing the content the instructor wants to get through. But the instructor really should *not* want to get through all the content. The instructor should want to find the sticking points where students are showing most interest so the class can really drill down into those specifics. The students will then realize that for everything else that is touched upon superficially there is drill-down. Students are tasked with comprehensive drill-downs on their own time, knowing that much more comprehensive drill-down will be achieved in class.

Instructors should be sensitive to sticking points. It may be a good practice to make PowerPoint presentations available online to the class. Here is an interaction: "You've got this presentation on your computer so dive into it in your own time. See this bullet here? This is the one that interests me today. Here is why." Then the students can see how the instructor teaches. They can experience how the instructor is willing to explore a topic in depth, pulling it from the list of other things that relate to it. These students can then get an idea how to teach when it is their turn to teach the instructor and the class.

Every victory must be celebrated. An instructor must celebrate small victories. Greatest among all small victories is trying. The more students try, the more they will discover correct answers or better yet correct questions. The only thing holding students back from correct answers is trying. Thus, Stephen Leacock's quote, "The harder I try, the luckier I get." It is etched in stone on the side of the Leacock Building on the McGill University campus in Montreal. Instructors can tell students after a great presentation, "I know how much work went into that while you were outside of class. Congratulations! It paid off." The instructor, in this case, wants students to know their efforts away from class are acknowledged through the lens of the presentation.

Future Research Directions

Future research that might contribute to this topic could include an experiment in which students create the curriculum for a department based upon need, followed by faculty modifying that curriculum based upon knowledge. A series of experiments in classroom management might involve videotaping student presentations and instructor presentations followed by analysis by students and instructors. Experiments in online curriculum could include the instructor posting the questions on the discussion board for the first half of the course and the students posting the questions on the discussion board for the second half of the course.

Conclusion

"Re-wiring Student Perceptions of What a Student Is" clearly begins with the re-wiring of the instructor. In a fast-paced technical world, change matters. Students come into the physical or online classroom with extraordinary tools. Their brilliance is acknowledged, unfocused, or untapped. If the instructor frees students to explore in creative delivery formats, students will be encouraged to step it up by their fellow students. In the same process, the instructor may discover a new excitement that can only come from being a student.

References

Arzola, G. (2000). Making a good team great. *Across the Board*, *37*(9), 44.

Festinger, L. (1957). *A theory of cognitive dissonance.* Evanston, IL: Row, Peterson and Company.

Gordon, D., and Meyers-Anderson, M. (1981). *Phoenix: The therapeutic patterns of Milton H. Erickson.* Capitola, CA: Meta Publications.

Maslow, A. (1946). A theory of human motivation. In P. Harriman (Ed.) *Twentieth century psychology.* New York, NY: Philosophical Library. (Reprinted from *Psychological Review*, 1946, *50*, 370-396).

Reeve, J. (2009). *Understanding motivation and emotion* (5th ed.). Hoboken, NJ: John Wiley & Sons, Inc.

PART TWO

ONLINE DELIVERY

Online and hybrid instructional delivery methods have become as common as in-class sessions. Yet many differing viewpoints are circulating regarding the best way to deliver online instruction.

Most would agree that to be effective, online instructors cannot merely transfer in-class activities to an online format. Online learning is a completely different methodology that involves the use of tools and strategies not found in traditional classrooms. Discussion boards, virtual team projects, interactions with and among remote students, and course cohesion are only a few of the aspects of online learning that require additional attention from faculty skilled in the use of this delivery method.

The chapters in Part Two identify proven practices in online delivery. Ranodda DeChambeau opens this section with a discussion of the nuances involved in hybrid delivery models by highlighting the advantages and challenges of this method. Dr. Maria Minor reviews the use of various technologies that can help reduce the isolation so often associated with online learning in an asynchronous environment. Keith Foe presents an analysis of some of the more popular options that can be used to include video clips in online classes.

Dr. Kelly Flores furthers the discussion of online and hybrid programs by presenting a number of practices that can help students succeed in these formats. Anna Cholewinska adds important motivational strategies to better engage learners in the online environment and Carla Weaver provides a number of specific strategies that instructors can use to ensure that their communication supports student learning.

Two chapters address the use of the case study method in online learning. Dr. Peggy Kasloff discusses the incorporation of case studies that utilize personal portfolios intended to engage students in active learning. Dr. Jean Ann French presents a number of recommendations for case-based learning that facilitates the real-life application of business lessons. Judy Hinrichs closes this section with a summary of recommendations from the literature and experiences from faculty regarding proven practices in the use of videoconferencing to join geographically disparate cohorts into a single classroom.

Mixed-Mode Course Design and Delivery

Ranodda DeChambeau, MBA, MEd
City University of Seattle
School of Management

Abstract

The student learning experience is undergoing an unprecedented transformation as the integration of technology becomes a major consideration when accessing delivery options. This paper will review the work of researchers as they explore the application of technology to learning. The model that is analyzed is the mixed-mode, hybrid, or blended learning that combines traditional face-to-face classroom time with significant online activities and resources. Perceptions of both students and instructors will be considered in conjunction with the theoretical support for this type of course delivery. Finally, the paper outlines the benefits of this model and the major considerations for design and implementation.

Introduction

The student learning experience is undergoing an unprecedented transformation. Technology has become the driver for the changing environment and is often considered both the problem and the solution to current learning delivery challenges. Adopting new learning technologies can result in a complex learning environment where discussions and other activities are presented to students as a blended learning experience. New communication technologies allow students to participate in discussions that are no longer restricted to the classroom. Instructors can start a topic before the students meet face-to-face and continue the discussion long after the class has ended. In a world where an increasing number of educational institutions offer online courses, it is time to stop and ask how changes in learning technologies have affected learning and whether technology is the problem or the solution.

The terms "mixed-mode," "hybrid," and "blended learning" may mean different things to different people; in this chapter the terms will be used interchangeably. Hybrid, blended, and mixed-mode learning have been defined by Hofmann and Miner (2008) as "using the best delivery methodologies available for a specific objective, including online, classroom-based instruction, electronic performance support, paper-based, and formal or informal on-the-job solutions among others" (p. 29). It is the nature of the learning experience that ultimately determines the "blend" of these components. Blended learning was developed as a very pragmatic concept. It was developed initially in organizational training to replace completely traditional face-to-face training with a mixture, or blend, of e-learning and traditional approaches.

Online learning has grown in popularity as busy learners search for ways to earn degrees without spending more time in the classroom. One trend in online education is the utilization of mixed-mode learning environments, primarily in higher educational institutions, which offer a combination of online and face-to-face instruction (Doering, 2006). The goal of mixed-mode learning is to improve the educational experience for students by joining together the best practices of in-class teaching with those of online learning to promote active independent learning and reduce class seat time. Mixed-mode courses offer many advantages over completely face-to-face or completely online courses, including convenience, interaction, flexibility, and similar levels of learning and retention. Research on the effectiveness of online education in general shows that students who learn at a distance do not learn any worse, or any better, than traditional students (Garnham & Kaleta, 2002).

From the point of view of instructional design, the choice of one learning method over another is hardly ever neutral although the general objectives of the face-to-face and online courses are essentially the same. In the adoption of the online approach rather than the traditional one, there are decisions to be made and problems to overcome. It is more complicated than simply adding technology to an existing program, as a re-working of the learning activities is often required (Ertmer, 2003). Blending traditional and online learning involves significant changes in both course modalities. These changes include 1) changes to the content of the curriculum; 2) changes to the organization of the modules; and 3) the development and use of major e-learning components (Boyle, 2005). Matching the delivery method to the learning objectives is the key to integrating technology into the online portion of the program.

According to Boyle (2005) organizations that lack experience creating blended learning often fail to align content with the most appropriate technology. For example, lecturing for forty minutes on how to create a Pivot Table in Excel is not effective because creation of the table requires hands-on practice. However, it is easy to demonstrate the topic using application sharing in a virtual classroom. Designers of blended curricula need to remember that each learning objective has different characteristics. Some objectives lend themselves better to activity-based training, while others tend to be more knowledge or information oriented, lending themselves to a more didactic approach. Going through the process of designing the best training approach on an objective-by-objective level allows for exploration of a blended solution. Objectives must also be viewed in light of the whole curriculum to ensure that they are integrated instead of each being its own independent learning. It's not about getting the technology right—it's about getting the instruction right.

Mixed-mode delivery offers positive and negative aspects for both the student and the instructor. To understand these elements more fully, it is helpful to understand how both the instructors and the students perceive the e-learning experience.

Faculty and Student Perceptions of E-learning

Garnham and Kaleta (2002) of the University of Wisconsin-Milwaukee found that the instructors they studied believed students learned more in the hybrid format than they did in traditional class sections. "Instructors reported that students wrote better papers, performed better on exams, produced higher quality projects, and were capable of more meaningful discussions on course material" (p. 2). The researchers supported their qualitative assessments with quantitative data from the University of Central Florida, which showed that students in hybrid courses achieved better grades than students in traditional face-to-face courses or in totally online courses. Data from the University of Central Florida also showed that student retention in hybrid courses was better than retention in totally online courses and was equivalent to that of face-to-face courses. In the same study Garnham and Kaleta (2002) captured these comments from instructors of hybrid courses:

1. My students have done better than I've ever seen; they are motivated, enthused, and doing their best work.
2. I sense a heightened level of enthusiasm in my students.
3. Introverts, who are quiet in the face-to-face class, really participate online.
4. I was tired of hearing myself talk. This gets so much more student interaction.
5. Discussions are good, both in and out of class.
6. The hybrid allowed me to do things in my course that I've always wanted to do and couldn't.

A study by Delialioglu and Yildirum (2007) found that students considered the mixed-mode course structure interesting and useful. The students especially liked courses that were neither fully online nor fully traditional. The students preferred to participate in learning activities in the classroom that practiced the information they read online. Finally, the sophistication of the website was important and the students reported that cognitive tools like glossaries in the course website made it more interesting than the standard electronic page-turning websites.

Delialioglu and Yildirum (2007) also asked students if the mixed-mode format allowed them to relate new information to their prior knowledge in the area studied. Their findings showed that the mixed-mode course was successful in relating previous knowledge to the newly acquired knowledge if the student had at least some previous knowledge in that subject. The course features that students felt supported their learning in the mixed-mode course, in order of importance, were:

- Homework and assignments provided through the website
- Announcements and additional links supplied through the website
- Quizzes given in the classroom
- Group work and classroom discussions conducted in the classroom
- Message Board in the course website.

Garnham and Kaleta (2002) found that 80 percent of the students would recommend a hybrid course to their friends and most appreciated the convenience and the freedom to work at home at their own pace. They also found that 69 percent of the students reported that they could control the pace of their own learning; 77 percent felt they could better organize their time; 61% stated that there should be more mixed-mode classes; and 67 percent disagreed that the time spent online would have been better spent in class.

An in-depth exploration of the mixed-mode or blended learning approach will aid program managers, course developers, and instructors in developing programs that more successfully meet the challenges and objectives of their programs.

Theoretical Support for Mixed-Mode Delivery Design

Support for the use of the mixed-mode design can be found in many schools of thought on adult learning, including that of Malcom Knowles, a pioneer in the area of adult learning theory.

Knowles (1984) identified characteristics of the adult learner (andragogy) that differed from the characteristics of child learners (pedagogy). Of the six major characteristics he identified, mixed-mode delivery supports two of them directly, and when incorporated with other course elements, supports all six. Briefly, Knowles's adult learning characteristics include the concepts that:

- Adults are autonomous and self-directed learners.
- Adults need to connect learning to their previous knowledge and experience.
- Adults are goal-oriented and must understand how the learning contributes to their goals.
- Adults are relevancy oriented; they must see the reason for learning something.
- Adults are practical learners, focusing on the elements of the lesson that they can use in the near future.
- Adults need to be shown respect and should be treated as equals in experience and knowledge and allowed to voice their opinions freely in class.

Mixed-mode design allows students to be highly autonomous and self-directed because much of their learning experience is outside of the controlled classroom environment and is at the discretion of the individual. The location and timing of online learning is in the control of the student and is typically done as a solitary activity when the online environment is asynchronous, which means that not all students are participating at the same time. Synchronous learning environments are less autonomous as the students interact at the same time, but the students retain control over the place they study and are allowed the ability to multi-task as they interact online.

The mixed-mode delivery model also respects the adult learner as it acknowledges the student's life as a whole and that being a student may be a relatively small part of one's commitments and schedule. Online discussion gives every student a voice, even those that are reluctant, for whatever reason, to participate fully in classroom face-to-face discussion. Online learning allows each student the time needed to respond and participate and respects the diverse learning styles that students bring to the classroom.

Good course design and quality instruction, whether it includes a mixed-mode delivery or not, needs to integrate the other characteristics of adult learners to fully enhance the adult learner's experience. The mixed-mode design does not restrict nor conflict with the incorporation of any of Knowles' other adult learning characteristics.

Merriam and Caffarella (1999) state in their foundational book *Learning in Adulthood: A Comprehensive Guide* that the overriding barriers of adults participating in educational endeavors were time, cost of education, and conflicting family responsibilities. The mixed-mode design addresses these barriers directly by allowing students to spend more time at home and less time in the classroom. Factoring in the time and costs of transportation, this design can be a less costly alternative for students. The cost of computer equipment and an Internet connection can mitigate any cost savings for the initial course. However, over time the student may see some cost savings.

Social Learning Constructivists argue that the traditional curriculum and the oral tradition of lectures within higher education are two central barriers to the implementation of blended learning. However, they believe that the social constructivist emphasis on self-governed work for students could remove these barriers. According to the social constructivist approach, learning is considered an active, social process in which individuals actively construct knowledge within the social environment. This means that learning necessitates the active and self-governed work of students (Vygotsky, 1978). The mixed-mode model allows students to self-govern their involvement in the learning activities while providing a strong social component in the classroom that supports the social processes needed to construct knowledge.

Social Learning Theory (Bandura, 1976) proposes that people learn from one another by observation, imitation, and modeling behavior. This theory has often been called a bridge between behaviorist and cognitive learning theories because it encompasses attention, memory, and motivation. Online only classes do not give students the ability to physically observe each other and learn from the social interactions in the same way. The mixed-mode delivery provides the opportunity for this social learning during the face-to-face sessions, while still supporting self-directed learning and flexibility in scheduling.

Mixed-Mode Delivery

The strengths and weaknesses of mixed-mode course delivery have been widely studied. One of the earliest arguments questioning technology's role in learning was pointed out by Clark (as cited by Delialioglu & Yildirim, 2007) who felt that focusing purely on technology would be the wrong approach and that learning should be the center of the educator's efforts. Many research studies show that integrating technology into instruction can definitely improve access to information, but that it does not improve learning in any significant way. Given that online and classroom delivery have equal impact on student learning, differing benefits and limitations accrue to both online and classroom course designs.

Classroom space and computer lab access is at a premium at many institutions that have insufficient physical resources to meet their expanding needs. Hybrid courses may allow institutions to maximize their available resources, allowing two classes to operate in one physical space. According to Ron Bleed, vice chancellor of Information Technologies at Maricopa Community College, hybrid course offerings may be the only way colleges and universities can keep up with the continuing population growth and the demands for lifelong learning (Gould, 2003). On a pure cost level, hybrids reduce paper and photocopying costs. In hybrid courses all course documents, including syllabi, lecture notes, assignment sheets, and other hard copy handouts are easily accessible to students on the course website.

While developing online course material is time consuming, hybrid course development can serve as a way for faculty to ease into distance learning formats without the burden of developing an entire course. In this way an institution can maximize the expertise of its faculty without incurring professional development costs.

Three overriding themes emerge from the literature on the benefits of online learning in a mixed-mode course design. These themes are centered on the benefits of collaboration, improved discussion and interaction, and student and instructor flexibility.

Collaboration

Harasim (1990) depicts peer interaction among students as a vital variable in learning and proposes that a collaborative learning process is necessary to engage the learner and promote the kind of learning necessary for present and future work preparation. Additional studies confirm that online interaction encourages collaborative environments and have determined that student collaboration can occur through a computer network. Most providers of online courses use asynchronous discussion groups to generate student-to-student and student-to-instructor interaction. Student-teacher interaction is enhanced as students do not have to rely on the instructor's physical "office hours" to meet. Instructors communicate consistently with students and can more easily be responsive to clarifications, questions, and student concerns.

The virtual environment aids in collaboration because it is a forum for continued interaction between students and the instructor. The asynchronous nature of the online portion allows students to collaborate even though they are not all at the same place and time. Collaborative efforts that may begin in the classroom can be continued without interruption through the online medium. The sharing of information in all its forms does not rely on the students "meeting up" to exchange physical documents. The centralization of electronic resources also supports environmental concerns about the overuse of paper products as students need only print those resources that are pertinent to them. Storing electronic information has become commonplace and students often prefer this method of organizing data.

Collaboration is enhanced by keeping a record of the collective learning of the class that can be reviewed at any time as needed. The opportunity for students to contribute comments, ideas, resources, and web links over the duration of the course and afterwards provides scope for dynamic knowledge sharing and knowledge creation. This may change the way students work and how they keep "notes" as they utilize the permanent record of conversations and ideas that are generated instead of capturing these same ideas by pen and paper.

Discussion

Discussion is a valuable tool in the teaching process, and a survey of online instructors found that forty-one of the forty-two respondents used discussion as a teaching method (Delfino & Persico, 2007). A criticism of online learning is that online courses lack the interaction to get the same benefits as a classroom discussion. Online discussion boards are asynchronous learning environments that offer students the opportunity to engage in dialogue. The utilization of discussion boards provides students an opportunity to share their thoughts with others in the class. Discussion boards establish a collaborative learning environment by allowing students to become acquainted with fellow classmates and develop rapport between students and instructors. Studies have found evidence that interaction between students in an asynchronous learning environment leads to a community of learners (Dalsgaard & Godsk, 2007).

Ellis and Calvo (2006) found that students who conceive of discussions as a useful way of learning more about the subject tend to engage in online discussions in a reflective and meaningful way. They also engage in face-to-face discussions with a similar intent. They found that students who approach discussions meaningfully hold positive perceptions of this type of learning experience. However, students who do not display an awareness of the link between their discussions and the learning outcomes tend to hold a negative perception of this type of learning experience.

The implications of this research for teaching practice are clear. At the level of the whole learning experience, a lot of preparation is necessary to help students learn through discussion. It is not enough to simply provide opportunities for meaningful discussions closely linked to the learning outcomes of the subject to the students. If students are not aware of the purpose of the discussions or they have negative perceptions of the learning context, then they are not likely to benefit from the discussions or perform well in the subject. Consequently more preparation is needed in helping students understand how to learn from the experience of others; how to use the postings of others to reflect on their own answers; how to stop worrying about appearing ignorant in their postings; and how to focus on the relationship between the discussions and the learning outcomes of the subject. Improving the clarity of the goals and standards is important in addressing the students' perceptions of their learning context, as does making a greater effort to understand the students' difficulties as they engage in their discussions. Another finding by Ells and Calvo (2006) is that postings stimulate follow-up face-to-face discussion and that online discussion engages students more actively in the whole course.

Other positive aspects to discussion include 1) discussion is not cut off at the end of the traditional class but can continue past the "given" time; 2) the student does not have to get the instructor's eye to make a comment but is free to comment at will; 3) it is more difficult for one person to dominate the debate; and 4) comments can be read and reread for clarity. Even the shyest student in the classroom is forced to have a voice online through discussion assignments. Students are given the time needed to format their thoughts and to express themselves in a thoughtful, controlled manner.

Flexibility

Flexibility manifests itself throughout the mixed-mode design. Scheduling and adapting to student learning styles are two of the major benefits.

The mixed-mode model allows students to participate from anywhere and at any time that they feel is their optimum learning time. For adult students who are typically juggling work, family, and other personal commitments, online classes fit into their schedule more easily than attending a regular weekly class in the evenings or on weekends. Those that travel frequently for business find this format allows them to be full participants in the class. The mixed-mode design does require that students be available at a predetermined time and place for the face-to-face class. However, since these meetings are far less frequent than in the traditional model, it is easier for students to work the classes into their schedules. As mentioned earlier the student also does not need to match the schedules of the instructor's office hours or the schedules of other students in order to collaborate on projects.

As adult learners, most students can learn in multiple styles, i.e., visual, auditory, kinesthetic, but often have a preferred style. The mixed-mode design allows the instructor to more easily incorporate a wider range of learning activities to meet the various learning preferences. For example, students can be directed to Internet sites like YouTube for instructional videos or to websites that contain information delivered through the use of podcasts for auditory learning. These types of technologies allow students to learn in the way that is most meaningful to them.

Mixed-mode design and delivery offers many benefits to the classroom experience and student learning by combining personalized opportunities for face-to-face interaction with the efficiency and flexibility of online learning. Some relevant aspects include instructor presentations, discussions, team building, communications skills, and student engagement and participation.

In a lecture factual information is presented in a direct logical manner, a method that is particularly useful in large groups and is a powerful learning tool that leads to unexpected insights by learners. By adding discussion to an instructor's lecture, students can question, clarify, and challenge what is being presented in real time and not have to wait for responses as they would in an online class. Online "lectures" typically take the form of written summaries or papers that the student reads independently without any interaction with the instructor. The ability to get the lecture information independently and directly from the instructor is one of the key advantages to the mixed-mode delivery model. The personality, enthusiasm, and delivery style of the instructor are part of the presentation of the material. Real-time interaction between the instructor and the student has the potential to promote student understanding at a deeper level, while the opportunity to take time to read, and possibly reread information presented, allows for individual variability in the rate of internalizing new information.

Online delivery has many benefits as discussed previously, but due to inappropriate designs, many online discussions fail to achieve desired learning outcomes. Online discussion also has the potential to promote critical thinking; however, it is a challenge to implement online discussions in a way that actualizes this potential.

Classrooms may support team learning more directly, allowing students to interact in person and to work through team issues. Virtual teams are possible, but they may benefit from at least an initial face-to-face group interaction. Student isolation is lessened as students build a learning community face-to-face and continue to develop the community online.

In many professions communication skills are important for success. As part of the work environment, the ability to speak proficiently in front of others is a requirement. This is a skill that may be more difficult to develop online. Many classes require presentations as part of their curriculum, which may be challenging with an all-online delivery method. The opportunity to give presentations and to get feedback is a vital benefit of many courses.

Posting introductory student bios online prior to the first class meeting helps to "break the ice" when the students meet for the first time. Students are often more expansive in the personal facts they share in writing than when asked to talk about themselves in front of the class. Students can also connect on similar interests prior to meeting in person. The student bios can also be used by the instructor as a way to group students for team activities and assignments, either by grouping students by similarities or by differences, depending on the purpose of team interaction.

In the typical classroom, some students are comfortable speaking up and participating freely in discussions and other students are not. There may be many reasons why a student does not readily participate in the discussion, including language barriers, intimidation from more vocal students, lack of confidence in their own ideas, or the lack of enthusiasm or interest in the class material. Larger classes are a challenge for instructors to gauge the participation of all students. The mixed-mode delivery allows students two options for participation, depending on what fits their learning preference and allows the instructor to gauge participation in more than one way.

The online environment makes it evident who is participating. The need to interact in writing increases student interaction, especially for those students that do not speak often in class. In this format students are not silenced by more talkative classmates or a verbal instructor. Also, the class does not "run out of time" for students to present their ideas. Participating online may be less intimidating than the classroom and students can also take longer to think through their ideas and contribute when they are ready. Students, especially those for whom English is not their first language, can write their online contributions in a Word document and run spell and grammar checks before posting it online. This allows them to fully consider what they want to say and to only add their comments when they are ready.

Tracking participation helps to target "at-risk" learners quickly. Students who hesitate to actively participate in classroom discussions may be at risk of failing the course. It is difficult for instructors to gauge these students' level of understanding based on their classroom participation. These same students may not be seen as at-risk, however, if they actively participate in the online discussion forums. By monitoring both the student's classroom and online participation, instructors can more readily identify the truly at-risk students so that the proper intervention(s) can be found.

While there are many advantages to mixed-mode, there are also limitations. An advantage to an all-online course as opposed to mixed-mode is the ability for students to be geographically dispersed. Many online programs are successful because they can be accessed by students no matter where they are in the world as long as they have adequate Internet connectivity. Because of the face-to-face component in mixed-mode delivery, students are confined to a specific geographic area, which limits the number of students who can participate.

Another limitation to online learning is that it is a relatively new delivery format, and both instructors and students are still establishing the best ways to use this method. While research in this topic dates back twenty years, there continues to be limited understanding of effective teaching and learning methods. Moving to online instruction has been a difficult transition for many institutions, instructors, and older students who have always learned in a traditional classroom setting. Many students, even younger ones, find online learning sterile and feel that it lacks the stimulation of the classroom.

Finally, there are still places in the world where the Internet is not available. This is becoming less of an issue, but for some students the availability of a stable and affordable Internet connection is a barrier to participation. Some students may also have limited access to updated computers and software that are needed to run the platform on which the online learning lives.

Mixed-Mode Design and Instruction Considerations

Many course designers are challenged by taking an existing traditionally designed course and adapting it to an online or mixed-mode format. In the process of transformation from classroom to online, there are five phases: 1) adjust the course design; 2) socialize the learners; 3) support student participation online; 4) sustain online interaction; and 5) sum up learning outcomes for the course. These phases are described by Walker and Arnold (2004) as follows:

Adjust the Course Design

Critics of online delivery often comment on the artificiality of the interaction and that the medium of virtual communication does not enhance the coursework or help the learning process. This suggests that the design of the courses can be improved, particularly the learning activities, to align them more closely with the use of the asynchronous communication tools. From a user's perspective, the effectiveness of the tools appears related to their alignment with the targeted learning method. When converting a classroom activity to work in online delivery, consider that students may need more detailed and comprehensive instruction about the purpose and outcomes of the activity because they will be read and not heard. The instructor will also want to minimize the number of questions, use visuals images whenever possible, and finally develop a forum in which to discuss specific assignments (Walker & Arnold, 2004).

Prepare learners for the virtual components of the course. Students often lack orientation regarding how to approach the online activities. Research has highlighted a range of factors which indicate many students are not properly prepared to embrace e-learning methods. Students are not always motivated to interact online when they could exchange ideas face-to-face. Students can also encounter technical problems, such as the log-in process, when attempting to access the site. Students need time to familiarize themselves with the virtual tools. In particular, first-time users often require assistance in developing the technical skills to function effectively online while others may lack the requisite learning skills and competencies to work effectively online. Students may also need some grounding in online etiquette, since taking an online course requires overcoming the lack of nonverbal communication. The Kent State Distance Education Department (2011) describes several important aspects of this etiquette:

1. Avoid language that may come across as strong or offensive. To ensure that your statements are not misinterpreted, review statements before posting to make sure that an outsider reader would not be offended. Humor and sarcasm may also be misinterpreted, so try to be as matter-of-fact as possible.
2. Stay on topic. Since online courses may require a great deal of reading, keep sentences brief so that readers do

not get lost in wordy paragraphs and miss the point of the statement.

3. Read first, write later. It is important to read all posts or comments of students and instructors before responding. This prevents repeating commentary or asking questions that have already been answered.

4. Review and then send. There is no taking back a comment that has already been sent, so double-check to make sure that your thoughts are clearly conveyed exactly as intended.

5. An online classroom is still a classroom and appropriate classroom behavior is still mandatory. Respect for fellow classmates and the instructors are important and expected.

6. Certain aspects of Internet communication are becoming conventional. For example, do not write using all capital letters, because it will appear as shouting. Also, the use of emoticons can be helpful when used to convey nonverbal feelings, for example: :-) or :-(; but avoid overusing them. Some acronyms such as LOL for "laughing out loud" or BTW for "by the way" are becoming more popular; but again, do not overuse them, and you may need to explain them the first time they are used.

7. Consider the privacy of others by asking permission prior to giving out a classmate's contact information.

8. No inappropriate material is acceptable. Do not forward virus warnings, chain letters, jokes, etc. to classmates or instructors.

Beyond these motivational and technical concerns, students need to generate a common sense of purpose in order to work collaboratively online. This sense of shared purpose is difficult to achieve when participants are accustomed to traditional study methods. Students need time to recognize virtual learning environments as spaces for ideas and information sharing.

It is important to support student participation online in the early stages of the course when they require more guidance and support. The need for technical support to help solve problems related to the uploading of reports or simply accessing the course site is important not only in the early stages of the course but throughout. Students also need guidance on how to express themselves online and may look to the instructor to encourage other students to respond to comments posted on the discussion board. Instructors can also play a proactive role by modeling targeted learning behavior (e.g., by posting new discussion themes; responding/referring to postings, integrating student responses, etc.).

Student participation may need to be sustained online during the later stages of the course when students typically become more confident and the participation of the instructor appears to be less important. However, the course instructor still needs to remain vigilant, monitoring the learning processes and ensuring that the interests of students in the course are maintained. Students also continue to need new articles and resources which add value to their learning to keep pulling them back online.

Instructors should sum up the learning outcomes at the end of the course. Students expect the instructor to identify the key outcomes of the in-class and the virtual learning, tying together the loose ends of the course. In this way the final class sessions can reinforce the lessons learned from the virtual phase of the course, with the instructor providing feedback on the research and collaborative learning activities. Students will then complete the course with a clear understanding of the learning outcomes and the relationship between the virtual and in-class learning processes.

Activities

Activities in a mixed-mode course build upon the tools available in an in-class course. Instructors now have more options for the delivery of learning activities (Caladine, 1999). Table 1 below outlines the tools available for each learning activity.

Table 1

Learning Activity	Mixed- Mode Course
Materials	Websites, online materials, also allows for the printing of materials.
Interaction with material	Multimedia, web browsing, glossary, homework, quizzes, classroom activities
Interaction with the teacher	Web announcements, forums, phone, face-to-face interaction, consultation, polling tools, webinars, videoconferencing
Interaction between students	Web forum, e-mail, group work, class discussions, projects, shared documents, webinars, videoconferencing, video chat rooms
Intra-action	Class discussion, group work, web forums

Researchers agree that the design, development, and implementation processes for a blended learning environment are different from those in a purely traditional, face-to-face lecture course or a purely online course. From the results of their studies, they make the following suggestions for the development and implementation of mixed-mode instruction:

- Don't mix only the technologies; mix the educational philosophies, theories, and instructional design methodologies. Each component must be evaluated and adapted for the mixed technology (Delialioglu & Yildirim, 2007).
- Start small and work backward from your final goals. What do you want students to be able to do at the end of the semester? When planning the integration of digital communications technologies, careful attention to learning objectives becomes even more important; this helps teachers avoid a counterproductive focus on the technologies themselves (Sands, 2002).

- Imagine interactivity rather than delivery. Simply posting materials on the web will not guarantee that students will engage with or and learn from them any more than having a student in a classroom guarantees his/her participation. Instructors need to offer activities that require students to perform basic academic tasks and that place them in conversation with each other, such as through responses to each others' summaries and analyses (Sands, 2002). While considering the appropriate delivery, first conceptualize the needed level of interactivity, and match the delivery method and the desired level of interactivity as best you can. For instance, if a high degree of analysis is needed, this discussion would best be conducted in the classroom, while the sharing of thoughts and experiences can be done effectively in an online discussion forum.
- Give special attention to student motivation in mixed-mode courses. Motivation and reward are very important for student learning, with intrinsic motivation the key element for success in a hybrid course (Delialioglu & Yildirim, 2007).
- Provide tools that support student understanding of the subject. The use of website items such as a glossary, site map, search function, and bookmarking increases the integration of both delivery methods.
- Use multimedia in the web components to enhance learning, including audio, video, and PowerPoint presentations (Delialioglu & Yildirim, 2007).
- Encourage and provide facilities for student-student and student-instructor communication. Besides the availability of online communication through discussion boards and e-mail, students communicate face-to-face on a regular basis (Garnham & Kaleta, 2002).
- Be prepared for a shift in the span of control over the way the course is managed. Since classroom time is reduced and everyone is online, opportunities to monitor and manage interactions move from the geographic space of the classroom to the temporal space of the week, month,

or whatever unit of time intervenes between classroom meetings (Sands, 2002).

- Be explicit about time-management issues and be prepared to teach new skills.
- Students who have spent the past two decades or so in traditional classroom settings will have to learn new skills to cope with the distribution of requirements over time and to cope with their new dependence on each other. If teachers create opportunities for interaction, then each participant becomes dependent on the participation of the others (Sands, 2002).
- Plan for effective use of classroom time and connect it to the online work. Many teachers bring to class one or two posted responses from students, project those responses using an overhead projector, and then discuss them with the class.
- Developing a hybrid course should be a collegial process. Discussing the course redesign problems and progress with colleagues is helpful for instructors when designing their first few courses. The opportunity to interact with an experienced hybrid course instructor can be especially valuable. An instructor with experience can answer questions, share "war stories" about what to expect when teaching a hybrid course, and give reassurance. (Garnham & Kaleta, 2002).

The role of the instructor is key to the successful implementation of this design. Delialioglu and Yildirim (2007) found that students in hybrid courses have very specific ideas about the role of the instructor and that this role is evolving in the following ways:

- From lecturer to consultant, guide, and resource provider;
- From having all the answers to expert questioners;
- From only providing structured student work to encouraging self-direction; and
- From a solitary teacher to a member of a learning team.

- Students perceive the role of the instructor as a guide and a facilitator of the classroom activities and need to communicate with the instructor in a friendly manner. The students should perceive their own role as "active" and the course as student-centered. The students interviewed by Delialioglyu and Yildirim also stated that the instructor was an important source of motivation for them and viewed the instructor as the person who:

- Outlined the important points of the course content (instructor as an information source);
- Motivated the students to come to class and read the content (instructor as a motivation source);
- Controlled their assignments, homework, and projects (instructor as an authority figure and feedback provider); and
- Helped them in doing their assignments, projects and classroom activities (instructor as a facilitator) (Delialioglu & Yildirim, 2007).

This evolving role of the instructor requires mixed-mode instructors to modify their traditional approach to both the classroom and their online delivery. For in-classroom instruction, instructors are advised to:

- Use the first week of class to focus on the technology, especially since some students may be concerned that they lack the necessary technology skills and access to fast connections.
- Present knowledge-based information through lecture/presentation during the classroom with follow up discussion on line.
- Prior to the lecture, have students prepare by reading basic hard-copy papers and online documents. The list of texts for this lecture/classroom session is made available on the course website.
- Consider outlining the lecture so it serves as a narrative that provides an overview of the topic, its basic theories,

and an introduction to the assignment and to the available online resources. The lecture itself becomes one of many resources available to the student.

- After the lecture, either online or in the classroom, have students work (individually or in groups) on solving the problem-based assignment using all the different resources, both from the lecture and on the course website.
- Use face-to-face discussion to explore the more complex concepts in the subject.
- Allow students class time to work out communication strategies for their online interactions.
- Use assignments that allow the students to present material to a live audience. This allows them to practice their oral communication and presentation skills.

For the online portion of the class, instructors are advised to:

- Be present in the online class. Plan the time it takes to be a consistent participant in the online discussions and introduction of ideas.
- Prepare discussion posts that invite questions, discussion, reflections, and responses.
- Create a supportive online course community.
- Focus on content resources, links to current events, and examples that are easily accessed through learner's computer.

Conclusion

The following conclusions about the use of the hybrid, blended or mixed-mode delivery model can be drawn from the literature and from experience. First, there are many ways to approach a hybrid course. When trying to answer, "How much of the course should be online?" and "What part of the course should go online?" there is no one answer. Mixed-mode course designs show enormous variety in how the face-to-face ratio to online time is distributed as well as how the schedule is followed. Instructors also design hybrid courses to accommodate their own teaching styles and course content. Therefore, learning activities taking place in and out of the classroom vary greatly.

Second, redesigning a traditional course into a hybrid takes time. Hybrid instructors should allow six months lead time for course development. Instructors surveyed by Garnham and Kaleta (2002) were universal in their advice to others developing hybrid courses: Start early and plan very carefully; hybridization is a lot of work.

Not all students grasp the hybrid concept readily. The hybrid model is new to many students, so they need a clear rationale for its use. Students may require repeated explanations about the model to understand why the instructor or institution chose it. Students not taking responsibility for their courses and students with poor time-management skills present problems that instructors may need to address. Many students don't perceive the time spent in lectures as "work," but they definitely see time spent online as work, even if it is time they would have spent in class in a traditional course (Garnham & Kaleta, 2002).

Having time flexibility in hybrid courses is popular. For the students the importance of time flexibility may outweigh any inconvenience caused by the technologies. Students strongly prefer using learning technologies that are available from home rather than in a computer lab (Garnham & Kaleta, 2002).

Finally, both instructors and students appear to like the hybrid course model. Despite the fact that this model is still evolving, it has proven to be a welcome alternative for many students and instructors because it has been found to increase student interactivity, improve student performance, and accomplish course goals that would not have been possible in traditional courses.

The power of the mixed-mode, hybrid, or blended course model lies in its flexibility and its educational effectiveness. Because it emphasizes active learning techniques while following accepted practices in adult learning theory, it increases student interaction with other students and the instructor. When designed and implemented carefully, it can be the "best of both worlds." It is clear that when course design is driven by learning objectives and not the technology, this use of technology can be the solution to some of the problems that are emerging as we try supply options that allow learning to occur in the time, place, and method that works best for the individual adult learner.

References

Bandura, A. (1976). *Social learning theory*. Englewood Cliffs, NJ: Prentice Hall.

Boyle, T. (2005). A Dynamic, systematic method for developing blended learning. *Education, Communication & Information, 5*(3), 221-232.

Caladine, R. (1999). *Teaching for flexible learning: Learning to apply the technology (MOLTA)*. Gilwern, Abergavenny: GSSE.

Dalsgaard, C., & Godsk, M. (2007). Transforming traditional lectures into problem-based blended learning: Challenges and experiences. *Open Learning, 22*(1), 29-42.

Doering, A. (2006). Adventure learning: Transformative hybrid online education. *Distance Education, 27*(2), 197-215.

Delfino, M., & Persico, D. (2007). Online or face-to-face? Experimenting with different techniques in teacher training. *Journal of Computer Assisted Learning, 23*(5), 351-365.

Delialioglu, O., & Yildirim, Z. (2007). Students' perceptions on effective dimensions of interactive learning in a blended learning environment. *Educational Technology & Society, 10*(2), 133-146.

Ellis, R. A., & Calvo, R. A. (2004). Learning through discussions in blended environments. *International Council for Educational Media*. Retrieved from http://www.tandf.co.uk/journals

Ertmer, P. (2003). Teacher pedagogical beliefs: The final frontier in our quest for technology integration? *Educational*

Technology Research and Development, 53(4), 25-39. doi: 10.1007/BF02504683

Garnham, C., & Kaleta., R. (2002, March). Introduction to hybrid courses. *Teaching with Technology Today, 8*(6). Retrieved from http://www.uwsa.edu/ttt/articles/garnham.htm.

Gould, T. (2003). Hybrid classes: Maximizing institutional resources and student learning. *ASCUE Conference*. Retrieved from http://courses.durhamtech.edu/tlc/www/html/learning-matters/hybrid.pdf.

Harasim, L. (1990). Shift happens: Online education as a new paradigm in learning. *The Internet and Higher Education, 3*(1-2), 41-61.

Hofmann, J., & Miner, N. (2008). Real blended learning stands up. *T+D, 62*(9), 28-31.

Kent State Distance Education (2011, February). Online etiquette. *Kent State University*. Retrieved from http://www.kent.edu/dl/technology/etiquette.cfm

Knowles, M. (1984). *The adult learner: A neglected species* (3rd Ed.). Houston, TX: Gulf Publishing.

Merriam & Caffarella (1999). *Learning in adulthood*. San Francisco, CA: Jossey-Bass.

Sands, P. (2002). Strategies for connecting online and face-to-face instruction in hybrid courses. *ASCUE Conference*. Retrieved from http://www.uwsa.edu/ttt/articles/sands2.htm

Vygotsky, L. S. (1978). *Mind in society: The development of higher psychological processes*. Cambridge, MA: Harvard University Press.

Walker, R., and Arnold, I. (2004). Introducing group-based asynchronous learning to business education: Reflections on effective course design and delivery. *Educational Media International, 41*(3), 253-262.

Technology in the Asynchronous Online World

Maria Minor, DM
City University of Seattle
School of Management

Abstract

Evolving technologies have impacted learning in the asynchronous and synchronous online world. An examination of the asynchronous online world is conducted and a review of the existing hypotheses surrounding learning is assessed. New technologies are assessed and suggestions are made as to how to use these technologies to create dynamic online classes.

Introduction

Online learning, distance learning, or virtual classroom are phrases which describe taking a class on the Internet. Delivering online education has its challenges and rewards. Traditional brick and mortar colleges and universities offer students face-to-face contact. Asynchronous online classes remove that element. However, technology can help instructors bridge the gap between face-to-face contact and online classes. The element of human interaction is not lost in the virtual world. Technologies such as PowerPoint, Instant Messaging, Skype, Jing, and Animoto can bring the classroom into the student's living room.

Jeffries (2011) traced distance learning back to the 1700s when correspondence courses originated. In 1892 Penn State University introduced one of the first correspondence courses to nontraditional students (Banas & Emory, 1998). These students could obtain degrees without attending on-ground classes. In the 1900s distance learning evolved to include a variety of technologies used to deliver education. Instructional media, such as tape recordings and interactive TV, were used to educate students unable to attend in a traditional classroom. The emergence of the Internet in the 1990s allowed colleges and universities to begin the creation and development of online classes.

Technologies used in online classes can be grouped into two categories: synchronous and asynchronous (Hrastinski, 2008). Synchronous learning requires all learners and instructors to be present at the same time. Classes are delivered through technologies such as web conferencing and live streaming, which allow users to connect into a live web conference. Asynchronous learning allows users to access material from a central site with no designated time assigned to it. E-mail, message boards, and blogs are the main modes of asynchronous communications (Hrastinski, 2008).

Some authors argue that the traditional classroom cannot be compared to an online classroom. These authors propose that the online classroom experience lacks vital elements that convey an effective learning experience, leaving students less engaged or motivated in the learning process (Bigelow, 1999; Clark, 2001; MacKinnon, 2000; Ponzurick., 2000; Thach, 1995). Other authors support the equivalency theory (Simonson, Schlosser &Hanson,

1999), which states that the closer the online classroom is to the traditional classroom, the more the results will emulate one another. Therefore, the results of face-to-face contact in a traditional classroom as compared to face-to-face contact via a form of technology should result in similar outcomes. If technology is used appropriately, the online experience can be as rich as the traditional classroom (Brower, 2003). According to Trier (1996) "interactive video versus videotape versus 'live' instructor has little effect on student achievement as long as the technology used to deliver the content is appropriate and all participants have access to the same technology" (para. 3).

In a study conducted by Hrastinski (2008), asynchronous and synchronous online learners were interviewed and a comparison was made of their opinions about the type of learning they received. An analysis was conducted on their perceptions of communication and the type of education they received.

The results of the study revealed that synchronous learners felt more motivated and aroused due to real-time conversation because it was similar to face-to-face contact. Whereas asynchronous learners believed they could reflect and cognitively process information more due to the lack of verbal and face-to-face interaction. Both groups thought their learning could be enriched and more effective if both types of e-learning were blended together.

Two hypotheses are in play concerning the impact of online learning on the student. The two hypotheses are Media Naturalness and Media Richness. Kock's (2005) hypothesis about Media Naturalness states that decreased face-to-face contact in learning increases cognitive ability. The Media Richness hypothesis postulates that humans prefer face-to-face contact that involves communication and technologies that deliver face-to-face contact, or as close as possible; this contact proves more effective (Daft & Lengle, 1986) A large number of studies exist that support both hypotheses. This leaves room for future studies to investigate e-learning that incorporates the use of technology that uses audio and video to bring in an enhanced form of human interaction in asynchronous learning.

Asynchronous Online Learning Technology

Audio

The use of audio in asynchronous classes can establish a caring environment and assist those who are auditory learners. Using various forms of audio software in the asynchronous classroom to engage learners, one can discover many positive outcomes. Software such as Jing and PowerPoint allows instructors to pre-record, save, and post those files to the online class or send them individually to students.

Jing software is owned by TechSmith (2011). The software has a wide variety of uses, including screen sharing and audio recording. Jing software is compatible with both Mac and Windows and can be downloaded in minutes. TechSmith (2011) offers a variety of packages available for sale with enhanced services like more audio recording time. The free downloaded version allows users to prerecord and capture a screen shot for up to five minutes.

Jing software allows instructors to provide weekly audio feedback to individual students, assisting them with both positive and constructive feedback. Using Jing or other audio software, along with the written comments in an assignment, allows a personalized touch. Sometimes written feedback can be perceived as harsh. Jing allows the instructor to connect with the student, personalize the feedback, and add that extra human element through verbal contact. Students enjoy listening to the feedback and find that the audio creates a connection with the instructor. The instructor becomes an actual person and not just one that sends weekly written feedback and posts grades.

Jing software also can be used to provide mini-lectures to students. A prerecorded lecture of five minutes or less can be used to highlight the assignments for the week, clarify information, and answer common questions students may have. A file can be attached in the announcement and made instantly available to all students.

Jing software is easy to learn due to the user-friendly icons. However, if some students find it difficult to learn, the instructor may want to post directions in the classroom.

Microsoft PowerPoint has a feature that allows sound to be embedded in a presentation. This feature allows an instructor to embed a story in a presentation that represents the material or can be used as an instructor's biography. Exhibit 1 is an example of how one slide with several pictures and sound can tell a story. In an online class, students can click on the sound button and hear the instructor speak.

Exhibit 1

The addition of sound to a PowerPoint slide is easy. A sound file can be created, saved, and attached in multiple presentations within minutes.. One can be creative and use this feature in multiple ways to build a dynamic classroom.

Animoto (2010) is a web application that allows the user to make videos using photographs and music. A free basic application version can be downloaded that allows the user to create a thirty-second video. This is an ideal application to use for biographies. The user uploads photographs, adds text, selects a background and music, and then sends it to Animoto (2010) to create the video. In a matter of minutes, an outstanding video is created and can be instantly exported to YouTube, Facebook, a personal website, or the online course. This is a simple tool used for creating dynamic lectures with all types of media. Assignments can be given that allow students to use Animoto (2010) as a substitute to PowerPoint. This technology has allowed the quality of presentations to reach new heights.

Live Video

The use of video in the asynchronous world can add a new dimension to the classroom. Technologies such as Skype and WebCam Central can present an interactive approach. WebCam allows a user to prerecord video messages and attach those messages as a video file in the classroom. This has been found to be a useful tool to replace written lectures; instructors can record their lectures and attach them to the classroom to be viewed at the student's convenience.

Skype is a software application that can be downloaded for no charge and used to make free video calls and to send instant messages to other Skype users (Skype, 2010). Additional features are available, such as the group video calling feature that allows multiple video calls to be merged together, much like a conference call. An instructor can use Skype to hold office hours and interact with students who are Skype users. If several students have the Skype group video calling feature, they can work on group projects together. Skype allows the asynchronous online world to enjoy virtual face-to-face, real-time contact.

Future Research

Opportunity exists for additional research to be conducted in the area of asynchronous learning. A review of the literature reveals that limited studies exist on the impact of technology in asynchronous learning. Both qualitative and quantitative analysis should be conducted in asynchronous online classes to support the levels of student satisfaction associated with each.

Surveying students in asynchronous classes and gathering data that identifies effective technological methods will be helpful in this process. Research could also be conducted to analyze the extent to which technology-enhanced learning has created a social, caring environment that contributes to a student's learning experience. This information would contribute additional support for proven practices that work in the asynchronous online world.

Conclusion

The use of technology in the asynchronous world can enhance the learning experience. A variety of technologies exist that can be used to create an interactive personal classroom. Several options exist for sharing audio and video to enhance adult learning in online modalities. Further studies are needed to identify the optimal ways that these technologies, as well as other emergent trends, can be used to further authentic student learning.

References

Animoto. (2011). Retrieved from http://animoto.com/

Banas, E, & Emory, F. (1998). History and issues of distance learning. *Public Administration Quarterly*, *22*(3), Retrieved from http://search.ebscohost.com/login.aspx?direct=true&db=bth&AN=2639947&site=ehost-live

Bigelow, J. D. 1999. The web as an organizational behavior learning medium. *Journal of Management Education*, 23, 635-650.

Brower, H. (2003). On emulating classroom. *Academy of Management Learning and Education*, *2*(1), Retrieved from http://ehis.ebscohost.com/ehost/pdfviewer/pdfviewer?hid=114&sid=490a3b70-2c18-4776-a0d0-614cb7f6d2b3%40sessionmgr115&vid=6

Clark, L. J. (2001). Web-based teaching: A new educational paradigm. *Intercom, 48,* 20-23.

Daft, R, & Lengel, R. (1986). Organizational information requirements, media richness and structural design. *Manage
Science, 32*(5), 554-571.

Hrastinski, S. (2008). Asynchronous & Synchronous e-learning.
Educate Quarterly, (4), 51-55.

Jeffries, M. (2011). *Research in distance education.* Informally
published manuscript, Educational Services, Distributed
Learning, Virtual, Retrieved from http://www.digitalschool.
net/edu/DL_history_mJeffries.html

Kock, N. (2005). Media richness or media naturalness? *The Evolution
Of IEEE Transaction On ProfessionalCommunication, 48*(2),
doi: 10.1109

MacKinnon, G. R. 2000. The dilemma of evaluating electronic
discussion groups. *Journal of Research on Computing in
Education, 33,* 125-132.

Ponzurick, T. G., France, K. R., & Logar, C. M. (2000). Delivering graduate marketing education: An analysis of face-to-face versus distance education. *Journal of Marketing Education, 22,*
180-188.

Skype. (2010). Retrieved from http://www.skype.com/intl/enus/
home/

Simonson, M., Schlosser, C, & Hanson, D. 1999. Theory and distance
education: A new discussion. *American Journal of Distance
Education, 13,* 60-75.

TechSmith, I. (2011). *Jing.* Retrieved from http://www.techsmith.
com/jing/

Thach, E. C, & Murphy, K. L. (1995). Competencies for Distance education professionals. *Educational technology Research and Development, 43,* 57-59.

Trier, Vicki (ed.) (1996). "Distance Education at a Glance: (Guide #10: Distance Education Research." Retrieved from http://www.uidaho.edu/evo/distlO.html.

16

The Use of Synchronized Audio, Video, and Slides to Enhance the Online Learning Experience

Keith Foe, MBA, CFP, CPA
City University of Seattle
School of Management

Abstract

Multimedia technologies are becoming more common in online education, and student response to materials presented in ways other than text is overwhelmingly positive. Multimedia presentations using synchronized audio, video, and slides can be quickly and easily created for a variety of uses, including introducing courses, explaining difficult concepts, and including supplemental material. Targeting these short (three–five minute) presentations to a single problem or example maximizes viewership while also effectively supplementing or clarifying course material. Software packages to create and publish these presentations are discussed along with specific examples of targeted presentations.

Introduction and Background

The online learning environment offers the well-documented advantage of flexibility in both time and space (El Mansour & Mupinga, 2007; Hurt, 2008; Nagel & Kotze, 2010). This flexibility allows students to take classes while balancing the demands of work, family, and other concerns. However, several disadvantages have also been shown to accompany online learning, including 1) lack of face-to-face contact (Hurt, 2008); 2) asynchronous communication (El Mansour, & Mupinga, 2007); 3) student difficulties interpreting an instructor's intent through written communication (Dykman & Davis, 2008); and 4) technology compatibility issues (Hurt, 2008). These disadvantages are inherent aspects of the online environment in general and will therefore never be eliminated entirely. They can, however, be mitigated by moving beyond what Nagel (2010) calls the "paper-behind-glass" style of online learning. This can be accomplished through the incorporation of targeted video presentations.

The use of multimedia technologies in both in-person and through online learning has also been well documented in the educational literature, with overwhelmingly positive student perceptions of lecture-based videos (Copley, 2007; Evans, 2008; Huntsberger & Stavitsky, 2007). To quantify the positive response to podcast videos in an in-person classroom environment, Dupagne, Millett, & Grinfeder (2009) determined that over 73 percent of students who viewed video podcasts of classroom lectures found them to be very helpful; 88 percent said that including the videos was a good idea; and 76 percent said that watching the videos was enjoyable. However, among the 261 students in the Dupagne, Millett, & Grinfeder (2009) study, only 41 percent on average viewed each video that was available and only 5 percent viewed all twelve videos that were available. Among the students who didn't watch the videos, 28 percent said that the videos were simply repeating lecture material, 18 percent said they didn't have enough time, and 10 percent had technology problems that didn't allow them to view the video.

Student response to podcast videos is even more positive in the online learning environment than it is in the traditional classroom (Murphy, 2000; Palmer, 2007). In a comparative study of on-campus and online course delivery, Palmer (2007) reports that 80 percent of students in the online course who watched supplemental videos found them to be useful, compared to 64 percent in the on-campus course. Furthermore, the number of students who viewed the videos in the online class was 90 percent compared to less than 50 percent in the on-campus course.

Online presentations with synchronized audio, video, and slides can be utilized as a method for alleviating the disadvantages associated with online learning while maximizing student viewership through targeting the presentations to specific problem-solving situations and minimizing technical difficulties.

Targeted Presentations with Synchronized Audio, Video, and Slides

Software Options

Several types of online presentations are common: audio only; voice-over slides; screen capture with audio; video with audio; and synchronized audio, video, and slides (Lawlor & Donnelly, 2010). It is reported in the literature that student attitudes toward any type of multimedia presentation in online learning are positive (Copley, 2007; Dupagne, 2009; Evans, 2008; Griffen, Mitchell, & Thompson, 2009; Huntsberger & Stavitsky, 2007). These studies, however, were all conducted in online or mixed-mode classes at institutions that are primarily classroom based and where instructors teach primarily in a traditional classroom setting with significant face-to-face interaction time. The unique nature of the fully online learning environment is that the instructor is often "faceless" to the students. To simulate the face-to-face learning experience, only presentation methods that included video of the instructor were evaluated in this work. The use of audio and video alone was excluded from consideration as it provided little more than a "spoken e-mail" to the students.

Several commercially available software packages are available at the time of publication that allow for the synchronization of audio, video, and slides, including Microsoft Producer for PowerPoint (2007), Momindum Studio (version 1.2.1, 2008), iPresent Presio (version 1.5, 2010), and Camtasia Studio (version 7.1, 2010). These programs accomplish the same task, but each has its own strengths and weaknesses as summarized in Table 1. All software was evaluated on a PC running the Microsoft Windows 7 operating system (Professional version, 2009).

Microsoft Producer for PowerPoint is extremely user-friendly and supports slide animations, but browser incompatibility issues and long load times (> 25 percent of the presentation length) make it difficult for many students to access and view presentations. Momindum Studio creates excellent presentations, but its user interface is not straightforward and several errors and bugs were experienced during testing. Camtasia Studio is the most complete and polished software package tested, with far more capabilities and options than the other programs, and it can produce presentations of extremely high quality. Navigating through all of these options, however, greatly increases the time it takes to create and publish a presentation. iPresent Presio produces high quality presentations with a professional look, is easy to use, and produces presentations with extremely fast (< 1 percent of the presentation length) load times.

It is worth noting, however, that software is frequently updated and that newer versions of these software packages could be significantly different from the description given here. Any instructor wishing to incorporate the methodologies presented in this chapter should carefully evaluate the available software options.

Software Package	Strengths	Weaknesses
Microsoft Producer For PowerPoint	Simplicity, ease of use Excellent user interface Compatible with slide animations	Incompatible with browsers other than Internet Explorer Long presentation load times
Momindum Studio	Compatible with all browsers Fast presentation load times	Difficult to use Incompatible with slide animations
Camtasia Studio	Many options and uses Compatible with all browsers Fast presentation load times Professional looking presentations	Requires skilled user Lengthy process to create and publish presentations
iPresent Presio	Simplicity, ease of use Compatible with all browsers Fast presentation load times Professional looking presentations	Incompatible with slide animations

Table 1. *Summary of the strengths and weaknesses of software to synchronize audio, video, and slides.*

Creation of presentations in iPresent Presio is a simple process, with step-by-step guidance in a logical order. The presenter must first create the slides to be presented in Microsoft PowerPoint and then import the PowerPoint file into iPresent. Video recording can be done with a webcam directly in iPresent Presio or recorded with any device capable of downloading the video to a computer (most digital cameras and camcorders) to be subsequently imported into the iPresent software. The presenter then synchronizes the slides to the video by watching the video and clicking on the screen to advance the slides at the appropriate time in the video. The presentation is then ready to be published to the web via an FTP server. The entire process for a five-minute video takes about an hour, although the bulk of that time is spent planning and creating succinct and meaningful slides. A screenshot of the final presentation can be seen in Figure 1.

Presentation Philosophy

While the creation of lecture-length presentations is certainly possible, literature shows that fewer than half of students watch them (Dupagne, 2009) and that a text-based method is still the best way to deliver most course materials (Berns, 2005). It is accepted in the literature (Berns, 2005; Buckley & Smith, 2008; Case & Hino, 2010; Young, 2008) that short videos (three–five minutes in length) targeted at a certain problem or specific topic are an effective method to supplement and clarify course material.

A specific example illustrates this philosophy. A homework assignment in a managerial finance course included a problem from a section that teaches a multitude of financing formulas and financial ratios. This specific problem, however, is solved through simple arithmetic, and students were struggling with trying to fit the question into one of the chapter's formulas. After seeing the students' frustration with the problem on the course discussion board, a presentation was quickly produced to help walk the students through the problem and alleviate their frustrations with it (see www.keithfoe.com/p6-4a/ for the presentation). Seeing and hearing the instructor in this type of targeted presentation allows students to easily infer from the instructor's body language and tone that the difficulties they've been having are understandable, and that they can easily solve the problem once they get started correctly.

Another example of the use of targeted presentations is as a course introduction at the beginning of each quarter (see http://www.keithfoe.com/Welcome/). These give the instructor a face and a voice from the very beginning of the course and set up a feeling of connection between the instructor and the student that is often absent in online education (El Mansour & Mupinga, 2007). The introductory presentation is also an excellent opportunity to cover the course policies, procedures, and expectations.

Other targeted presentations have been produced to explain difficult concepts in the course textbook, to expand upon inadequately covered material, to add relevant material that isn't covered in the text, and to provide hints for topics that will be on upcoming exams.

Student Feedback

Exclusively positive student feedback, both direct and indirect, has been received in response to the use of synchronized audio, video, and slide presentations in this author's online courses. Direct comments from students include

"The video instructions were a memorable and clever touch."
"The videos were great! Would love to see more of those in my courses."
"I really value the video tutorials."
"The videos were very helpful and well timed."
"The introduction video was a great help in getting started. Every course should have one!"

Conclusion

The use of targeted presentations with synchronized audio, video, and slides has the ability to mitigate many of the disadvantages associated with the online learning environment. The presentations allow for the simulation of face-to-face contact, while audio along with video provides for more insight into an instructor's intent than simple text can provide. El Mansour points out that asynchronous communication in online classes "tends to remove any feelings of connection between the student and instructor" (2007). Though the videos are still communicated to students in an asynchronous fashion, the inclusion of audio and video in the presentations restores much of this perceived connection. Finally, though technology and compatibility issues may never be completely removed from the online learning environment, an evaluation of software to create the presentations has been performed to minimize these issues and maximize compatibility across multiple computer platforms.

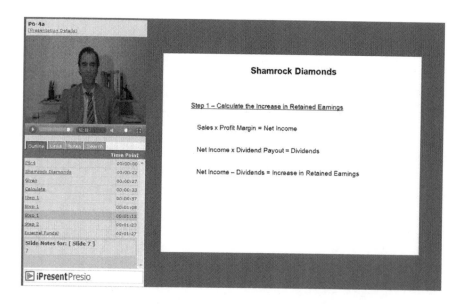

Figure 1. *Screenshot of a published presentation in iPresent Presio.*

References

Berns, S. (2005). Streaming audio, video level the online playing field. *Distance Education Report, 9,* 5-6.

Buckley, W. & Smith A. (2008). Application of multimedia technologies to enhance distance learning. *Review, 39,* 57-65.

Camtasia Studio (Version 7.1) [Software]. (2010) Available from www.camtasia.com.

Case, P. & Hino, J. (2010). A powerful teaching tool: Self-produced videos. *Journal of Extension, 48,* 1-3.

Copley, J. (2007). Audio and video podcasts of lectures for campus-based students: Production and evaluation of student use. *Innovations in Education and Teaching International, 44,* 386-395.

Dupagne, M., Millette, D. M., & Grinfeder, K. (2009). Effectiveness of video podcast use as a revision tool. *Journalism & Mass Communication Educator, 64,* 54-70.

Dykman, C. A. & Davis, C. K. (2008). Online education forum – part three: A quality online educational experience. *Journal of Information Systems Education, 19,* 281-289.

El Mansour, B. & Mupinga D. M. (2007). Students' positive and negative experiences in hybrid and online classes. *College Student Journal, 41,* 242-248.

Evans, C. (2008). The effectiveness of M-learning in the form of podcast revision lectures in higher education. *Computers & Education, 50,* 495.

Griffen, D. K., Mitchell, D., & Thompson, S. J. (2009). Podcasting by synchronising PowerPoint and voice: What are the pedagogical benefits? *Computers & Education, 53,* 532-539.

Huntsberger, M. & Stavitsky, A. (2007). The new pedagogy: Incorporating podcasting into journalism education. *Journalism & Mass Communication Educator, 61,* 397-410.

Hurt, J. (2008). The advantages and disadvantages of teaching and learning on-line. *The Delta Kappa Gamma Bulletin, 74,* 5-11.

iPresent Presio (Version 1.5) [Software]. (2010) Retrieved from www.iPresent.net.

Lawlor, B. and Donnelly, R. (2010). Using podcasts to support communication skills development: A case study for content format preferences among postgraduate research students. *Computers & Education, 54,* 962-971.

Microsoft Producer for PowerPoint 2007 [Software]. Retrieved from www.microsoft.com.

Momindum Studio (Version 1.2.1) [Software]. (2008) Retrieved from www.momindum.com/products/studio/.

Murphy, T.H. (2000). An evaluation of distance education course design for general soils. *Journal of Agricultural Education, 41,* 103-113.

Nagel, L. and Kotze T. G. (2010). Supersizing e-learning: What a CoI survey reveals about teaching presence in a large online class. *Internet and Higher Education, 13,* 45-51.

Palmer, S. (2007). An evaluation of streaming digital video resources in on- and off-campus engineering management education. *Computers and Education, 49,* 297-308.

Young, J. R. (2008). To spice up course work, professors make their own videos. *The Education Digest, 74,* 48-50.

Implementing Online and Hybrid Programs and Courses: Benefits, Challenges, and Proven Practices

Kelly A. Flores, EdD
City University of Seattle
School of Management

Abstract

As leaders of learning institutions seek to shift courses and programs to hybrid and online delivery formats, they need to carefully consider the benefits and challenges of implementing these options. This chapter offers proven practices and lessons learned from program leaders at a university which has long used online and hybrid modes of instruction. The experiences of these program leaders, faculty, and students reinforce the growing research on the many benefits of online and hybrid delivery. Taking steps to establish organizational readiness, implement change management principles, and proactively overcome faculty and student resistance will increase the chances of successful implementation.

Introduction

Many researchers have engaged in controversial discussions on the philosophical approaches to learning in online and hybrid formats. Debates continue on the effectiveness, benefits, and limitations of online and hybrid delivery, and faculty and students continue to challenge curricular approaches in these formats.

Historically, curriculum design in all delivery modes has followed a pedagogical, or teacher-centered, framework (Honigsfeld & Dunn, 2006). Since the late 1970s, the leaders of some nontraditional institutions have shifted the curriculum design to reflect the classic works of Knowles (1980) on the needs of adult learners through student-centered learning, or andragogy (Domask, 2007). As access to technology has increased, curriculum design discussions have evolved to include ways to enhance the online experience by offering multiple pathways to obtain content and feedback (Mupinga, Nora, & Yaw, 2006).

In 2003, 34 percent of institutions of higher education in the United States had complete online degree programs (Allen & Seaman, 2005). Some schools have online programs with the same requirements, classes, and teachers as their traditional programs. The alternative is attractive for many students, including the minimally tapped market of students who have little time but have the funds, as online programs typically cost more than traditional classroom programs (Endres, Chowdhury, Frye, & Hurtubis, 2009). Curriculum developers in online and hybrid programs need to be aware of the benefits and challenges that come with distance learning and should become familiar with strategies that have historically been successful in overcoming the challenges.

Hybrid and Online Delivery

Benefits of Hybrid and Online Delivery

Hannon (2009) discussed several benefits to online courses, including asynchronous components for students in multiple time zones, the enhancement of student learning through online discussions, and online access to course materials. After evaluating research on the topic, Appana (2008) noted the main benefits of online learning include "new markets, economic benefits, international partnerships, reduced time to market, educational benefits, anonymity, student interaction and satisfaction, growth in faculty learning curve, and 'rich' feedback and evaluation" (p. 7). Nontraditional learners have reiterated what Solnik (2007) and Kiriakidis (2008) found: they appreciate the flexibility of being able to access class anytime; they benefit from collaborating with their peers around the world; and they enjoy having the opportunity to share best practices and experiences.

Online and hybrid programs have been shown to promote learning effectiveness when online learning is blended with local experiences. This approach accommodates diverse student populations and learning styles and allows theory and practice to be combined with locally relevant issues providing real-world learning experiences (Moloney, Hickey, Bergin, Boccia, & Polley, 2007). As an example, at City University of Seattle (CityU), courses and programs are taught at multiple campuses around the world. With online and hybrid course offerings, students are able to choose the delivery mode most compatible with their learning preferences and learn from instructors located in other countries. Many CityU students appreciate collaborating with students and faculty members who bring international perspectives from across borders. Students can choose to travel to other countries to engage in international learning or learn online from geographically dispersed instructors who bring real-world, international experiences to the online classroom.

Lim, Morris, and Kupritz (2007) compared hybrid-learning models with online-only models and found several benefits of hybrid learning: lower instructional difficulty level, lower perceived workload, higher perceived support, and higher learner satisfaction. Durrington, Berryhill, and Swafford (2006) demonstrated that hybrid and online learning could be as effective as traditional classroom instruction when the technologies are appropriate for the instruction, when instructors provide timely feedback to students, and when levels of student interactivity are high. Tanner, Noser, and Totaro (2009) conducted a study that indicated that students in online courses might achieve even better results than their classroom-based counterparts.

From an instructor or program manager's perspective, the following benefits of offering courses in online or blended formats have been documented: (a) improved faculty support, (b) effective delivery of student assistance, (c) increased ability to share electronic course materials, (d) greater sharing of faculty workload, (e) promotion of virtual learning communities, (f) increased facilitation of student feedback, and (g) more effective program management (Tang & Byrne, 2007).

Many CityU program managers find that they are able to better manage their online and hybrid programs and courses by having ready access to the online classroom experiences. Using performance dashboards offered through CityU's learning management system, program managers are alerted to potential concerns by reviewing how often instructors are present in the online classroom, how responsive they are in the discussion forums, and even how well they are doing in providing rich, formative feedback designed to help students improve their work. Also through the learning management system and other conferencing options, CityU program managers are able to conduct interactive sessions among instructors teaching similar courses to share ideas and best practices, and continue to improve the courses and programs.

Challenges of Hybrid and Online Delivery

Owen and Allardice (2008) acknowledged the following limitations with implementing hybrid and online delivery formats: (a) a lack of expertise at management level, (b) the presence of few champions in senior management, and (c) a lack of management and faculty buy-in. Other limitations include (d) a failure to bridge the gap between pedagogic design and technology at a college level, (e) a lack of relevant training, (f) a lack of policies based on needs analysis and field research, and (g) a resistance to changing paradigms.

Leaders face many of these challenges in implementing online and hybrid programs. Strong advocacy and support provided by senior management in shifting to online and hybrid delivery allows program leaders who were early adopters to begin integrating technology into their programs and designing course content in online modalities. Gaining insight from lessons learned, leaders can begin policy discussions, implement change management principles, and provide supplemental faculty development workshops to provide needed support to make the institutional shift to online and hybrid learning models.

Appana (2008) articulated several potential limitations found in online learning, including the need for startup funding, adequate time, organizational preparedness, student readiness, differing stages of team development, crisis management, faculty learning curve, members with limited language skills, technical support, team effort, synchronous- or asynchronous-classroom contexts, costs, accessibility to course materials, delayed feedback, and evaluation and assessment.

Leaders at CityU took steps to prepare the organization for online and hybrid delivery. The selection of the learning management system came only after conducting a comprehensive cost-benefit analysis of multiple options. A team was established to support the use of the learning management system and ensure adequate faculty and student preparation. Ongoing professional development workshops have been offered to equip faculty with basic and advanced skills in using the system, in addition to learning and sharing strategies for effectively teaching through the online platform.

Implementing Hybrid and Online Programs

According to Li and Lui (2005), designing the online experience for students by integrating technology can take many forms, from simply providing an online resource for content and course materials to providing a space for students to display their best work. Garrison and Cleveland-Innes (2005) encouraged developers to integrate technology to promote higher learning by ensuring that learners' needs are addressed and motivating learners to invest themselves and spend time on their work. The authors also recommended challenging learners to reflect on their own learning, become aware of why they do what they do, and to engage with content in multiple contexts.

Amrein-Beardsley, Foulger, and Toth (2007) noted that adult learners value the following characteristics in the hybrid courses: (a) guidance through course announcements, course information documents, and information on specific assignments; (b) some degree of individualization, self-direction, variety, and a learning community; (c) two-way communication, including feedback and confirmation; and (d) learning outcomes that allow for self-direction based on real-world needs. CityU program leaders and course managers strive to ensure consistency in the student experience by providing them with course information in just-in-time formats. Learning communities are offered through team work and discussions, and students are encouraged to take ownership of their learning by making the assessments relevant and meaningful to their current and future work.

At CityU, faculty members are reflective practitioners, actively working in the fields in which they teach. Online and hybrid delivery modes provide many options for engaging with learners and promoting higher learning through discussion boards, integration of videos and podcasts, and using wikis and blogs to collaborate and foster collective intellectual inquiry. Students benefit from multiple ways of learning through technology in addition to gaining insights from the diverse perspectives of their peers who are geographically dispersed.

Overcoming Resistance

Online interaction should help students reach higher learning, which can include looking at content in a new way, addressing learners' needs, motivating learners to spend time, challenging learners to understand their own learning, and framing understanding in multiple contexts (Garrison & Cleveland-Innes, 2005). The goal of program developers and faculty should be to ensure that high-level learning takes place, regardless of the delivery mode. Moser (2007) noted, "If blended learning is to be successfully integrated, a bottom-up approach informed by socio-cultural principles is essential, whereby faculty feel ownership in the decision-making and development process" (p. 68).

The following seven strategies are recommended for gaining faculty buy-in for distance learning initiatives: (a) empower departments to accept more responsibility for distance learning, (b) provide research and information for faculty about the benefits of hybrid and online delivery, and (c) encourage faculty to start small and begin incorporating technology into their classrooms. Institutions are encouraged to (d) provide incentives for faculty who integrate technology into their classrooms, (e) improve training and instructional support for these initiatives, (f) build a stronger distance education faculty community through virtual faculty lounges and other forums, and (g) encourage scholarship and research on hybrid and online learning (Seven Strategies, 2004).

CityU leaders have struggled to manage the challenges faced with moving to online and hybrid delivery options. Program managers took ownership of their programs and conducted market analyses to determine the best time to move to online and hybrid options and meet the changing needs of their students. Faculty members were encouraged to start integrating technology in small ways, and these technology options have expanded over time. Faculty development options were provided for faculty who desired to learn more about integrating technology and how to improve their online presence. Ongoing support for research and scholarship continues to surface new ideas and opportunities to share best practices.

Overcoming Faculty Resistance

Many faculty members are resistant to integrating online coursework into their programs and have voiced concerns that academic quality will diminish. Educational scholars who believe that face-to-face interaction is required for adults to learn echo these concerns. Muilenburg and Berge (2005) believed that online learning is impersonal and more beneficial to educational institutions than to students. Gorski (2004) noted, "Effective teaching and learning emerge from strong pedagogy, high levels of expectations for all students, and a classroom approach that centers and empowers those students, not any particular technology or medium" (p. 37). Gorski continued, "The Internet can contribute to effective and progressive teaching and learning" (p. 37), but noted that online education should not be a total replacement of the human teacher. Hannon (2009) noted that these are common concerns that faculty can overcome through gaining comfort with technology and by sharing best practices.

For the successful implementation of online and hybrid programs, faculty development and support systems need to be in place for the instructors. Wang (2007) recommended developing facilitators who can enhance online learning through expertise in content, online social process, structure management, and technical modeling. In each of the roles, faculty need to develop new strategies, have opportunities to share best practices, and obtain support from experts in the field.

CityU continues to expand its faculty development offerings to support faculty in their efforts to teach their subject matter in online and hybrid delivery modes. In-person, hybrid, and online workshops are offered each year—and sometimes twice a year—to provide opportunities for faculty members to learn new skills and share ideas with their colleagues. Exemplar models have been evaluated and selected by peer-review teams, and best practices have been disseminated among program leaders and course developers. Over time more faculty members have become comfortable with technology options and have opted to teach in online and hybrid delivery modes.

Overcoming Student Resistance

Online courses are not for everyone. Solnick (2007) recognized the following drawbacks to online learning: conversation does not flow as freely online; students can feel anxious when they do not receive immediate feedback; and technology challenges can frustrate and discourage students from persevering. Mupinga et al. (2006) discussed several sources of negative affective responses, including (a) students' familiarity with the learning environment, (b) students' skills and confidence with computer technology, and (c) students' preferred learning styles. O'Neil and Fisher (2008) reinforced that online learning works well for learners who are comfortable using technology and are independent, well organized, and disciplined. If a learner is not organized or disciplined, needs constant instructor reassurance, or craves face-to-face interaction, online learning might not be the best choice.

CityU advisors are equipped with information on how to evaluate students' motives, learning styles, commitment to interacting with others, and computer competence to help them make the best decisions about taking online courses (O'Neil & Fisher, 2008). Initially many learners choose online learning for the freedom afforded in asynchronous environments, although more learners are choosing online models of learning as their primary learning environment (Stein, Wanstreet, Calvin, Overtoom, & Wheaton, 2005). Some students are advised to start with hybrid course offerings until they become more comfortable with technology, while other students are advised to take courses fully online. These recommendations are made only after careful evaluation of each student's needs and abilities.

Sufficient student support is necessary in the online environment. Although the operational structure of hybrid and online programs is more important than the technical expertise of the student (Stein et al., 2005), learner satisfaction is often the primary motivator for online learning (Dennen, Darabi, & Smith, 2007). Students need to feel supported in their learning experience through faculty and peer interaction, technology support, and regular constructive feedback.

Gould (2006) encouraged faculty to use the following seven strategies to improve student satisfaction in online courses: (a) post the course syllabus online, (b) administer a learning styles inventory, (c) explain the importance of group work, (d) use team contracts for team collaboration, (e) use various assessments and learning activities, (f) be flexible, and (g) provide frequent inter-action. Shepherd, Alpert, and Koeller (2007) further suggested that faculty establish a tone of excellence, treat each student as an individual, and add emotion through descriptive, positive lan-guage. At CityU, faculty members are encouraged to apply these best practices and are evaluated on these criteria, in addition to many others.

Future Research Directions

Learners in well-designed online and hybrid programs with appropriate levels of interaction and feedback and adequate fac-ulty and student support can achieve the same outcomes and learning goals as those learning in the classroom face-to-face (Durrington, Berryhill, & Swafford, 2006). Yet the research does not clearly indicate which curriculum design practices in online and hybrid formats best achieve the outcomes and learning goals. Martell (2007) revealed that many schools are lagging in the use of appropriate assessment strategies and are struggling to use assessment data to continue to improve programs. Martell recom-mended that when assessing the quality of business curricula, pro-gram managers seek the answers to the following four questions: (a) what are their learning goals, (b) how and where did they assess these learning goals, (c) what did they find out from the results, and (d) what are they going to change? The results could reveal curriculum design strategies that are successful and those that are not. Future research could be conducted using assessment data to determine which curriculum design practices in online and hybrid formats best achieve the outcomes and learning goals.

Conclusion

Taking steps to establish organizational readiness, implement change management principles, and proactively overcoming fac-ulty and student resistance will increase the chances of successful implementation.

CityU program leaders and faculty have learned many lessons by moving programs and courses into online and hybrid delivery formats. There are many challenges that need to be considered and overcome to be successful in implementing these formats. However, the experience of CityU program leaders, faculty, and students reinforces the growing research on the many benefits of online and hybrid delivery.

References

Allen, I. E., & Seaman, J. (2005). *Growing by degrees: Online education in the United States.* Retrieved from http://www.sloan-c.org/resources/growing_by_degrees.pdf

Amrein-Beardsley, A., Foulger, T. S., & Toth, M. (2007). Examining the development of a hybrid degree program: Using student and instructor data to inform decision-making. International Society for Technology in Education, 39, 331-357.

Appana, S. (2008). A review of benefits and limitations of online learning in the context of the student, the instructor, and the tenured faculty. *International Journal on E-Learning, 7,* 5-22.

Dennen, V. P., Darabi, A. A., & Smith, L. J. (2007). Instructor-learner interaction in online courses: The relative perceived importance of particular instructor actions on performance and satisfaction. *Distance Education, 28,* 65-79.

Domask, J. J. (2007). Achieving goals in higher education: An experiential approach to sustainability studies. *International Journal of Sustainability in Higher Education, 8,* 53-68.

Durrington, V. A., Berryhill, A., & Swafford, J. (2006). Strategies for enhancing student interactivity in an online environment. *College Teaching, 54,* 190-193.

Endres, M. L., Chowdhury, S., Frye, C., & Hurtubis, C. A. (2009). The multifaceted nature of online MBA student satisfaction and impacts on behavioral intentions. *Journal of Education for Business, 84*, 304-312.

Garrison, D. R., & Cleveland-Innes, M. (2005). Facilitating cognitive presence in online learning: Interaction is not enough. *American Journal of Distance Education, 19*, 133 – 148.

Gorski, P. C. (2004). Multicultural education and progressive pedagogy in the online information age. *Multicultural Perspectives, 6*(4), 37-48.

Gould, M. (2006). Seven ways to improve student satisfaction in online courses. *Distance Education Report, 10*(12), 7-7.

Hannon, J. (2009). Breaking down online teaching: Innovation and resistance. *Australasian Journal of Educational Technology, 25*, 14-29.

Honigsfeld, A., & Dunn, R. (2006). Learning style characteristics of adult learners. *Delta Kappa Gamma Bulletin, 72*(2), 14-31.

Kiriakidis, P. (2008). Online learner satisfaction: Learner-instructor discourse. *College Teaching Methods & Styles Journal, 4*, 11-18.

Knowles, M. (1980). *The modern practice of adult education: From pedagogy to andragogy.* Englewood Cliffs, NJ: Prentice Hall.

Li, S., & Lui, D. (2005). The online top-down modeling model. *Quarterly Review of Distance Education, 6*, 343-359.

Lim, D. H., Morris, M. L., & Kupritz, V. W. (2007). Online vs. blended learning: Differences in instructional outcomes and learner satisfaction. *Journal of Asynchronous Learning Networks, 11*(2), 1-17. Retrieved from http://www.sloan-c.org/publications/jaln/v11n2/pdf/v11n2_lim.pdf

Martell, K. (2007). Assessing student learning: Are business schools making the grade? *Journal of Education for Business, 82,* 189-196.

Moloney, J. F., Hickey, C. P., Bergin, A. L., Boccia, J., & Polley, K. (2007). Characteristics of successful local blended programs in the context of the Sloan-C pillars. *Journal of Asynchronous Learning Networks, 11.* Retrieved from http://www.sloan-c. org/publications/jaln/v11n1/pdf/v11n1_5moloney.pdf

Moser, F. Z. (2007). Faculty adoption of educational technology. *Educause Quarterly, 1,* 66-69. Retrieved from http://net. educause.edu/ir/library/pdf/eqm07111.pdf

Muilenburg, L. Y., & Berge, Z. L. (2005). Student barriers to online learning: A factor analytic study. *Distance Education, 26,* 29-48.

Mupinga, D. M., Nora, R. T., & Yaw, D. C. (2006, March 18). The learning styles, expectations, and needs of online students. Retrieved from http://www.redorbit.com/news/technology/433632/the_learning_styles_expectations_and_needs_of_online_students/

O'Neil, C., & Fisher, C. (2008). Should I take this course online? *Journal of Nursing Education, 47*(2), 53-59.

Owen, H., & Allardice, R. (2008). Managing the implementation of blended e-learning initiatives with the unconverted in a climate of institutionally driven change. *International Journal of Learning, 14,* 179-191.

Shepherd, C., Alpert, M., & Koeller, M. (2007). Increasing the efficacy of educators teaching online. *International Journal of Social Sciences, 2,* 173-179. Retrieved from http://66.102.1.104/scholar?q=cache:0v7RgNdE9pgJ:scholar.google.com/+Tips+and+tricks+for+teaching+online:+How+to+teach+like+a+pro&hl=en

Solnik, C. (2007, September 14). Debating the pros and cons of an online education. *Long Island Business News.*

Stein, D. S., Wanstreet, C. E., Calvin, J., Overtoom, C., & Wheaton, J. E. (2005). Bridging the transactional distance gap in online learning environments. *The American Journal of Distance Learning. 19*, 105-118.

Tang, M., & Byrne, R. (2007). Regular versus online versus blended: A qualitative description of the advantages of the electronic models and a quantitative evaluation. *International Journal on E-Learning, 6*, 257-266.

Tanner, J. R., Noser, T. C., & Totaro, M. W. (2009). Business faculty and undergraduate students' perceptions of online learning: A comparative study. *Journal of Information Systems Education, 20*, 29-40.

Wang, Q. (2008). Student-facilitators' roles in moderating online discussions. *British Journal of Educational Technology, 39*, 859-874.

Proven Approaches to Motivating Engagement by Students in Online Classes

Anna Cholewinska, MA
City University of Seattle
Division of Arts and Sciences

Abstract

An instructor's role in motivating students may be more important in online than in any other format of classes. Online classes can still be viewed as isolating for students who have to learn on their own and present their knowledge through participation in various activities on the discussion board. Students do not always have enough self-motivation to contribute consistently and thoughtfully in activities. Thus, involving students in collaboration seems to be one of the more perplexing tasks with which instructors have to deal. Even so, several proven approaches are available for encouraging students to participate in online class activities.

Introduction

Participation in online activities can easily be imposed upon students through curriculum design. Engagement in class activities could be simply included as one of required and graded assessments, and students may view it as more or less important depending on the percentage of their final grade for that course. This approach, while successful in driving students to participate, most likely will result in students' minimal engagement in discussions or online activities. Additionally, the quality of contribution may not be as high as it could be if instructors were to use other, more positive methods of motivating and engaging students.

Highly successful instructors do not rely on curriculum requirements only to facilitate a quality class. They engage students in activities and are actively involved in the facilitation of discussions. They post interesting and complex questions, show other aspects of discussed topics, incorporate new ideas, provide real-life applications, and share their own professional experiences in discussions as they work to create a supportive classroom environment.

Background

The impact of an instructor's presence on the dynamics of the class is a highly researched topic among those studying higher education. Mandernach, Gonzales, and Garret (2006) emphasize that the instructor's presence is central to the effectiveness of online learning. They point out that a delicate balance needs to be found in online classes, as too much interaction leads to student feelings of being overburdened, while too little interaction may cause isolation and feelings of not being heard. Mandernach, Dailey-Herbert, and Donnelli-Sallee (2007) add that in online courses students could only notice the presence of instructors when they visibly participated in discussions by submitting posts to the threaded discussions. This is also a reason why Burgess and Strong (2003) stress that "each online class must be a reliable and robust teacher-present environment, that is in effect, always in session throughout the term" (p. 2).

A supportive classroom environment is a broad term that describes various instructor behaviors. It includes friendly ice-breaking activities at the very beginning of the quarter when students introduce themselves to their classmates and learn about expectations in the class. In the online delivery format, those activities may also be conducted by posting a self-introduction with a photo or scavenger hunts that would make students search for details about their class.

Creating a supportive classroom is not a new concept and is very important in any classroom setting. Vella (1994) described twelve principles of effective adult learning, including safety in the environment and process; respect for learners as subjects of their own learning; and teamwork or working in small groups. While she discussed these in the context of a traditional classroom, the online environment is not that different. In fact, creating a supportive classroom may be viewed as even more critical in this format as students' online learning is still often viewed as very isolating and anonymous (Bambara, Harbour, Davies, & Athey, 2009; McInnerney & Roberts, 2004). Therefore, creating a safe learning environment helps students overcome anxieties about online learning and learn to participate with no fear that they will be ignored, ridiculed, or exposed to others as negative examples. Through positive classroom experiences, students realize that instructors are available and will assist them in their learning. Such positive activities also include offering periodic summaries of what was already taught in the class, detailed feedback on student performance, and help for those students who need to improve. Finally, as pointed out by Heuer and King (2004), instructors can model student behavior by setting a positive example for collaboration and discussion participation. They also coach students, providing them encouragement, support, motivation, and feedback. Highly engaged instructors, who are visibly present to students through posts and comments, observe similar behavior in their students who also actively participate in discussions, incorporate new ideas into their posts, and in general do not limit their presence and contribution to mere fulfillment of basic requirements for engagement in course activities.

Quantity and quality of student interaction in online courses depends, however, not just on the active engagement of instructors; it also depends on the quality of the instructor's engagement. Instructors cannot limit their interactions to scattered and short comments to students. Their role as facilitators starts with soliciting complex and interesting problems or questions that compel students to use course concepts and to make references to concepts learned in previous courses or professional experience. Moreover, it is the instructor's role to move discussions to a further level by emphasizing the advantages and disadvantages of students' approaches and alternative viewpoints as well as the results and the importance of their standpoint. Simultaneously, instructors facilitating online activities advocate clarity of response by persuading students to be elaborate in their posts. As Maor (2003) points out, online instructors need to be ready to intervene in the discussion when it stalls or goes off track and ensure that student postings are professional and scholarly and that they serve as experiences that connect the students to one another.

Observations from courses taught at City University of Seattle appear to support the findings presented in the literature. Analysis of courses taught by twelve Division of Arts and Sciences instructors showed that the level of student engagement depended significantly on the instructor's engagement. In all classes, most of the students began with a very positive attitude; they engaged and made an effort to participate in class activities. By the third week of the quarter, students started to show signs of differentiating between highly engaging classes in which instructors did not rely on curricular requirements only and courses that were much less engaging where instructors merely expected students to fulfill minimum requirements for participation. In the latter the number of student posts started dropping from the first and second week highs. This trend continued until the very end of the quarter. Students typically posted only on two different days, and some submitted all posts on one day. None of the students exceeded the minimum required number of posts, and some of the students submitted less than the minimum required number of posts. In extreme cases students chose not to participate at all. Similarly, qualitative analysis of student posts in such classes showed that student responses were very short, with no or very few connections between concepts learned in the current session and those learned in previous sessions or previous courses; students did not make an effort to use materials other than textbook resources or real-life situations to illustrate or support their posts in the discussion. Overall, course quality seemed very low.

At the same time, students in classes with active facilitation of discussion were very engaged. Most of the students posted more than the required number of times and typically a high number of posts continued throughout the entire quarter. Students posted on more than two days, and none of the students posted on one day. While the quality of the posts varied between classes and students, generally it was relatively high; in each class there was evidence of students connecting concepts from various sessions and classes as well as using various examples to support claims in the discussion.

Proven Practices

When City University of Seattle started offering online courses over a decade ago, no specific guidelines existed for student and instructor participation. Even though participation in online activities, such as threaded discussions, was built into those courses as a graded assessment, it was not clear what it really meant in terms of timeline. In 2004 the first set of guidelines was created for Division of Arts and Sciences students. Those guidelines included clear expectations for timely submission of posts. More specifically, a three–four rule was created. It required students to post their initial responses to an instructor's questions no later than the end of the third day of the weekly session and then to participate in student-to-student and student-to-instructor discussions during the remaining four days. That simple rule significantly changed the dynamic of the discussions.

In 2006 the CityU Online Coordinating Committee (OCC) introduced a set of guidelines for all instructors and students. Those guidelines described the timelines for submission to threaded discussions, the number of posts required in the discussion (original response and at least two posts in student-to-student discussion), and the quality of the discussion (using writing conventions, not limiting posts to short comments such as "good job"), and the response time to e-mails and inquiries, etc. Implementation of these guidelines increased the level of participation in many courses. For example, in the first psychology courses offered online, there were less than 100 posts per session in a class with 12–16 students. This number increased to about 120 posts per week after the first set of guidelines was introduced and then jumped again to more than 150 posts after guidelines for online instructors and students were implemented. Currently, it is not unusual to see more than 200 posts each week in classes of similar size.

Clear guidelines for students help them understand that online discussion does not happen on its own. At the same time, guidelines for instructors help them realize that they need to be active as well as to model student behavior. Instructors who moved from message posting to engaging in discussions helped students to do the same. As a result students felt that they learned more from those instructors. This was reflected in student comments and evaluations. As noted before the evidence in the literature about online education is clear: it is instructors who shape the course and the student-to-student and student-to-instructor interactions. While there is no "one-size-fits-all" rule indicating the optimal level of interaction, students need to see active instructors, and instructors need to find a balance between encouragement and the activities, depending on the nature of their classes, group composition, etc. (Dennen, 2005).

The required level of participation in online threaded discussions was just a small part of the success in increasing student engagement in course activities. As Dallimore, Hertenstein, and Platt (2004) note, non-voluntary participation is not an effective way to increase participation. It has to be accompanied by other practices to keep students interested in courses and course activities as well as to help them feel safe to share. CityU created a set of best practices in collaboration with the most successful instructors who shared their ideas about teaching online. The perception of isolation, from other students as well as the instructor, is one of the main student complaints about online courses (Bambara, Harbour, Davies, & Athey, 2009; McInnerney & Roberts, 2004). Therefore, all CityU instructors are required to post their profiles in class shells so students know how to find them. While the profiles in early online courses were very short and limited to contact information and office hours, most instructors now submit their photo and include personal information about themselves. Additionally, to make interaction in class more personal, many instructors require students to submit their photos as part of the introductory assignment. Similarly, instructors are strongly recommended to greet all students in the course by replying to their introductory posts. These practices ease initial fears about a class and make students feel welcome and comfortable as seen by the number of posts in the introductory activity.

While the quantity of interaction could be relatively easily prescribed by requirements built into the curriculum, it is much more difficult to define the quality of participation. One way to ensure quality is to create rubrics that specifically describe how activities will be assessed. The OCC created a rubric that is used in all online courses. In addition to being graded for timeliness and the number of posts in the discussion, students are also graded based on the depth of their posts, their use of concepts from the course, and the way that they support them with evidence from the required textbook and additional sources. However, it is important to emphasize that even the best rubric will not prevent students from discussing unrelated issues, and, as Maor (2003) pointed out, instructors need to be ready to intervene in such situations. Additionally, as the literature suggests, instructors need to model professional discussions in which students learn from instructors and fellow students. Through questions and comments to student posts, instructors need to shape discussions that will help students learn course concepts. However, what is most important is that instructors need to make discussions relevant to students' experiences and other course activities (Dennen, 2005). The CityU "practitioner/instructor" model seems to encourage that practice. In combination with questions based on case studies, vignettes, or current events, faculty add their practical experiences throughout the discussions and online activities whenever appropriate.

The best instructors are practitioners who regularly use their professional experience, share articles with students, and encourage them to do the same. Documentaries and news are often used as examples for the discussions in psychology and social sciences classes. The best instructors contribute significantly to the discussion, accounting for about 20–25 percent of the total number of posts each session. Students looking for a model of online behavior see their instructors engaged, asking questions, and making relevant connections between theory and practice.

While in general this is a desired model, it is important to realize potential problems. The literature about online education cautions about overactive instructors who can be viewed as a threat to student learning. They can easily dominate discussions, which can prevent or discourage students from participating (Dennen, 2005; Mandernach, Gonzales, & Garrett, 2006; Palloff & Pratt, 2001). Instructors need to find that right balance between being too absent and being too active. Moderation and balance are the keys to a successful class, and this balance may differ based on many factors, such as discipline, class (introductory *vs.* advanced) topic, group dynamics, etc. There is no magic number of posts that could be recommended for all instructors who are teaching online. To avoid bias and instructor-dominated discussion, some instructors choose not to participate in discussions until students post their original responses to session questions. They observe discussions at the beginning of the week and start posting their comments in the middle of the week, allowing students to freely express themselves in their initial posts. Then through various questions, they show students different sides of the discussed issues. Finally, while it is recommended that instructors make relevant connections between theory and real-life examples, it is difficult at times to keep students focused on the course concepts. Instructors constantly need to observe discussions to make sure that real life examples and applications are simply used to illustrate or support discussed theories and concepts rather than allowing them to dominate the class objectives. Otherwise discussion might become useless or at times even uncomfortable for students to participate.

Future Research Directions

There is a great need for future systematic research that would investigate ways to motivate online students to participate in class activities. Motivation is a very complex concept. Many variables impact motivation, starting with intrinsic factors such as student motivation for taking courses, personal situations, personality of the students, etc. and ending with extrinsic factors such as the personality of an instructor, group dynamics, the composition of the class, the type or level of the class (elective *vs.* required, introductory *vs.* advanced), or the relevance of topics discussed to students' experiences. It would be beneficial to conduct a longitudinal study of different groups of students to better understand the correlation of these factors with student motivation.

Online learning can be very engaging and beneficial for students. In a supportive online classroom, less formal activities are seamlessly combined with formal and academic discussions while instructors find a delicate balance between being too active and too absent.

References

Bambara, C. S., Harbour, C. P., Davies, T. G., & Athey, S. (2009). The lived experience of community college students enrolled in high-risk online courses. *Community College Review, 36*(3), 219-238.

Burgess, L. A., & Strong, S. D. (2003). Trends in online education: Case study at Southwest Missouri State University. *Journal of Industrial Technology, 19*(3). Retrieved from http://atmae.org/jit/Articles/burgess041403.pdf

Dallimore, E. J., Hertenstein, J. H., & Platt, M. B. (2004). Classroom participation and discussion effectiveness: Student-generated strategies. *Communication Education, 53*(1), 103-115.

Dennen, V. P. (2005). From message posting to learning dialogues: Factors affecting learner participation in asynchronous discussion. *Distance Education, 26*(1), 127-148.

Heuer, B. P., & King, K. P. (2004). Leading the band: The role of the instructor in online leaning for educators. *The Journal of Interactive and Online Learning, 3*(1). Retrieved from http://www.ncolr.org/jiol/issues/pdf/3.1.5.pdf

McInnerney, J. M., & Roberts, T. S. (2004). Online learning: Social interaction and the creation of a sense of community. *Educational Technology & Society, 7*(3), 73-81.

Mandernach, B. J., Dailey-Hebert, A., & Donnelli-Sallee, E. (2007). Frequency and time investment of instructors' participation in threaded discussions in the online classroom. *Journal of Interactive Online Learning, 6*(1). Retrieved from http://www.ncolr.org/jiol/issues/pdf/6.1.1.pdf

Mandernach, B. J., Gonzales, R. M., & Garrett, A. L. (2006). An examination of the instructor presence via threaded discussion participation. *Journal of Online Learning and Teaching, 2*(4). Retrieved from http://jolt.merlot.org/vol2no4mandernach.htm

Maor, D. (2003). The teacher's role in developing interaction and reflection in an online learning community. *Education Media International, 40*(1/2), 127-137.

Palloff, R. M., & Pratt, K. (2001). *Lessons from the cyberspace classroom: the realities of online teaching.* San Francisco, CA: Jossey-Bass.

Vella, J. (1994). Learning to listen, learning to teach: The power of dialogue in educating adults. San Francisco, CA: Jossey-Bass.

Creating a Supportive Online Classroom Environment

Carla Weaver, MA, MSC
City University of Seattle
School of Management

Abstract

Effective classroom management is necessary to create a supportive learning environment where students can learn in a meaningful way, especially in an online environment. Research, education and training, consulting and online teaching experience have all helped to develop techniques for an effective and supportive online classroom: communicate clearly and often; set expectations; offer constructive and timely feedback; build rapport; be present; respect, encourage, and motivate students; reach out to them; build community; and keep course content relevant.

Introduction

"Effective classroom management is necessary to create a supportive learning environment and a supportive learning environment is essential if students' learning experiences are to be meaningful." (Curtis, 2008, p. 77). The keys to effective classroom management for a supportive online learning environment are clear communication and responsiveness from the instructor. While students appreciate the convenience and flexibility of online learning, they also want to enjoy the benefits of an in-class experience. Much of the available literature emphasizes students interacting with the course content. However, in addition to the content of the course, students seem to want interaction with their fellow students and instructors. This social interaction is important, and instructors can emphasize and facilitate interaction. Without it, online learning can become merely a self-paced, individualized approach to learning. Effective coaching and management by an online instructor facilitates collaborative problem solving amongst students. While there is little conclusive proof that interaction improves learning outcomes, it enriches the learning experience by contributing to motivation and course completion rates (Chalmers, 1999).

Collison, Elbaum, Haavind, & Tinker (2003) described three roles for instructors in online courses: guide-on-the-side, instructor/project leader, and group process facilitator. The "guide-on-the-side," or coach approach, gives the instructor an opportunity to coach and assist students to engage in dialogue that allows them to be the prime influencers on the culture of the online classroom. Online instructors also act as project managers or team leaders within the course by being in control of the feedback and content and by facilitating peer support. Collison et al. also encourage online instructors to facilitate process by "Leading introductory, community building activities, providing virtual 'hand-holding' to the 'digitally-challenged'" (Collison, et al, 2003, p. 49) as well as acknowledging the diversity of the participants. While students in online classes should be computer literate, often an instructor will find first-time online students getting used to the virtual classroom concept and not as computer literate as they could be, so patience and encouragement are required to help these students make the transition to online learning. This role also includes facilitating the discussions and communicating one-on-one with students via e-mail and telephone (Collison, et al, 2003).

Best Practices for Supporting Online Classrooms

Communicate Clearly and Often

Experience shows that instructors should communicate clearly and often throughout the duration of an online course. The first communication should be a timely welcome letter from the instructor to each student welcoming the student to the course. Even though one e-mail may be distributed to all, an individual e-mail to each student rather than a group e-mail helps to build rapport. This e-mail should be sent out a few days before the course start date, or at the very latest, early on the first day of the course. It fulfills several purposes. First, it introduces the instructor to the students and welcomes them to the class. It also sets the tone for the course by including information that the instructor deems most important, such as pointing out important assignments, describing how to succeed in the course, directing students to the syllabus, and advising them about how to get started in the course. By sending the welcome letter as an e-mail, students receive the communication in their e-mail inboxes and are more likely to read it sooner than if it is posted in the course as an announcement. It also ensures that students who don't know how to access the course will get the information, and it should contain instructions about how to access the course and get started in order to help those who may not be clear about how to do that. Following is an example of the Getting Started section of a welcome e-mail:

Now, let's get started:

1. *Access the course at [insert course URL].*
2. *Use your login information and select the [insert course name and number here].*

3. *Please go to the discussion board by clicking on the Discussion Board tab on the left of your screen. Select the forum for the student introductory assignment, and write and post a brief description of your background and interests, your international business experience, something of interest about you, and your expectations from this course.*
4. *When you see your classmates' introductions, please respond to them.*
5. *Begin working on the Session 1 discussion forum. If you have any questions, post them in the Q&A discussion forum.*

Consistent communication reduces confusion. Instructors should post regularly to the course by making regular announcements and discussion posts. Approximately two announcements a week will build student confidence that the instructor is fully engaged in the course. The first announcement can welcome students to the session for that week and indicate the learning objectives and topic for discussion that will be covered, as well as reminding students about the assignments that will be due. If the instructor's experience has been that students are unclear about certain aspects of the assignment, an e-mail giving tips about how to approach the assignment is appropriate. At the end of the week, the instructor also posts an announcement letting students know that discussion grades and/or assignment grades have been posted and summarizes the material covered in those previous discussions and assignments.

An instructor learns from experience in teaching a specific course how to improve communication and instructions by observing how students respond to instructions and what questions they ask. This observation will help to improve communication over time so that an instructor can provide clear instructions to students for all aspects of the course. This includes learning objectives, assignment instructions, discussion topics, grading rubrics, assignment and discussion feedback, and announcements. In short, all communication must be clear and specific.

Set Clear Expectations

Setting clear expectations at the outset of each online course helps students to be better prepared for the course. It is important to tell students what is expected from them. This can be accomplished through several tools in the course. First, the course learning objectives should be clearly described and listed, so that students know what they will be expected to achieve. Assignments should be designed to help students meet the course learning objectives. As the course progresses, an effective instructor manages the discussion board in the course to ensure that the learning objectives are covered in the discussion.

A syllabus for the course is a contract between student and instructor, clearly outlining the course learning objectives, assignments, course schedule, and grading expectations. Students should be instructed to review the syllabus early in the course and to ask questions to ensure that they understand the course requirements. Communication should be given that students are expected to print out the syllabus and course schedule and keep them handy so that they can refer to them as needed. Having the course schedule in a format that is easy to assimilate at a glance helps students to see the course requirements easily and also to keep on track of assignment due dates.

At some schools curriculum guides and syllabi are prepared by the department and can be edited by instructors, so each instructor is able to ensure that the syllabus and its included course schedule are posted in the course and easy to access. Other schools may provide more or less freedom to faculty in this area.

For consistency in grading, experience has shown that having grading rubrics for all assignments helps to keep grading consistent. When these are included in the course, it is advisable to remind students about them when they are working on the assignments so that they keep them in mind as they prepare their assignments. This can be done by posting an announcement to refer students to the syllabus and grading rubrics or by posting the grading rubrics in the announcement.

Students need to know and understand the expectations for participating in the discussion forums. Typically, discussion participation should be evaluated with both qualitative and quantitative feedback. For students to be able to make their best contributions to the discussion, instructors should inform them what they need to do to earn full points for participating. The instructor should inform them how frequently they should participate and should specify the approximate length and number of posts and type of content. Additionally, discussion participation should count toward the final grade to ensure that students actively participate to enhance their learning (Bender, 2003).

Providing good communication and setting expectations also involves telling students what they can expect from the instructor. This can be accomplished by including the information in the welcome e-mail or by posting a separate announcement that lets students know when the instructor is online, when grades will be returned, how the instructor will participate in the course, and how long it will take to respond to students' queries.

Offer Constructive and Timely Feedback

Effective online instructors offer constructive and timely feedback by responding to student posts on the discussion board and student e-mails daily. Students should be advised that the instructor will respond to e-mails within twenty-four hours. If they know that they may not get a response for twenty-four hours, they are more likely to be proactive in looking ahead to make sure that their questions are answered before they need the information to meet deadlines. Timely feedback has more impact while the content and participation are fresh in students' minds, so student participation in discussion boards should be graded within forty-eight hours of the end of the week. Longer assignments should be graded within the week that they are submitted. Each week, an announcement to students indicating when they can expect to receive their grades for the previous week's assignments keeps them informed and manages their expectations.

The Center for the Enhancement of Learning and Teaching (October, 2008) reminds us that everyone likes to succeed, so it is important that feedback be positive and clear. One way to begin feedback is to congratulate students for what they have done well. Tell the student what he or she did right before launching into what was not right. In fact, telling students how to improve is more positive than sharing what was wrong with the assignment. Students who did not do well on an assignment can be invited to contact the instructor during his/her office hours to discuss the feedback in person and receive extra help (Center for Enhancement of Learning & Teaching, 2008). A hypothetical example of positive feedback follows:

> *"[Mary], you did a great job of describing what is meant by globalization. To strengthen your answer, you could have also included a description of the major forces that have driven globalization and a discussion of the changing nature of our economy."*

Students who read the grading rubrics will expect to be graded by them, so instructors should relate feedback to the rubrics. This can be accomplished by directly referencing the rubrics in student feedback by either including a table or grid with the rubrics and the assigned grade for each rubric or by referring to the rubrics in the comments.

After an assignment or week's discussion participation is complete, summaries and samples can be posted for student review and exam preparation. For example, at the end of each week, module, or unit, it is helpful if the instructor posts a summary of the content and the important points that relate to the learning objectives for that portion of the course. For assignments such as case studies or written assignments, a sample of a model or very good assignment can be posted for students to review. Experience has shown that it is helpful to post some accompanying comments to be clear about expectations. This avoids the confusion that can result in the case where more than one approach to the right answer is possible, such as with a case study. Posting a sample along with comments indicating that there were multiple correct approaches to an assignment will help expand students' perspectives.

Build Rapport

All communications with students, from the welcome e-mail to assignment feedback, are opportunities to build rapport if done effectively. It is helpful to ensure that all communications are positive, professional, clear, and friendly. The tone of communications must be professional to establish respect for the faculty member but also friendly and respectful to students. Using the student's name in e-mails and assignment feedback makes communication more friendly and personal even though an instructor may cut and paste some standard comments. For example, an instructor might develop and format some feedback about how to improve the bibliography for the assignment and insert that comment into several students' assignments, but it can be made personal by adding the student's name and/or assignment topic. For example,

> *"[Tom], you have included a number of good references in your bibliography for your research on [starting a business in India]. However, be sure to check your APA manual to put your citations into correct APA format, and also be sure to start your bibliography on a new page."*

A good way to build rapport with students is to contact them by e-mail or phone at regular intervals to ask them how they are doing or if they need any help. At the end of the first week, midway through the course, and again toward the end of the course are good times to be in touch with students. In an online course, it would be easy for students to conclude that the instructor does not care or isn't present if there is little or no contact. By phoning or e-mailing regularly to check in on students, they realize that the instructor is a real person who cares about their progress in the course.

Posting regular announcements also helps to build rapport because it gives the impression to students that the instructor is anticipating their needs and questions. It makes a far better impression to post a timely announcement rather than the student having to post a question and wait twenty-four hours for an answer when he/she could have been working on the assignment that generated the question.

Use a friendly tone when communicating with students and use encouraging language. For example:

Hi Brendan,

Thank you for your e-mail with the questions about your grade for last week's case study. I understand that you're disappointed in your grade. I've reviewed your assignment again to make sure that I didn't miss anything, but having done so I am comfortable that your grade is fair and accurate according to the assignment grading rubrics. I've included some additional feedback inside the attached file to help clarify the assignment for you. Please review my additional comments, and then let me know if you have any further questions.

Finally, the process of posting a photo in the course that shows the instructor smiling and looking approachable and professional, along with an introduction that relates the instructor's credentials, will garner the students' respect for the faculty member, while also sending a friendly and approachable message. In their introductions instructors might include some personal information, such as mentioning a hobby, a love for travel, information about family or pets, to reinforce that a real live person is facilitating the course.

Be Present

Instructors should regularly post to the discussion board, four to six days per week, to carefully manage the discussion in order to cover learning objectives and to demonstrate presence in the classroom. It is not enough to look at or read the posts in the discussions; if students don't see their instructor regularly posting to the discussion board they may assume that the instructor is not engaged in the course. If instructors cannot post daily, they should advise the class at the beginning of the course when to expect them to be online, and it should be consistent. For example,

"I will be in the course six days a week, and I usually do my online work either from about nine to eleven a.m. or else later in the evening. I take Saturdays off, so you won't see me on Saturdays, but you will see me in the course on the other six days of the week."

It has already been mentioned that timely responses to student questions and e-mails helps to build rapport and demonstrates the instructor's presence in the classroom.

It is important that instructors grade and return assignments in a timely manner. A good guideline is to return discussion participation grades within forty-eight hours of the end of the week and written assignments within the week. Forcing a student to wait an excessive amount of time for an assignment to be graded and returned can leave the impression that the instructor is not present or available.

Motivate, Respect, and Encourage

Creating a Safe and Supportive Learning Environment: Supporting Adult Learners (n.d.) states that motivation is important to student success and that students can be motivated by making them active participants in their learning by asking them to write, create, design, and problem solve. Whenever possible it is best to offer students some choice in their learning by allowing them to select between two options, such as to answer question A or B, or to choose their own research project topic. When students have the freedom to choose to invest their time in something that is most interesting to them, experience has shown that they remain more motivated. Variety also keeps students interested and motivated, so it is best to incorporate different learning strategies such as brainstorming, discussions, demonstrations, case studies, presentations, or team work. Different communication tools and learning activities also facilitate better comprehension for students with different learning styles (Literacy Source, n.d.).

Collison, Elbaum, Haavind, & Tinker (2003) recommend that instructors guide the direction of the discussion, help to sort out key points, and help students to focus on the learning objectives in order to focus class discussions. They also recommend that instructors allow students the opportunity for multiple points of view. Additionally, instructors should organize the discussion threads so that they are easy to follow and don't become overwhelming. This can be accomplished by providing some instructions to students about how to manage their posts and also by setting an example when posting. Depending on the learning platform used, instructions will vary.

Students should be encouraged to demonstrate their learning and knowledge. This can be accomplished by designing assignments that require students to apply the course concepts rather than simply repeating information. Case studies and Internet "field trips" are good examples of applied assignments that allow students this opportunity to demonstrate their learning (Collison, Elbaum, Haavind, & Tinker, 2003).

An instructor who is enthusiastic about the course keeps students motivated. Instructors can encourage students to participate in the discussions by enticing them with easy questions at the beginning of the week when they may not yet have had an opportunity to complete the readings. This can then draw them in to the more challenging and difficult questions as the discussion progresses. Instructors should praise students for their responses to encourage them to post again. Students should also be asked to offer their own experience, expertise, examples, and opinions in discussions to support the concepts covered in the assigned readings. Lastly, instructors should thank them for sharing their experience.

Collison et al. (2003) identified some patterns of discussion that most commonly occur in online courses: social, argumentative, and pragmatic forms. They state that social and argumentative discussions tend to inhibit discussion while a pragmatic approach encourages a more productive discussion that helps students to meet learning objectives, builds community, and ensures a respectful environment. It is important to regularly monitor the discussions to keep posts relevant and pragmatic (Collison et al., 2003).

Occasionally students may post unprofessional or argumentative comments in a discussion forum. It is important to address this immediately by contacting the student outside the classroom by e-mail or telephone to let him/her know that it is not acceptable to post derogatory, argumentative, or unprofessional comments in the discussions. This type of behavior can intimidate or discourage other students from posting or can develop into an out of control or off-topic discussion. To avoid this type of behavior in discussions, some description of what is considered civil and professional conduct in the discussions can be posted in an announcement to let students know what is expected of them in their postings (Bender, 2003).

And, finally, instructors must practice patience. If students don't understand something the first time, instructors should find another way to explain it by using a different communication tool (chat, phone) or different words. Respect all students by using a positive, friendly tone in all communications and feedback. Some students can be challenging, but no matter how challenging they are or how frustrated an instructor might become with a student, it is always important to be respectful and encouraging in communication with students. When frustrated with a student, it's a good idea to draft a response and save it for later review before sending it.

Reach Out

Students are often too shy, embarrassed, or reserved to ask for help, so when an instructor observes that a student is having difficulty in the course, it is best to reach out to students by e-mail or telephone and offer help. Signs that students may be having difficulty include poor performance on assignments, quizzes, or exams; incorrect information posted on the discussion board; absence from the course; or consistently late assignments. Some additional points to consider when reaching out to students include:

- It is a best practice for building rapport to check in by e-mail or phone with *all* students on a regular basis to see how the course is going and offer assistance if needed.

Sending regular announcements and e-mailing them to the students so they don't miss them may also prompt students to respond with questions or feedback.

- When possible an optional survey can be incorporated into the discussion forum midway through the course to solicit feedback from students. This offers students an opportunity to provide feedback about both the course and the instructor while time remains to make changes for the last half of the course.
- Having regular office hours and encouraging students to call if they need help makes instructors available to offer assistance. Instructors can offer to meet in a chat room or on the phone if a two-way conversation will be more effective to accomplish what's needed.
- A discussion forum for questions and answers about the course should be included and checked regularly and responded to in a timely manner. By positioning this discussion forum at the top of the discussion board the instructor will ensure that questions are not missed.
- Students experiencing difficulty in a course can be encouraged to work together in informal groups. Those having more difficulty may be encouraged to contact student services or advising for additional help with language issues or to get outside tutoring (Center for Enhancement of Learning & Teaching, 2008).

Sample assignments or tips for completing the assignments should be posted when appropriate. This can be done by announcement when an instructor anticipates that students may have questions about an assignment; or if several students have asked the same question, all students should receive the clarification while working on the assignment. For a final exam, a special discussion forum can be set up to answer questions about how to prepare. This is in addition to any proactive communication on the part of the instructor that offers specific guidance regarding the content that will be included on the final exam (Center for Enhancement of Learning & Teaching, 2008).

Build Community

The dropout rates in online courses are significantly higher than in traditional courses, and a primary reason is the feeling of isolation among online students; to encourage students not to drop out, instructors can help to build a supportive community for their students (Vesely, Bloom, & Sherlock, 2007).

Vesely, Bloom and Sherlock (2007) point out that the concept of learning communities has been discussed for more than two decades and that research shows that functioning in a community enhances learning by community members. Community has been defined in the education literature in many different ways. Vesely, Bloom and Sherlock summarize common elements of community as follows:

1. A sense of shared purpose;
2. Establishment of boundaries defining who is a member and who is not;
3. Establishment and enforcement of rules/policies regarding community behavior;
4. Interaction among members; and
5. A level of trust, respect, and support among community members (p. 2).

Collison et al. (2003) stated that students desire a sense of community within the online learning environment and that the instructor can guide students through their dialog. In discussion forums students should be encouraged to directly respond to each other's posts rather than simply posting a monologue. When discussions are interactive, students build rapport and a sense of community and consequently learn more because they are actually discussing the course concepts rather than posting individual posts that do not relate to each other.

Instructors can create a class conversation area using a chat room or discussion forum to encourage students to help and support each other. Students can be encouraged to communicate with each other outside the online classroom by exchanging e-mails if they so choose. Some learning management systems facilitate sending e-mails from inside the course so that students and instructors can easily communicate.

Team assignments can be used when appropriate and should be carefully monitored to ensure success. Not all students enjoy working on team assignments, as they are concerned that their teammates may not contribute equally to the workload or will produce work that is of a lesser standard, thereby impacting the team's evaluation. Team assignments also take more time to complete. Teams can be successful if the instructor sets clear expectations, makes suggestions about how to function effectively as a team, and monitors the team discussions daily. The instructor may need to follow up with students who do not start participating early to ensure that the team gets started and that everyone participates. No grades should be given for individual submissions and students must participate on the team to receive a grade.

Keep the Material Relevant

An instructor can make the content of an online course come alive by incorporating his or her practical experience into the course. This can be done in the discussions by offering examples to support the course concepts being discussed. Students can also bring their experience to the course, especially students who have strong work experience or when the student body is diverse in cultural and geographic backgrounds. Students should be encouraged to share their experience; instructors can provide exercises that facilitate researching relevant current events, current research, or current processes.

Questions in online discussions should be stimulating and open ended. Select topics that offer an opportunity to share personal experiences and build on the concepts in the assigned readings. Avoid closed-ended questions that can be answered with a yes or no answer. Instructors can encourage students to respond with succinct and clear comments. Posts that are too long may discourage other students from participating in the discussion or responding to the specific long comments (Bender, 2003).

Conclusion

Students who feel encouraged, respected, and supported in their online courses are more likely to continue and to succeed. Teaching online is different from teaching in a physical classroom, and different practices are relevant to anyone who is currently teaching online or who may be transitioning from a physical classroom to a virtual classroom or teaching a hybrid course.

Implementing best practices online techniques will enhance the online experience for both faculty and students by providing an effective and supportive online classroom:

- communicate clearly and often
- set expectations
- offer constructive and timely feedback
- build rapport
- be present
- respect, encourage, and motivate students
- reach out to them
- build community
- keep course content relevant.

Utilizing these practices should create an effective online experience for students that will result in better learning and higher retention rates in online courses.

References

Bender, T. (2003). *Discussion Based Online Teaching to Enhance Student Learning*, Stylus

Center for Enhancement of Learning & Teaching. (2008). *Five Suggestions for Creating a Supportive Learning Environment.* CELT Tip Sheets.

Chalmers, M. (1999). *Creating a supportive learning environment online*, Retrieved from http://forum.education.

tas.gov.au/webforum/education/cgi-bin/ultimatebb.
cgi?ubb=get_topic;f=103;t=000011

Collison, G., Elbaum, B., Haavind, S., & Tinker, R., (2003). *Facilitating online learning: Effective strategies for moderators,* Retrieved from http://www.ifets.info/journals/6_2/8.html.

Literacy Source (n.d.) *Creating a safe and supportive learning environment: Supporting adult learners.* (n.d.). *Literacy Online,* Retrieved from http://sites.google.com/site/literacyonline/support/creating-a-safe-and-supportive-learning-environment

Curtis, E. (2008) *Creating supportive learning environments.* In D.J. Tangen, D.C. Bland, R.S. Spooner-Lane, T.L. Sedgley, A.G. Mergler, L. Mercer, & E.M. Curtis, (Eds.) Engaging diverse learners. (pp. 77-96). Frenchs Forest, NSW: Pearson Education

Vesely, P., Bloom, L., Sherlock, J. (2007). Key elements of building online community: Comparing faculty and student perceptions. *Journal of Online Learning and Teaching, 3*(3). Retrieved from http://jolt.merlot.org/vol3no3/vesely.htm

Active Online Learning: Implementing the Case Study/Personal Portfolio Method

Peggy Kasloff, EdD
City University of Seattle
School of Management

Abstract

Students in online classrooms must be prepared with the skills necessary to be successful in the twenty-first century. Pink (2005) stressed that educators must provide learning that not only engages the left-brain thinkers but also the right-brained thinkers who will create and problem solve. To meet that goal, and at the same time challenge learners to develop critical thinking skills, the case study method was employed and examined. This chapter explores the use of the traditional case study method expanded to include personal portfolio entries that lay the foundation for active learning.

Introduction

Preparing students to be successful in the real world of the twenty-first century boardroom, the twenty-first century class-room, the twenty-first century medical operating room, or in fact anywhere in the twenty-first century workplace, must be the foremost goal of every educational institution. With the grow-ing number of students opting for online programs, educators must develop learning strategies that ensure that online students develop the skills needed in the twenty-first century including the higher-level thinking skills needed to be a creative and criti-cal thinker (Pink, 2005). According to Barrett and Moore (2011), "Problems have always mobilised and stimulated thinking and learning; they energise our activity and focus our attention" (p. 3). Educators must find strategies to harness that energy and curios-ity to arm students with the skills needed to be effective problem solvers.

Utilizing relevant and thought-provoking case studies chal-lenges students to think deeply, analyze, synthesize, and cre-ate solutions that can later be applied to other similar situations (Chen & Bradshaw, 2007; Zach & Agosto, 2009). Much literature exists on the value of using the problem-based learning approach in the classroom (Ballantyne & Knowles, 2007; Barret & Moore, 2011; Young, 2006; Zach & Agosto, 2009), and now more than ever, there is a growing need to apply this learning strategy to the online classroom. "Online instructors are encouraged to focus on real-world application of course material and promote growth of practical skills in their students (Riha & Robles-Piña, 2009, para. 12).

It is equally important to ensure that students are equipped with strong interpersonal skills to enable them to work collabo-ratively in teams. According to Kemp (2006) these skills can be developed in the online classroom. With creative, goal-oriented planning, instructors can facilitate an online course that motivates, challenges, and stimulates learners while preparing them for real world situations and experiences (Zach & Agosto, 2009).

Creativity, another skill needed for success, needs also to be developed in the online classroom (Mintu-Wimsatt, Sadler, & Ingram, 2007). Keebler (2009) stated that the "online learning environment must provide the means for students to collaborate in an open environment to share their ideas, reflect, and explore alternative perspectives" (para. 15). The kinds of activities that were most beneficial for learners were ones that encouraged collaboration (Ruey, 2010). Lock and Redmond (2006) wrote that "the social and collaborative nature of learning is important in education in the twenty-first century," and according to Ruey (2010) providing a constructivist classroom environment leads to a "more collaborative, authentic, and responsible" (para. 21) online learning experience.

During the past decade, the number of online students increased dramatically, and more institutions are incorporating this method of instruction than in previous years (Braun, 2008). In the report *Class Difference$* published by the Sloan Consortium (2010), "The most recent estimate, for fall 2009, shows an increase of twenty-one percent over fall 2008 to a total of 5.6 million online students" (p.8). With the increasing number of online students, educators must be able to adjust to the online learning environment by adapting themselves to the demands of the online forum in order to provide the highest quality of education to all learners. Within the framework of a course outline, instructors must modify the course assignments to meet the needs of students.

The Online Adult Learner

Unfortunately a "one-size-fits-all" theory of adult learning does not exist; however, to better understand how adults learn, instructors should become familiar with the various characteristics and needs of adult learners (Cercone, 2008). It is also important to realize that a learning theory does not address the best way to teach, but understanding how adults learn helps instructors become more effective with their approach to instruction in an adult learning community (Swan, 2005). The various models of adult learning outline different facets of learning that should be addressed when dealing with adult learners (Merriam, Caffarella, & Baumgartner, 2007). Teaching adults is different from teaching children, though the reasons may not be clear.

Much research has been conducted on andragogy, the art of teaching adults (Martin, 2009). Knowles and Associates (1984) outlined the characteristics of adult learners. Adults have matured and are now self-directed human beings. They are independent and need ample room to be involved and responsible for their own learning. Based on adult learning needs, and to encourage a deeper level of understanding of content (Hackmann, 2004), instructors should take on the role of guide, instead of "sage on the stage" (Gueldenzoph & May, 2002; Hackmann, 2004).

Another characteristic of adult learners is that they carry with them a plethora of experiences which must be included and valued by the instructor (Cercone, 2008). According to Gould (2009), Piaget, an early constructivist theorist, determined that for new learning to occur there must be some previous basis on which to attach the new learning. These are called schemata (Gould, 2009). Therefore, if new concepts are relevant and relate to adult experiences, effective learning should result. The most effective learning is meaningful and can be applied to their work or personal experiences (Cercone, 2008). To that end instructors must design the course activities that are real-world issues leading to significant learning. Gould (2009) suggested that discussion, case study, and problem-solving activities are valuable approaches to adult learning.

In addition, adult learners do well when the goals are outlined, enabling them to realize that what they learn will be advantageous to their personal goals. Adults are ready to gain new knowledge and want to immediately find ways to apply their new learning (Cercone, 2008). The best case scenario occurs when an online student is able to develop a plan that can then be used in his or her workplace. That kind of immediate satisfaction results in a very positive learning experience for the adult. Effective instructors should be flexible in allowing students the breadth of a topic. Adults are internally motivated to learn (Gould, 2009) and, as mature learners, they will often reflect on their learning (Jones, Connolly, Gear & Read, 2006).

As we know, no two adults are the same. They possess degrees of the adult learners' traits, and because of this instructors must recognize the differences and make accommodations to meet the learning needs of all the students. Andragogy does not address the process of learning but offers a baseline of adult learning traits that play into successful learning (Cercone, 2008). What has emerged from the research in this area, however, is that adults thrive in an experiential, self-directed learning environment. Rudestam and Schoenholtz-Read (2010) wrote that "learners are actively attempting to create meaning" (p. 100). Therefore, the instructors must provide a student-centered classroom environment in which active learning is the foundation. The students take the lead role and the instructor assumes the role of facilitator (Martin, 2009). Students will be challenged to take the initiative to develop their higher order thinking skills and collaborative, social skills in order to be successful. A student-centered, hands-on learning environment is an effective strategy used to prepare students for the twenty-first century workplace. Rhia and Robles-Pina (2009) stated that "online instructors are encouraged to focus a real-world application of course material and promote growth of practical skills in their students" (para. 12). Andragogy helps us understand that adult learning is more about the process than about the content of the subject (Holyoke & Larson, 2009).

Constructivism

According to Cercone (2008), "There is no one theory that explains how adults learn, just as there is no one theory that explains all human learning" (para. 16). However, to provide an effective and challenging online experience, educators must continue to examine the traits of adult learners. "One of the challenges of teaching in an online course is the development and inclusion of materials that teach the concepts in a meaningful manner (Engleman & Schmidt, 2007, para. 4). Building an online environment where expectations are high, rigor of content is emphasized

(Engelman & Schmidt, 2007), and higher-level thinking skills are essential, should be facilitated by the instructor (Mandernach, Forrest, Babutzke, & Manker, 2009). In addition, preparing students to be successful in the workplace requires strong skills of collaboration and communication (Zach & Agosto, 2009).

The constructivist theorist Vygotsky focused on building meaning from socially interactive, goal-directed activities (Eun, 2008). In the constructivist approach, learning is based on experiences and ideas. Learners become active as they discuss, debate, and solve problems collaboratively (Ruey, 2010). In doing so, adult learners have the opportunity to utilize their past experiences to solve future issues. In addition, they develop and strengthen their communication and collaboration skills. Students are engaged, motivated, and empowered to direct their own learning as they strive to reach both short-term and long-term goals. The very nature of the constructivist approach to learning aligns with the characteristics of adult learners (Knowles & Associates, 1984).

Problem-based Learning

Imagine how an instructor can create an exciting, dynamic, and energizing online classroom experience. How can one provide activities that will meet the needs of adult learners, while at the same time ensure that the rigor of the content is not forgotten? Is it possible to change students from being passive learners just going through the motions to earn the course credit to enthusiastic problem solvers with a passion to learn and create? These important questions may determine the success of meeting the mark of excellence for online learning in order to sustain the growing number of students who will choose the online classroom experience instead of the traditional classroom.

Before moving forward in the understanding of problem-based learning, it is important to differentiate between a cooperative team learning project and a collaborative team learning project. Many online courses have a component of team work. However, experience has shown that these team assignments are often carried out as cooperative learning assignments where each student takes a part of the task and completes it independently of the other team members. Then all the isolated parts are put together into a final product. In many cases an experienced instructor can identify who wrote each piece. Collaborative work, according to Hennessy and Evans (2006), "due to its formal structure and clearly defined outcomes, generally requires basic recall or, at best, synthesis of facts" (para. 15). Contrast this with an assignment in which all team members actively work together to plan, discuss, debate, and design a final artifact that is seamless and is a composite of the entire team's contributions (Hennessy & Evans, 2006). Collaboration, an approach where the students are required to take charge of their learning, is mirrored in boardrooms in all types of organizations. Collaboration brings about an energy and a synergy that result in a product that surpasses what one person alone could have created (Gomez, Wu, & Passerini, 2009; Slotte, & Tynjala, 2005).

Collaboration provides opportunities for students to share information, create connections, and build online communities of learning (Zach & Agosto, 2009). Abrams (2005) explained that a connection exists between collaboration and increased critical thinking skills. Moreover, Ashcraft, Treadwell, and Kumar (2008) stated that "collaborative learning. . .whereby students interact and build on each other's ideas is constructivist in nature" (p. 110). It follows that the constructivist approach, which involves collaborative learning, could be used as a strategy for building strong higher-level thinking skills. Lock and Redmond (2006) emphasized that "online learning needs to be constructivist-learner-centered and collaborative" (p.234).

Problem-based learning, a method based on the social constructivist approach (Gomez, Wu, & Passerini, 2009; Hmelo-Silver & Barrows, 2006), was first discovered in the 1960s at McMaster University in Ontario, Canada (Tripathy, 2008), where it was found that students could learn basic science in small groups. The activities they used were problem-based tutorials that replaced the traditional lectures (Barret & Moore, 2011). Years later, in the mid 1980s, Harvard Medical School developed courses where students spent time on problem-based learning activities (Torp & Sage, 2002). Compared with the traditional methods of learning, problem-based learning is more authentic, motivating, challenging, and comprehensive (Hmelo-Silver, 2004). Barret and Moore (2011) stated that "future programs must provide graduates with sufficient domain-specific technical knowledge and the transferable skills essential to succeed in their future programs. Problem-based learning will do that!" (p. 87).

Problem-based learning, a cooperative and collaborative method of learning, is a learner-centered approach that encourages student discovery and inquiry (Schroeder-Moreno, 2010). Students control their own learning, thereby becoming more responsible and self-directed active learners (Ruey, 2010). Problem-based learning encourages learners to use reasoning skills to analyze and solve problems that exist in the real world. By working in small groups, they not only add different perspectives (Ko & Rossen, 2010) but also develop stronger collaboration and communication skills (Palloff & Pratt, 2005). Savery (2006) described the problem-based learning method as "learner-centered that empowers learners to conduct research, integrate theory and practice, and apply knowledge and skills to develop a viable solution to a defined problem" (para. 4). Higher-order thinkers and problem solvers who collaborate and communicate clearly are those who are sought after by successful companies (Zach & Agosto, 2009). Effective online instruction must provide opportunities for students to engage collaboratively in real-world situations where they must communicate and interact effectively with others. Connecting theory with practice lays the foundation for a more valuable online course (Young, 2006).

Online instruction has been shown to be equal to, or even more conducive to, the problem-based method of learning than face-to-face environments (Rollag, 2010). Asynchronous learning enables students to take the time to think and rethink before they respond or share their ideas with the group. In addition, the ongoing discussion is documented, thus allowing students to review the information that has been shared. Shy personalities who may have difficulty in face-to-face social situations may find the online learning environment more comfortable (Rollag, 2010). Online learning may also assist in developing creativity, a skill sought after by many employers in the corporate world (Mintu-Wimsatt,

Sadler, & Ingram, 2007). Moreover, research has shown that the online environment helps students develop collaborative skills (Kemp, 2006).

Taking into consideration the needs of the online adult learner and the skills that are critical for success in organizations in the twenty-first century, instructors should develop teaching activities and utilize instructional strategies that will address both those areas. Research has proven that the problem-based learning method has been successful since the 1960s, and according to Savery (2006), ". . .more than ever, higher-order thinking skills, self-regulated learning habits, and problem-solving skills are necessary for all students" (para. 24). Therefore, before implementing any new teaching strategy, instructors must examine the roles they play in the online classroom and what drives their instruction. Do they still lecture and provide basic learning activities that result in recall and rote responses, or do they challenge their students to become engaged and active learners by presenting activities that demand analysis, critique, evaluation, synthesis, and application?

Problem-based learning clearly delineates the roles for the students and the instructors. First and foremost, the instructor must become the facilitator, providing students with clear expectations and explanations of how the course will proceed and what they must do to be successful (Hmelo-Silver & Barrows, 2006). Instructors, although now on the side, still play a vital role in the environment. They must continue to be involved by providing guidance and effective feedback (Mintu-Wimsatt, Sadler, & Ingram, 2007). Instructors must encourage discussion and promote critical thinking by applying strong facilitation skills. Interacting with the students and empowering them to become active, critical thinkers positively affect the overall quality of the learning. The need to stay connected with students is very important in the online environment, perhaps even more than in the face-to-face classroom (Mandernach, Forrest, Babutzke, & Manker, 2009). Research has shown that students who feel that the instructor is present and supportive have a more successful learning experience (Young, 2006). Students also perform better when they maintain a connection with the online instructor (Schroeder-Moreno, 2010).

In addition, students become responsible for their own learning. As a collaborative group, they must engage in the problems that provoke debate, discussion, and conversations that result in the creation of new ideas and learning (Hennessy & Evans, 2006). The learners share their knowledge and ideas in their social interactions (Gomez, Wu, & Passerini, 2009; Ruey, 2010). Students learn by discussing ideas, reflecting on their own ideas and those of others, and negotiating until they create a workable solution (Ko & Rossen, 2010). Ruey (2010) believed that the constructivist instructional approach encourages adult learners to develop the skills that are needed to interact in meaningful learning in an online learning community classroom. Online learning environments must not promote passive learners who lack energy and excitement. Adult online learning must be engaging, challenging, and relevant. It must encourage higher-level thinking, creative problem solving, and a passion for collaboration. One of the tools that empowers students to meet those goals is the online case study method that is based on personal portfolio entries outlining the experiences of the adult learners.

Case Studies

Case studies have their roots in constructivism (Webb, Gill, & Poe, 2005) and have been used extensively as teaching tools in medicine, business, law, psychology and other disciplines (Tripathy, 2008). Following the work of Vygotsky, a theorist who stressed the importance of experiential learning, case studies have become a basic part of adult learning (Rollag, 2010). Case studies were developed based on problem-based learning and constructivism (Ballantyne & Knowles, 2007) in order to stimulate the use of critical thinking and application (Tripathy, 2008). Although case studies were first used in face-to-face classrooms, they have been proven to be highly successful in online learning environments (Rollag, 2010).

Case studies represent real-world scenarios that present situations or problems that do not have one specific solution; thus, they are open for "…critical thinking and analysis, inferencing skills, comparison and contrast, evaluation, and internalization of concepts and principles" (Bonk & Zang, 2008, p. 109). Students are expected to analyze the case and determine possible solutions. In addition, they are then required to communicate their ideas to others (Ellet, 2007). Being able to critically analyze and support decisions promotes higher level thinking and problem-solving skills. Figure 1 outlines the steps in the case study method as well as the corresponding higher-level thinking skills that the learners must apply. Using that model the group begins with the problem and strategically works through all the steps. The most powerful result of

Figure 1. *Case Study Sequence - Step by Step*

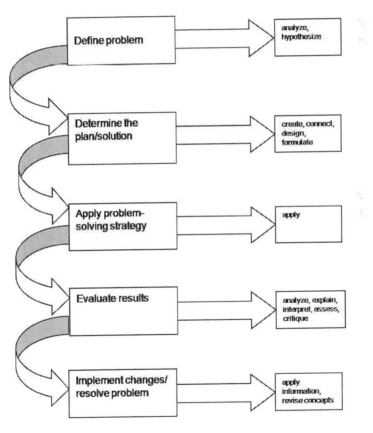

applying this step-by-step method is that a number of higher-level thinking skills are applied in a collaborative manner. Although there is no specific design used to develop case studies (Tripathy, 2008), Ellet (2007) shared that "...they all have a common purpose: to represent reality, to convey a situation with all its cross currents and rough edges. . ." (p. 13). They are stories that represent situations that are really part of the workplace and give students the opportunity to apply theories and concepts learned in class to situations that they might face in the workplace. Case studies can be fictional or factual situations, but they must be realistic and open to many solutions (Tripathy, 2008).

Online education presents a number of issues directly related to the fact that there is no face-to-face communication, which can affect the quality of learning. However, a skilled instructor can create an exciting, challenging online environment where students become passionate about their learning and develop skills that will be useful in any workplace. Too often, however, online learning becomes dull and repetitive, and students just go through the motions, completing the weekly assignments until the course is completed. They may earn the credit for the course, but they will likely forget what they have learned.

Compare that learning environment with one in which the students are actively engaged, debating a number of possible solutions to a problem. Instructors who use the case study instructional method provide a forum where learners can develop higher-order thinking skills, communicate their ideas, and support their strategies (Vonderwell, Liang, & Alderman, 2007). However, even though the students are in control of their own learning, the instructor plays a very important role as facilitator, being present to guide students, scaffold learning, and provide timely, effective feedback (Palloff & Pratt, 2005). Instructors' comments and probing questions may also encourage student reflection (Lee, Lee, Liu, Bonk, & Magjuka, 2009).

Piloting the Case Study/Personal Portfolio Method

In a particular online graduate program, students had never been exposed to the case study method. In the middle of the course, the instructor proposed a pilot for any students who were interested. They could continue with the regular syllabus, which was already outlined, or they could try the case study method. Most of the students had no idea what that entailed, but they decided to give it a try. With almost all the students on this track, the instructor posted the case study and a few leading questions. Before too long the discussions came alive. The students took on the roles of the characters in the case and became animated and argumentative. They debated and supported the reasons for their comments, while other students tried to influence their thinking. It appeared to be highly effective! The students were learning! The instructor, who in the past always needed to push and prod for participation, was now able to hover above the discussion board, facilitating only when necessary but always available to support and guide. Although the number of posts did not increase for all students, the quality and depth of the responses did improve.

Implementing the case study method made a difference. Feedback from students supported the success of this change. In some cases students enjoyed the flexibility and creativity that resulted from working with the study. In other cases students were quick to apply the case study situation to their personal experiences, and in doing so they uncovered an immediate relevant connection between the course and what they were doing in their own workplaces. No longer was this just a discussion question to answer by parroting the textbook. They found meaning in the different applications derived from the case study. In addition, the students explored the various perspectives presented in the discussion, and although they often agreed with one another, situations arose that initiated discussion on a higher level. Compared with the traditional classroom activities of reading, lectures, discussion questions, and assignments, the case study method was more stimulating and engaging.

However, after a number of trials using the case study method, this instructional format was enhanced and improved with the addition of the students' personal experiences. Adult learning theory emphasized that instructors must recognize and appreciate the personal experiences that adult learners bring to the course. Therefore, the students were asked to keep portfolio entries describing those experiences.

Standard portfolio entries can be compared to journal entries. Each entry was expected to be a reflection on a specific incident that the student experienced. Length or writing style was not emphasized for these portfolio entries. Each week the students were required to post one of these entries on the discussion board where fellow students would comment and react to the various scenarios. Once again the discussion reached another level. In addition, students bonded and formed supportive relationships with each other. They offered comments and suggestions and shared and supported one another. Slowly it became evident that these entries began to elicit more social interactions, which are very important in an online classroom (Eun, 2008). Although the students did not provide specific feedback and comments on the addition of the portfolio entries, their level of engagement provided evidence that learning was improving in a number of ways. According to McHann and Frost (2010), although journaling has not been widely used in business education, history demonstrates many examples of how leaders have found it to be a very helpful tool by which the employees can learn and grow. Educators also engage in reflective practices as a means of improving their skills. According to Hord and Sommers (2008), "The process of reflection can help stimulate conversations that allow us to reflect on what we are doing, what results we are getting, and how we might do things differently" (p. 88). McHann and Frost (2010) added that "with some methodological development, this tool can be put to powerful use to teach application and inculcate habits of learning by doing" (para. 33).

The addition of the case study and then the portfolio entries added a real world flavor to the course. However, one additional change was left to implement. Assuming students were able to relate to the case studies written by others, how much better would they relate to cases that they would create themselves? What if they included their own portfolio entries in those self-created case studies? McHann and Frost (2010) supported this idea and shared that the traditional case study was simply not enough and should be replaced with a case study in which the students'

". . .lives and work experiences become the living case study in which they learn deeply, existentially, and memorably the content of a given course" (para. 50). To complete these case studies, students would need to implement "higher-level thinking skills, self-regulated learning habits, and problem-solving skills" (Savery, 2006, para.24), which are skills needed in the twenty-first century workplace. Figure 2 outlines the steps of the case study/portfolio method. In addition, the higher-level thinking skills associated with each step are listed. Each of the large circles in the figure represent a specific step that is critical to the successful approach of problem solving, using the skills as outlined in each of the smaller circles. Adult students found this method relevant because they were able to insert their own experiences as they prepared their case studies. Following the sequence of the steps, students were empowered to not only build their case but also present and analyze it in a group setting, thus enriching their own ideas.

Figure 2. *Case Study/Personal Portfolio Method*

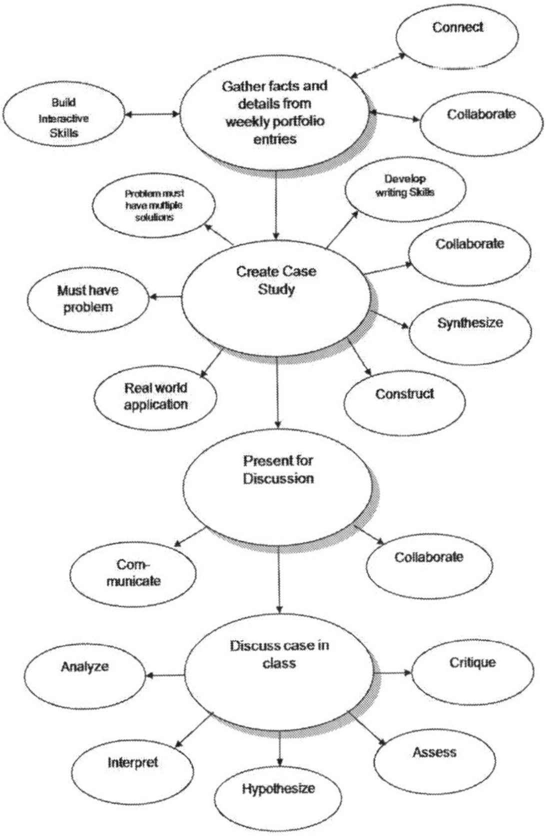

Lessons Learned

Best practices of educational instruction are successfully carried out when instructors fully understand the learning goals and plan for what the students must learn and then how they can apply that learning (Rollag, 2010). Students need to be given clear instructions and directions in

order to carry out their assignment. Rollag (2010) stressed that clear guidelines on learning objectives must be presented to students. Without them students become confused and frustrated. Online presentation adds to the importance for instructors to be very clear and concise and to provide specific examples on what is expected. Another important lesson learned is that because students are so often involved with only surface learning, they are severely challenged when asked to incorporate activities with higher-level thinking skills. To bridge that gap, instructors must be prepared to scaffold the learning (Bennett, 2010) until the students are gradually ready to work on their own. Instructors should model the expectation for the students. For the most part, instructors will find that even though the case study based on personal portfolio entries is an effective teaching strategy, every group of students will be different, and therefore the instructor must be prepared to differentiate to ensure successful learning for all.

Lastly, the cycle of learning cannot be complete without reflection on the concepts learned and the outcomes of the case study analysis and discussion (Lee et al., 2009). Engaging in this process can be conducted individually or collaboratively within the group. In either case this is the opportunity for students to take the new learning and incorporate it into their schemata. Instructors cannot forget that students seek feedback and critical assessment. Therefore, instructors must determine which evaluation method would be most effective. Palloff and Pratt (2005) emphasized that "Collaborative work should be assessed collaboratively" (p.53). However, the instructor must have the final word on the grade, regardless of what input is given by the learners. Alternative assessments might include asking the students to summarize their learning in an essay or apply their solutions to everyday situations in the news. Bringing closure to each case study must occur to complete the learning cycle.

As more students elect to learn in the online classroom environment, instructors must continue to find creative teaching strategies. The case study built on personal portfolio entries is one such methodology. However, one of the challenges with this teaching activity is that it is very time intensive. However, the dividends that result from implementing a case study-based-on-portfolio strategy are well worth the efforts.

References

Abrams, Z. (2005). Asynchronous CMC, collaboration and the development of critical thinking in a graduate seminar in applied linguistics. *Canadian Journal of Learning and Technology, 31*(2).

Allen, E., & Seaman, J. (2010). Class differences. *Online education in the United States, 2010*. Retrieved from http://sloanconsortium.org/publications/survey/pdf/class_differences.pdf

Ashcraft, D., Treadwell, T., & Kumar, V.K. (2008). Collaborative online learning: A constructivist example. *Journal of Online Learning and Teaching, 4*(1).

Ballantyne, N., & Knowles, A. (2007). Enhancing student learning with case-based learning objects in a problem-based learning context: The views of social work students in Scotland and Canada. *Journal of Online Learning and Teaching, 3*(4).

Barrett, T., & Moore, S. (Eds.). (2011). *New approaches to problem-based learning*. New York, NY: Routledge.

Bennett, S. (2010). Investigating strategies for using related cases to support design problem solving. *Education Tech Research Development, 58*.

Bonk, C., & Zhang, K. (2008). *Empowering online learning*. San Francisco, CA: Jossey-Bass.

Braun, T. (2008). Making a choice: The perceptions and attitudes of online graduate students. *Journal of Technology and Teacher Education, 16*(1).

Cercone, K. (2008). Characteristics of adult learners with implications for online learning design. *Association for the Advancement of Computing in Education Journal, 16*(2), 137-159.

Chen, C-H., Bradshaw, A. (2007). The effect of web-based question prompts on scaffolding knowledge integration and ill-structured problem solving. *Journal of Research on Technology in Education, 39*(4), 359-375.

Ellet, W. (2007). *The case study handbook. How to read, discuss, and write persuasively about cases*. Boston, MA: Harvard Business Press.

Engleman, M., & Schmidt, M. (2007). Testing an experimental universally designed learning unit in a graduate level online teacher education course. *Journal of Online Learning and Teaching, 3*(2).

Eun, B. (2008). Making connections: Grounding professional development in the developmental theories of Vygotsky. *The Teacher Educator, 43*(2), 134-155.

Gomez, E., Wu, D., & Passerini, K. (2009). Traditional, hybrid, and online teamwork: Lessons from the field. *Communications of the Association for Information Systems, 25*, 395-412.

Gould, J. (2009). *Learning theory and classroom practice in the lifelong learning sector*. Great Britain: Bell & Bain Ltd., Glasgow.

Gueldenzoph, L., & May, G. (2002). Collaborative peer evaluation: Best practices for group member assessments. *Business Communication Quarterly, 65*(1), 9-20.

Hackmann, D. (2004). Constructivism and block scheduling: Making the connection. *Phi Delta Kappan, 85*(9).

Hennessy, D., & Evans, R. (2006). Small-group learning in the community college classroom. *The Community College Enterprise, 12*(1).

Hmelo-Silver, C. (2004). Problem-based learning: What and how do students learn? *Educational Psychology Review, 16*(3).

Hmelo-Silver, C., & Barrows, H. (2006). Goals and strategies of a problem-based learning facilitator. *The Interdisciplinary Journal of Problem-based Learning, 1*(1).

Holyoke, L., & Larson, E. (2009). Engaging the adult learner generational mix. *Journal of Adult Education, 38*(1).

Hord, S., & Sommers, W. (2008). *Leading professional learning communities.* Thousand Oaks, CA: Corwin Press.

Jones, C., Connolly, M., Gear, A., & Read, M. (2006). Collaborative learning with group interactive technology: A case study with postgraduate students. *Management Learning, 37*(3), 377-396.

Keebler, D. (2009). Online teaching strategy: A position paper. *Journal of Online Learning and Teaching, 5*(3).

Kemp, L. (2006). Learning about teamwork in an online study environment. *Journal of Online Learning and Teaching, 2*(1).

Knowles, M. and Associates. (1984). *Andragogy in action. Applying modern principles of adult learning.* San Francisco, CA: Jossey-Bass.

Ko, S., & Rossen, S. (2010). *Teaching online. A practical guide* (3rd ed.). New York, NY: Routledge.

Lee, S-H., Lee, J., Liu, X., Bonk, C., & Magjuka, R. (2009). A review of case-based learning practices in an online MBA program: A program-level case study. *Educational Technology & Society, 12*(3), 178-190.

Lock, J., & Redmond, P. (2006). International online collaboration: Modeling online learning and teaching. *Journal of Online Learning and Teaching, 2*(4).

Mandernach, B.J., Forrest, K., Babutzke, J., & Manker, L. (2009). The role of instructor interactivity in promoting critical thinking in online and face-to-face classrooms. *Journal of Online Learning and Teaching, 5*(1).

Martin, J. (2009). Developing course material for online adult instruction. *Journal of Online Learning and Teaching, 5*(2).

McHann, J., & Frost, L. (2010). Integrating experiential learning into business courses: Using learning journals to create living case studies. *American Journal of Business Education, 3*(8).

Merriam, S., Caffarella, R., & Baumgartner, L. (2007). *Learning in adulthood. A comprehensive guide* (3rd ed.). San Francisco, CA: Jossey-Bass.

Mintu-Wimsatt, A., Sadler, T., & Ingram, K. (2007). Creativity in online courses: Perceptions of MBA students. *Journal of Online Learning and Teaching, 3*(4).

Palloff, R., & Pratt, K. (2005). *Collaborating online. Learning together in community.* San Francisco, CA: Jossey-Bass.

Pink, D. (2005). *A whole new mind. Moving from the information age to the conceptual age.* New York, NY: Riverhead Books.

Riha, M., Robles-Pina, R. (2009). The influence of multiple intelligence theory on web-based learning. *Journal of online learning and teaching, 5*(1).

Rollag, K. (2010). Teaching business cases online through discussion boards: Strategies and best practices. *Journal of Management Education, 34*(4), 499-526.

Rudestam, K. & Schoenholtz-Read, J. (2010). *Handbook of online learning* (2nd ed.). Los Angeles, CA: SAGE.

Ruey, S. (2010). A case study of constructivist instructional strategies for adult online learning. *British Journal of Educational Technology, 41*(5), 706-720.

Savery, J. (2006). Overview of problem-based learning: Definitions and distinctions. *The Interdisciplinary Journal of Problem-based Learning, 1*(1).

Schroeder-Moreno, M. (2010). Enhancing active and interactive learning online. Lessons learned from an online introductory agroecology course. *NACTA Journal, 54*(1).

Slotte, V., & Tynjala, P. (2005). Communication and collaborative learning at work: Views expressed on a cross-cultural E-learning course. *International Journal on Elearning, 4*(2).

Swan, K. (2005). A constructivist model for thinking about learning online. In J. Bourne & J.C. Moore (Eds.). *Elements of Quality Online Education: Engaging Communities.* Needham, MA: Sloan-C.

Torp, L., & Sage, S. (2002). *Problems as possibilities: Problem-based learning for K-16 education.* Alexandria, VA: Association for Supervision and Curriculum Development.

Tripathy, M. (2008). Case methodology for adult learning: A critical review of theory and practice. *Asian Journal of Management Cases, 5*(1), 5-19.

Vonderwell, S., Liang, X., & Alderman, K. (2007). Asynchronous discussions and assessment in online learning. *Journal of Research on Technology in Education, 39*(3), 309-328.

Webb, N. et al. (2005). *Web alignment tool. Wisconsin Center of Educational Research.* Retrieved from http://www.pdesas.org/main/fileview/Instruction_Depth_of_Knowledge.pdf

Webb, H., Gill, G., & Poe, G. (2005). Teaching with the case method online: Pure versus hybrid approaches. *Decision Sciences Journal of Innovative Education, 3*(2).

Young, S. (2006). Student views of effective online teaching in higher education. *The American Journal of Distance Education, 20*(2), 65-77.

Zach, L., & Agosto, D. (2009). Using the online learning environment to develop real-life collaboration and knowledge-sharing skills: A theoretical discussion and framework for online course design. *Journal of Online Learning and Teaching, 5(4).*

Utilizing Case Study Analysis in Online Learning

Jean Ann French, DBA
City University of Seattle
School of Management

Abstract

There are quality learning theories and pedagogies that attract and retain online adult learners using case-based learning as the course design. Proven practices for undergraduate- and graduate-level business management studies are identified along with the challenges that are presented by the online environment. Recommendations are made for instructional design and approaches to successfully engage adult learners in a relevant manner for real-life application of business management concepts and learned skills.

Introduction

When Harvard Business School initially formed, it was determined that text books were not sufficient for instruction at a more advanced level in the graduate school. The problem was resolved by having faculty interview corporate professionals and record the cases they presented (Copeland, 1954). As the practice developed, various learning objectives were identified which led to the *Harvard Business Review* series being developed and used as a supplement to text books. Other institutions that publish cases include the Richard Ivey School of Business, the Darden School at the University of Virginia, INSEAD, and the European Case Clearing House.

A program-level case study was conducted as a review of case-based learning practices for an online MBA program by Lee, Lee, Liu, Bonk, and Magjuka (2009). These authors believe that the field of business requires multifaceted practices for real-world problems as much, or more than, any other field. A business school expects that application skills and knowledge available to students will be comparable to the skills and knowledge possessed by business professionals. Therefore, creating learning experiences where knowledge can be acquired, organized, and applied is critical. Case-based learning facilitates learning and real-world applicability, a primary concern in the field of business education.

Background

Case study analysis is a methodology that has been supported by theorists for more than one hundred years. Vygotsky and Dewey were the founding fathers of "learning by doing," which became the foundation of problem-based learning (PBL) and constructivism. Case analysis is used in the social and human sciences for study and research. Case study analysis was popularized in business schools by Harvard and is an effective way to learn strategic management and business assessment (Copeland, 1954). The foundation theories and the dynamics of learning facilitation for the adult learner need to be examined to better understand successful instruction of case study analysis.

Ruey (2010) conducted a case study in constructivist strategies for adult online learning. His study included the following theories of constructivist learning:

- Dewey (1938) believed that individual development is dependent upon the existing social environmental context and argued that students should learn from the genuine world through continuous interaction with others.
- Scott (2001) asserted that a constructivist, dialogical instructional approach should focus on learning about "why" and "how."
- Palincsar (1998) defined the constructivist learning environment as being one where students are encouraged to actively engage in learning by discussing, arguing, negotiating ideas, and collaboratively solving problems, and where instructors serve as facilitators.

PBL has its roots in experience-based education, which is a component of Dewey's (1938) "learn by doing" theory. Hmelo-Silver's (2004) study in PBL defines, describes, and summarizes the methodology succinctly:

> Psychological research and theory suggests that by having students learn through the experience of solving problems, they can learn both content and thinking strategies. Problem-based learning (PBL) is an instructional method in which students learn through facilitated problem solving. In PBL, student learning centers on a complex problem that does not have a single correct answer. Students work in collaborative groups to identify what they need to learn to solve a problem. They engage in self-directed learning (SDL) and then apply their new knowledge to the problem and reflect on what they learned and the effectiveness of the strategies employed. The teacher acts to facilitate the learning process rather than to provide knowledge. The goals of PBL include helping students develop:

1. Flexible knowledge
2. Effective problem-solving skills
3. Self-directed learning skills
4. Effective collaboration skills
5. Intrinsic motivation (p. 235)

Case-based learning is used in several other professions, including law, the social sciences, and medicine. The study of cases offers the instructor and the student a welcome relief from lecture and an opportunity for active learning and collaboration. Case-based learning was described by Helms (2006) as a method that involves studying actual business situations written as in-depth presentations of companies, and studying markets and strategic decisions to improve the problem-solving abilities of managers and/or students. Cases are typically used to investigate real-life situations where there are multiple issues to consider and various alternatives to solve the case issues presented.

By employing real-life business problems and solutions in case studies, instructors and adult learners can explore their business management skill sets. Lee, et al. (2009) believed that cases direct students to discuss and debate issues dynamically. Williams (2004) summarizes the benefits of case use for teaching and learning by stating that it allows learners to:

- Apply theoretical knowledge to real school contexts
- Reason critically about complex situations and recommend courses of action
- Develop self-knowledge and recognize own assumptions
- Clarify personal beliefs about teaching
- Compare and evaluate their own and other's perspectives
- Develop the practice of reflection (p. 20).

Lee, et al. (2009) asserted that graduate business education has relied upon case-based learning and that many business schools have adopted this approach as a central teaching and learning method. The constructivist approach prompts a shift in traditional instructor/student relationships.

Constructivist theory, problem-based learning, and case-based learning prompt the instructor to serve as a facilitator instead of a teacher. A teacher gives a lecture from the text, while a facilitator assists the learners in their efforts to reach their own understanding of the material. During a lecture the learner plays a passive role. By implementing experiential learning practices, the learner can take an active role in the learning process. The emphasis turns away from the instructor and the content and towards the learner (Gamoran, Secada, & Marrett, 1998). Rhodes and Bellamy (1999) have clearly defined this new facilitator/learner relationship by saying that a teacher tells, a facilitator asks, and a teacher lectures from the front while a facilitator supports from the back. An instructor gives answers according to a set curriculum while a facilitator provides guidelines and creates the environment for the learner to arrive at his or her own conclusions.

Ruey (2010) believes that the facilitator takes on a mentoring role and has the important role of ensuring that the learners engage in critical reflection. Higher-order thinking and giving adequate feedback are critical to the active learning dynamics. Timely, meaningful feedback is decisive to the instructional quality of the online course (Gaytan & McEwen, 2007). "Because of various characteristics of adult learners, an important role of the facilitator is to satisfy learners" diverse learning needs and learning anticipation" (Ruey, 2010, p. 717).

The education of adult learners via an online medium presents unique challenges and opportunities. Online schooling is cost effective, time efficient, and flexible. A report by Moore and Kearsely (2005) indicates that most adult learners are between the ages of twenty-five and fifty. Park and Choi (2009) performed a study to determine the factors that influence adult learners' decisions to drop out or persist in online learning. According to Meister (2002), 70 percent of adult learners enrolled in a corporate online program did not complete. Park and Choi (2009) believe that the numbers are misleading and that careful interpretation is required due to unique characteristics and situations that online, adult learners have. What cannot be controlled but needs to be considered are the following adult learner issues that may contribute to such high dropout rates:

- Do not receive support from their family and/or peers
- Do not receive support from their employer
- Job/career changes
- Workload
- Financial stress
- Time constraints
- Lack of motivation, due to lack of rewards (Park and Choi, 2009)

As educators the issues that can be controlled and can have a possible impact on the adult learners' decisions to persist in online programs include:
- Course design, which leads to student satisfaction:
  - Relevance to learners' jobs
  - Relevance to learners' lives
  - Opportunities to apply newly acquired knowledge to real situations
  - Skills and knowledge obtained from the course are useful
  - Materials and cases closely related to learners' interests, experiences, and goals
  - Assignments that are practical and applicable to the students' life or work
- Instructor communications, which provide motivation for the student to persist:
  - Paying extra attention to counter lack of family, peer, or employer support
  - Supporting the student in getting help when needed
  - Allowing learners to choose learning methods and strategies
  - Allowing learners to assist in setting goals and expectations

Park and Choi (2009) concluded, "Instructional designers should systematically analyze external factors surrounding learners and use the analysis results to initiate learning and motivate learners" (p. 215).

Adults learn differently than children or adolescents because youth have fewer experiences; therefore, their brains can create new structures when they learn. Inversely, adult learners have existing structures due to their years of experience and previously learned lessons (Caffarella, 2001). Huang (2002) discusses how constructivism works for adult learners in online learning environments by calling upon the adult learning theory of Knowles (Knowles, Holton, & Swanson, 1998). Knowles, Holton and Swanson (1998) identified six principles of adult learning theory, which they collectively referred to as andragogy. The first principle is the learner's need to know "how learning will be conducted, what learning will occur, and why learning is important" (Knowles et al., 1998, p. 133). Second, self-directed learning is the ability to take control of the techniques and of the purposes of learning. Third, prior experience impacts learning in creating individual differences, providing rich resources, creating biases, and providing adults with self-identity. The fourth principle is readiness to learn, as adults become ready to learn when their life situations create a need to learn. The fifth principle is orientation to learning in that adults prefer a problem-solving orientation to learning and learn best when knowledge is presented in a real-life context. Finally, the sixth principle is motivation to learn, particularly when learners can gain the new knowledge to help them solve important problems in their life. Constructivism and andragogy are similar in stressing ownership of the learning process by learners, experiential learning, and a problem-solving approach to learning (Knowles et al., 1998).

Online learning, distance learning, and technology are often in conflict with adult learners constructivist, problem-based, and case-based learning approaches. Huang (2002) identified issues that online educators face with adult learning styles:

- *Humanity and the learner's isolation:* Many distance educators attempt to use advanced technologies and don't realize that technology and social context are equally important.
- *Quality and authenticity in the learner's experience:* Adult learners usually have strong self-direction in learning;

therefore, some learning takes place beyond the instructor's scope in the online learning environment.

- *Physical distance vs. conventional classrooms:* The learner's autonomy meets the expectation of the constructivist approach; however, the instructor's role becomes that of a facilitator.
- *Adult learning emphasizes learner-centered instruction:* Online classrooms rely on discussion boards and team projects to connect the students; therefore, collaborative learning is in conflict with individual differences. Social constructivism occurs when experienced students help inexperienced learners by collaborative learning.

Online technologies are reducing the barriers of distance education that result from interactive or communication problems. Instructional designers must meet the challenge to create online environments that suit the adult learner. Constructivist principles provide ideas to help instructors create learner-centered and collaborative systems that support critical reflection and experiential processes (Jonassen, Davidson, Collins, Campbell, & Haag, 1995).

Case-based Learning Proven Practices

In academia there are two primary classifications of case studies as defined by the American Heritage Dictionary: 1) A detailed analysis of a person or group, especially as a model of medical, psychiatric, psychological, or social phenomena, and 2) A detailed intensive study of a unit, such as a corporation or a corporate division, that stresses factors contributing to its success or failure.

Case studies are written to be analyzed or to demonstrate specific business situations; therefore, cases can be part of the curriculum for undergraduate and graduate degrees. The focus of business cases offers a large range of topics within corporations from Fortune 500 to startup companies. Some of the areas that have been the subject of case study and analysis include ethics, leadership, management, finance, corporate social responsibility, operations, organizational learning, reorganization, culture and change, decision making, marketing, human resources, mergers and acquisitions, strategies for growth, and communication. Business case studies play an important role for adult learners in developing their analytical skills and problem solving applications.

Based on learning theories and andragogy parameters, case study and case analysis are one of the most effective ways for the adult learner to relate to course work. The student identifies with the business situations presented in the cases, as many are employed in companies that experience similar problems. The mature student, or students who have work experience, are motivated and engaged when the subject matter relates to real life. Many students are quick to share their experiences to help explain the problem to other students. In the online environment, this shared experience in group discussions can be the beginning and ongoing foundation for class interaction. The primary motivation of adult learners to engage in case studies can be to apply a solution or lesson to their workplace. The course work has now become relevant to students by being directly applicable.

Case studies come in many sizes, shapes, and forms in that some are short stories with a few questions at the end to stimulate a discussion, while some may be up to ten pages in length with charts, graphs, and financials.

Short case studies are good options for weekly online discussion questions. This type of question and answer format creates an interaction among the students and teaches single lessons that can be viewed from different perspectives on the same topic. Students can be asked to challenge each other with their interpretations of cause and effect.

Larger case studies can be used in case analysis and can support lessons in strategic management problem solving. Case studies are useful as major and minor assignments and can be completed by students as individuals or in teams. An analysis can be reported in many formats, using a variety of processes, and yielding countless outcomes. But the core of a case analysis has four primary functions:

1. The Problem
2. Analyses

3. Alternatives
4. Recommendations

A case study analysis assignment must stand on its own, which requires an introduction of the corporate case and a summary regarding follow-up or evaluation. The students have an opportunity to improve writing skills by succinctly describing the case in the introduction without restating the entire case. To assist students the following guideline serves as a basic outline and content description for a stand alone case analysis:

- *The Introduction:* Provides background, historical, and current information that sets the framework for the problem being analyzed. The author/student needs to define his/her perspective, i.e., department head, officer, consultant, etc.
- *The Problem:* Identifies one major problem, as many corporations are rife with problems. The student must discern the difference between symptoms and problems.
- *The Analyses:* Uses the analytical tool that best addresses the problem and will offer potential solutions. Available tools include Porter's five-forces model of industry competition analysis, value-chain analysis, and financial ratio analysis.
- *The Alternatives:* (Sometimes referred to as alternative solutions.) Identifies a minimum of three alternatives and no more than four potential solutions, which give the writer the opportunity to put forth options from different categories of solutions; e.g., cost effective/short term, long term for the greater good, external market impact, internal culture/moral impact, the company's vision, mission, and objectives, and stakeholder relations.
- *The Recommendations:* Outlines the course of action recommended and is often a blend of two alternatives. The recommendations must be supported by the analysis and should describe the course of action and how best to implement the solution.

- *The Conclusion:* Summarizes the recommendations and allows for tying together any loose ends and establishing maintenance or evaluation of the implementation.

Case-based learning stimulates adult online learners by allowing them to use their creativity in problem-solving current issues that resonate with them. Including collaborative structures in the online course design enables the distance learners to develop community similar to the classroom environment.

Student Application

Case study methodology can be used in all business courses, online and in the classroom, for undergraduate and graduate study. It can be organized in teams or by individuals. The adult distance learner requires an incentive for engagement. Case studies are written about current companies facing current issues which connect the employed student to the course. By using case studies as weekly discussions, individual analysis, and/or team assignments, mature students can be drawn into the course work by fellow students through relevant issues that are most likely to impact their workplace and career.

Adult learning experts believe that the emphasis should be on learner-centered instruction (Knowles et al., 1998), while social constructivists McDonald and Gibson (1998) contend that knowledge is constructed by social interaction, i.e., team and group assignments, which create collaborative learning. Ruey's (2010) study confirmed the following benefits for online adult learners in a constructivist-based course:

- Acquiring new concepts from course materials
- Obtaining different thoughts from reading peer postings, e.g., viewpoints and experiences
- Increasing confidence in dealing with routine work tasks
- Appling learned concepts to real-life practices
- Becoming more responsible, self-directed learners

The online environment creates a particular challenge for adult learners, as it permits a student to become isolated. Chen (1997) found that adult distance learners are highly autonomous, self-directed, motivated, and individually different. However, the use of case studies for class discussion and team assignments online can accomplish positive learning experiences, such as the development of critical thinking, and social and interpersonal skills by offering a collaborative environment. Huang (2002) characterized online discussion groups as discussion oriented, authentic, project based, inquiry focused, and collaborative, thereby creating a better learning environment.

Instructor as Facilitator

The design of case-based learning for adult learners demands a paradigm shift for the instructor. The "instructor becomes a facilitator" concept (Bellamy, 1999; Gamoran, Secada, & Marrett, 1998; Palincsar, 1998; Rhodes & Hmelo-Silver, 2004; Ruey, 2010) is the focus of many theorists and stimulates the facilitator to take on a mentoring role guiding learners' self-directed, high-quality learning skills. Salmon (2002) developed a five-stage model to facilitate online teaching and learning that includes varied facilitation skills and activities. The five stages are:

1. Access and motivation—setting up the system, welcoming, and encouraging
2. Socialization—establishing cultural, social learning environments
3. Information exchange—facilitating, supporting use of course materials
4. Knowledge construction—conferencing, moderating process
5. Development stages—helping achieve personal goals

Huang (2002), from a social constructivist perspective, outlines six instructional principles for consideration:

1. Interactive learning—interacting with the instructor and peers rather than engaging in isolated learning
2. Collaborative learning—engaging in collaborative knowledge construction, social negotiation, and reflection
3. Facilitating learning—providing a safe, positive learning environment for sharing ideas and thoughts
4. Authentic learning—connecting learning content to real-life experience
5. Student-centered learning—emphasizing self-directed, experiential learning
6. High-quality learning—stressing critical thinking skills and learners' reflection on their own lives

As a facilitator and mentor, the instructor must be sensitive to the diverse learning needs of the adult, online learner and anticipate those needs. Another important responsibility is to monitor the learner's engagement in critical reflection and higher-order thinking. This responsibility is readily resolved with timely and relevant feedback in online postings and assignment critiques. Ruey (2010) effectively summarizes the facilitator's mentoring role as being pivotal in the process when he/she helps learners articulate their learning desires and objectives and assists individual learners to achieve learning goals in a reflective method.

Challenges of Case Approaches in Online Instruction

Kearsley (1998) offered a word of caution for distance educators when he said, "Educators fail to understand that distance education is really about creating a different kind of structure for learning and teaching, not the use of technology" (p. 49). Lee, et al. (2009) alerted the instructor to be aware that the technology can disrupt students if they have to manage tasks and tool functions while learning the course material. When case-based learning is adopted for online course work, the instructor must be knowledgeable about how the technology will enhance or detract from the students' learning. Harvard Business School and the University of Virginia's Darden Graduate School of Business Administration, two top-ranked MBA programs, were the basis of a study on successful case discussion leadership by Smith (2010). Smith (2010) outlined the characteristics of successful leadership discussion and included the following challenges for instructors:

- Over-focus on the case facts, computations, and details, preventing the instructor from ensuring effective discussion.
- Over-focus and knowledge of the case calculations leading to strict coverage and adherence to the material rather than allowing the class to participate freely.
- Diminished student motivation.
- Students who want a simple takeaway or direct answers, which minimizes self-discovery in group discussions.
- Instructors' inability to give up control and accept the unknown outcomes and direction of the case discussion.
- Effectively balancing the quantity of material covered with the optimal quality, depth, and retention of the material by the students.
- Cases selected that are poorly written or don't fit the focus of the course work (Smith, 2010).

Lee, et al. (2009) reviewed case-based learning practices for online MBA programs and cautioned instructors that technology can burden students with managing tasks and tool functions while learning the course material. It is often recommended that weekly discussions be monitored closely for full participation and that instructor responses stimulate students.

Active Learning and "Live" Cases

An exciting expansion on experiential learning is active learning. Hamer (2000) and Camarero, Rodriguez, & San Jose (2010) describe active learning as seeking to engage student involvement with the course concepts by encouraging them to apply theory to real-life situations. Active learning creates a paradigm where instructors become designers of the learning environment and where the students are active in their own learning process.

This concept parallels case-based learning where the instructor becomes the facilitator.

Camarero, et al. (2010) from the University of Valladolid studied the learning effectiveness of live cases in a classroom setting. Their experiment involved students working with a "live" company on a real marketing problem. Live case development is rather difficult in that the instructor must preplan the activity and host by carefully outlining the concepts and skills to be learned from the case. Camarero, et al. (2010) discovered at the time of company assignment that students had a preference for companies they were already familiar with, thereby reducing the instructor's control over the concept and skills outcome. This type of live case study and active learning seems difficult enough in a classroom environment. Questions remain as to whether it might transfer to distance learning without significant research, design, and development.

A similar live case experiment was employed in the MBA-level course People and Systems in Organizations in the classroom. The difference being that the students, working in a team, opted for a case problem presented by one of the student's employers. In this particular class, Wells Fargo and T-Mobile were the companies that became the focus of the studies. The engagement and enthusiasm of the students was phenomenal, which confirms constructivist theory and experiential learning andragogy for adult learners. Transferring the live case study from classroom to online will require further research and exploration, but this method could have significant merit. It may not be an option for the undergraduate, but graduate-level studies would embrace the applicability of the live case study. The following objectives are likely outcomes of such an application:

- Students put theoretical concepts into practice
- Improve understanding of relevance and applicability of theoretical concepts
- Increase critical thinking
- Improve strategic analysis and problem-solving skills
- Develop leadership and team building skills
- Develop managerial skills

Another benefit of such an approach is the learning process in creating the case features that lead to the identification of the problem, which results in a solution for at least one student from the team to submit to the employer. An entire course could be structured with this type of case study, which would allow each team member to develop and deliver the company case to the team. The development of the case could serve as an individual assignment, and the live case study results could be packaged as a proposal for the case company by the employed student as another individual assignment.

Ruey's (2010) study indicated that learners suffered from lack of motivation that may have been stimulated by lack of critical performance feedback in the online environment. Huang (2002) discussed the importance of educators recognizing that technology and social context are equally important for distance learning. The online learning environment allows for isolation of the adult learner; therefore, it becomes imperative for the instructor to develop some humanity in the delivery of the course. Distance educators attempt to employ state-of-the-art technologies, such as web, video, and teleconferencing, but at some point the use of technology becomes the learning process and not the course material.

Conference calls can be difficult for the same reason that students take online courses—scheduling. Although it can be a significant burden on the instructor, perhaps at least one phone call to each online student at the beginning of the session would put a voice with the name. Another technique to enhance social relationships online is the posting of individual pictures in the student and faculty introductions. The weekly discussions have a similarity to blogging or the social network systems that are so popular today. The development of a pseudo-social network environment for online learners is worth further investigation.

Conclusion

Case-based learning for undergraduate and graduate adult learners is a proven practice that constructivist and experiential educators can successfully use to teach students the principles and strategies of business. The adult learner prefers learning processes that have a practical rather than an academic purpose. Through the constructivist, problem-solving, case-based, experiential, and active learning approaches that have been demonstrated in this chapter, mature students can apply their learning to their real lives.

The greater challenge comes from transferring the classroom dynamics to the online environment and creating the paradigm shift from instructor to facilitator. Lee, et al. (2009) stated, "A key educational challenge of online courses and programs is how to develop pedagogically effective technologically mediated environments that enhance the quality of education" (p. 188). Designing an online environment that parallels social networking sites to attract and motivate the adult learner with relevant company cases, including live case development, may be the solution for enhancing, enrolling, and retaining distance learners.

References

Caffarella, R. S. (2001). *Planning programs for adult learners: A practical guide for educators, trainers, and staff developers* (2 ed.). San Francisco: Jossey-Bass, Inc.

Camarero, C., Rodriguez, J., & San Jose, R. (2010). A comparison of the learning effectiveness of live cases and classroom projects. *International Journal of Management Education. 8*(3), 83-94.

Chen, L. L. (1997). *Distance learners in higher education: institutional responses for quality outcomes.* Atwood Publishing. Madison.

Copeland, M. (1954). *The Genesis of the Case Method in Business Administration.* The Case Method at the Harvard Business School. ed. Malcolm P. McNair. New York: McGraw-Hill.

Dewey, J. (1938). *John Dewey experience and education* London: Collier Books.

Gamoran, A., Secada, W.G., & Marrett, C.A. (1998). The organizational context of teaching and learning: changing theoretical perspectives. Hallinan, M.T. (Eds). Handbook of Sociology of Education.

Gaytan, J., & McEwen, B. C. (2007). Effective online instructional and assessment strategies. *American Journal of Distance Education. 21*(3), 117-132.

Hamer, L. O. (2000). The additive effects of semi-structured classroom activities on student learning: An application of classroom-based experiential learning techniques. *Journal of Marketing Education, 22*, 25-34.

Helms, M. M. (2006). Case method of analysis. In M. M. Helms (Ed.), *Encyclopedia of management* (pp. 67-69). Farmington Hills, MI: Gale Cengage.

Hmelo-Silver, C. E. (2004). Problem-based learning: What and how do students learn? *Educational Psychology Review, 16*(3), 235-266.

Huang, H. (2002). Toward constructivism for adult learners in online learning environments. *British Journal of Educational Technology, 33*(1), 27-37.

Jonassen, D., Davidson, M., Collins, M., Campbell, J., & Haag, B. B. (1995). Constructivism and computer-mediated communication in distance education. *The American Journal of Distance Education, 9*(2), 7-23.

Kearsley, G. (1998). Educational technology: A critique. *Educational Technology, 38*(2), 47-51.

Knowles, M. S., Holton III, E. F., & Swanson, R. A. (1998). *The Adult Learner* (5th ed). Gulf, TX.

Lee, S., Lee, J., Liu, X., Bonk, C. J., & Magjuka, R. J. (2009). A review of case-based learning practices in an online MBA program: A program-level case study. *Educational Technology & Society, 12*(3), 178-190.

McDonald, J. & Gibson, C. C. (1998). Interpersonal dynamics and group development in computer conferencing. *The American Journal of Distance Education, 12*(1), 6-24.

Meister, J. (2002). *Pillars of e-learning success.* New York, NY: Corporate University Xchange.

Moore, M. G., & Kearsley, G. (2005). *Distance education: A systems view* (2nd ed.). Belmont, CA: Wadsworth Publishing Company.

Palincsar, A. S. (1998). Social constructivist perspectives on teaching and learning. *Annual Review Psychology, 49*, 345-375.

Park, J., & Choi, H. J. (2009). Factors influencing adult learners' decision to dropout or persist in online learning. *Journal of Educational Technology & Society, 12*(4), 207-217.

Rhodes, L.K. & Bellamy, G.T. (1999). Choices and consequences in the renewal of teacher education. *Journal of Teacher Education, 50*(1), 17-25.

Ruey, S. (2010). A case study of constructivist instructional strategies for adult online learning. *British Journal of Educational Technology, 41*(5), 706-720.

Salmon, G. (2002). *E-tivities: The key to active online learning.* New York: RoutledgeFalmer.

Scott, B. (2001). Conversation theory: a constructivist, dialogical approach to educational technology. *Cybernetics and Human Knowing, 8*(4), 25-46.

Smith, R. A. (2010). Professors' use of case discussion leadership at Harvard and Darden MBA programs: Characteristics of a successful case discussion. *Academy of Educational Leadership Journal, 14*(2), 13-32.

Williams, M. (2004). *Exploring the effects of a multimedia case-based learning environment in pre-service science teacher education in Jamaica.* Unpublished doctoral dissertation, University of Twente, The Netherlands.

The Art and Science of Videoconference Instruction

Judy Hinrichs, MEd
City University of Seattle
Gordon Albright School of Education and Division of Arts and Sciences

Abstract

Videoconference instruction is a relatively new addition to the portfolio of delivery modes for instruction. This article summarizes recommendations from the literature and the experiences of faculty and students with the goal of providing both technical and pedagogical guidance for future successful learning experiences and the expansion of this modality.

Introduction

City University of Seattle (CityU) began using videoconference instruction for instructional delivery in 2003 in its Bachelor of Arts in Education program in Hawaii with the purpose of developing Certified Special Education Teachers who were residents of the state and were located in geographic areas that were difficult to reach. Due to the networking of all of the public schools throughout the state, the Hawaii program used both the Local Area Network (LAN) and the Wireless Access Network to provide direct videoconferencing instruction at school district offices, school libraries, school classrooms, or other available sites on the islands. CityU is currently engaged in efforts to utilize this delivery mode to enhance instruction in other locations and other programs throughout the university. Videoconference equipment linked through the K-20 system in Washington State was installed in two locations in 2009. This system provides a high speed connection between sites for both video and data. It is part of a network that connects all K-20 school locations in the state of Washington as well as all libraries and hospitals in the state. CityU expanded the installation of supporting equipment to three additional sites in 2011. It is increasingly being used to enhance meetings and conversations among faculty located at those sites as well as for course delivery. Through this network, members can videoconference multiple locations by accessing the network or can conduct point to point connection without a direct connection to the network. Thus, participation in this consortium provides flexibility for a variety of uses, including individual and large group meetings as well as the conduct of classes and workshops from both internal and external locations.

Following a brief definition of terms and a review of the field of videoconference instruction, this article will focus on two areas: (1) instructional strategies teachers can use to establish effective learning in this environment and (2) effective utilization of the technical environment unique to this delivery mode.

History of Distance Education

"Distance Learning in general has been around for over 100 years, beginning in the 1980s as a means for (mostly) women to take advantage of educational opportunities and have access to learning that was otherwise denied them" (Greenberg, 2004, p. 6). Since then there have been a variety of methods for delivering education at a distance, beginning with correspondence courses in which students studied independently and submitted assignments by mail. The first public use of video communication itself was the unsuccessful motion video telephone developed by AT&T and shown at the New York World's Fair in 1964, and the earliest instructional use of television systems (videoconferencing) was in the late 1960s by Stanford University (Noll, 1997). New technologies now offer the opportunity to extend the power, efficacy, and reach of distance learning to individuals and groups of students of all ages, all locations and all learning styles through a variety of synchronous and asynchronous delivery modes.

Lawson (2010) defines videoconferencing as "synchronous audio and video communication through computer or telephone networks between two or more geographically dispersed sites." It can be used one-to-one, one-to-many, or many-to-many. At City University of Seattle, a university with multiple campuses across Washington State and around the world, the use of videoconferencing has many applications, including small and large group meetings, classroom instruction, conferences and workshops, and special events such as guest speakers for courses offered in different locations. It brings another synchronous dimension to the asynchronous technology-supported instruction that has been introduced in recent years, primarily through the university's learning management system.

Experiences with videoconferencing document some advantages over other instructional technologies in use. It can increase access to education for small groups of geographically dispersed students and enable small cohorts or individuals to participate at multiple sites and be aggregated with one instructor to meet minimum effective class size. It can provide expanded access to excellent teachers or guest lecturers in specialized content areas. In Hawaii nationally recognized content-specific instructors who were located on the various islands throughout the state provided a strong and diverse team of instructors, benefitting the students on all the islands. This reduced travel requirements and costs. Another advantage of videoconference instruction is that class sessions can be auto-recorded and made available for repeated practice or learning by students. Participants were able to access replays of any of the lectures, debates, and student project presentations throughout their program as they prepared for examinations, reviewed research projects, or made up for a missed class. One instructor in Hawaii commented, "In tandem with the Polycom system, every session was secured and stored for later use and review by the instructors, students, and others via the CD and DVD formats. Through the use of the videoconferencing Polycom system, all barriers for instruction and learning were lowered for students."

As an instructor review tool, recorded sessions can give valuable feedback to faculty on which to base future modifications to the curriculum or instruction. It is also "environmentally friendly" as reported by another Hawaiian instructor, as most of the major parts of the instruction were done in a paperless format. All instructional materials, student presentations, assignments, projects, and papers were presented and submitted electronically. The environmental savings in travel alone, in addition to the time, cost, and family disruption associated with it, were substantial factors. A third instructor and field supervisor commented that, "The videoconferencing capability provides opportunities to recruit a wide diversity of potential Special Education teachers on all of the islands. Without the technology used in videoconferencing, these same students would not have had the opportunity to complete their professional teaching degree."

Instructional staff can also use this mode to interact with each other and share resources and strategies. In Hawaii the faculty conducted interactive meetings with the benefit of conducting administrative work efficiently and also of sharing specific instructional strategies with each other throughout the four cohorts conducted there.

Videoconferencing has other uses which can provide valuable support or access to instruction for students. Through video-chat systems such as Skype individual students can sometimes access classes that they cannot attend in person because of an emergency or other planned absence if an instructor is willing to set up and support that access.

The effectiveness of the videoconference delivery mode relies on the application of sound instructional techniques as is true in face-to-face instructional delivery, along with adaptive techniques to maximize its potential and minimize any perceived disadvantages. The body of research supports the premise that learning can occur just as well through videoconferencing or other technology-supported distance learning as it can face-to-face (Webster & Hackley, 1997). Spooner (2009) found that student ratings of instructor effectiveness were not affected by delivery mode, with distance delivery instructors rating no worse than the same instructor in a face-to-face classroom format on campus. Greenberg (2009), in examining the body of research on videoconferencing, reports that results indicate that videoconferencing stacks up well against traditional classrooms for delivering instruction. It can create a social presence and more comfortable learning environment for learning (Tyler, 1999). The synchronous nature of videoconferencing makes it a superior distance-education technology for business, education, and other social disciplines in which interpersonal skills are a large component of the learning outcomes expected of students (Olson, 2003).

Experiences with Videoconference Instruction

Ensuring effective teaching and learning begins with the selection of courses within programs that best lend themselves to a videoconference environment. Attention to content and pedagogy, in addition to careful selection of the teaching faculty, help maximize this opportunity for success. Courses previously taught face-to-face or in mixed mode will likely need modifications when taught using videoconferencing, so advance planning is critical. The university has moved gradually over the past three years to introduce new elements of technology-supported learning into all of its courses. This has helped prepare instructors and students for alternative modes of delivery, and many are now ready to take the next step to synchronous technology-supported instruction. Admittedly, the decision to offer a course via videoconferencing may at times be influenced by the number of students enrolled at various sites or by instructor availability. Curriculum needs to be evaluated to determine when, where, and if to offer courses either fully online, mixed mode, or through videoconferencing to select the best delivery modes for a particular course or activity.

When selecting a course to offer through videoconferencing, it is important that faculty carefully select the course content that would most effectively be delivered in that medium. University experience in the Hawaii program required that all courses be delivered via videoconferencing since students from the different Hawaiian Islands needed to network for their entire program. When implementing videoconferencing in Washington where instruction was traditionally offered in locations face-to-face, faculty had more opportunity to individualize the selection process. They analyzed course content in an effort to identify courses that would most lend themselves to a successful first experience for instructors and students. The selected courses were taught, monitored, and subsequently evaluated by students, instructors, and administrative faculty. Experiences in these courses will continue to enhance familiarity with equipment, course preparation, and delivery.

As faculty prepare to deliver videoconference instruction, the principles of effective teaching which influence and affect learning in all delivery modes have relevance and importance. Instructors in all modalities seek to build this relevance and meaning into instructional activities through creating a set for learning; providing for formative assessments throughout the course; providing dispersed individual and group practice of new skills; and providing active, student-centered learning.

Many universities use videoconference instruction as a way to deliver lectures to wider audiences or to make lectures available to students who wish to watch them again. However, when the expectation is that all learners will be actively engaged in the learning process rather than passive recipients of lectures or instructor presentations, the passive approach to just watching a lecture is insufficient. One of the major challenges faced by those faculty members who wish to utilize videoconferencing with these expectations is to introduce as much interactivity into the instruction as possible—both between instructor and students and among students. There are sound pedagogical reasons for this approach. The literature consistently documents that students in more interactive courses have more positive attitudes and that these attitudes influence their learning (Rangecroft, 1998). Hayden (1999) supports student-centered learning and suggests that the technology needs to be paired with "constructivist instructional strategies"— strategies that promote active learning and lead students to construct new concepts based on their current and past knowledge. Some effective constructivist learning strategies include shared discovery, team learning, collaborative learning, distributed communities of practice, and accessible experts. Students can also view "real-life" filmed experiences during videoconference sessions, enhancing the relevance of their learning. For example, in teacher preparation programs, they can view prerecorded learning and teaching experiences in real K–12 classrooms to support their classroom-based learning.

The structure and use of time is key to designing student-centered lessons. Amirian (2003) as cited in Greenberg (2004) posits that interaction is the key component to support a more social learning environment as it facilitates the formation of a sense of community using the technology. One way to achieve that is for educators to use the "fifteen-minute rule," limiting lecture time to no more than fifteen minutes and following these sessions immediately with activity involving the students. Cyrs and Conway (1997) further recommend that students should be involved in interactive activities from 30 to 50 percent of the time.

Planning the Lesson

Preparation time for a first-time videoconference instructor may be more time-consuming than for a class that was previously taught in face-to-face format. It may take three to five times longer, and for a repeat instructor two to three times longer, to allow for the preparation of visual materials and creation of interactive experiences (Cyrs & Conway, 1997).

The University of Malta (2007) recommends that videoconferencing lessons always be planned with *interaction* in mind. The videoconference lesson has the potential of being able to focus more on collaborative learning than on the traditional didactic process. A lesson plan for a videoconference session should include the following:

- Expected learning outcomes
- Methodology and activities
- Materials and audiovisual resources
- Time (duration of each planned activity)
- Notes (support handouts and additional notes to be supplied before or after the session)

Faculty at CityU are expected to incorporate this lesson planning and also to embrace principles of student involvement in their planning. They receive their initial training in this through the New Faculty Orientation (NFO). There they complete an Instructional Plan and also have students complete a mid-course evaluation which, in addition to an observation of their teaching by their Primary Supervisor, gives them guidance upon which to adjust instruction if needed. This feedback is used by instructors and administrative faculty as they make modifications to the delivery of future videoconference courses.

Faculty are encouraged to schedule videoconference sessions with short breaks each hour. Lectures, if used, should be a maximum of fifteen to twenty minutes in duration followed by a change element, such as a learning activity or a shift of focus to another location (Davies, n.d.). Audiovisual materials prepared for students should either be projected on a separate screen at the videoconference locations and/or posted and available to students on the learning management system well ahead of the class session so they can be retrieved and printed before class if necessary, avoiding the experience of some students in earlier sessions who reported that materials were posted as they were driving to class in the morning and therefore unavailable for them to access and print if needed.

Conducting the Lesson

Generally recognized aspects of effective instruction apply to videoconference instruction as well. Instructors should carefully prepare the lesson opening and closing (set and closure), beginning each lesson with an activity that engages student interest and increases motivation for ensuing parts. At the beginning of the course, this activity should help to create a sense of community among all participants by helping them get to know each other. Other important practices to incorporate include planning for dispersed practice sessions; providing formative feedback; asking direct and indirect questions to both check for understanding and provide for reflection; and closing the lesson with an opportunity to summarize and reflect on learning.

Instructors can build on student engagement in a variety of ways. As in face-to-face classroom sessions, guest speakers can provide interest and relevance, provide real life examples, and make a significant contribution to student learning when aligned with the course goals. Local and nationally recognized experts are sometimes available through videoconference that would otherwise be inaccessible to instructors and students. Other strategies to consider incorporating into lessons include involving students in demonstrations or presentations; analysis of case studies; using cooperative learning techniques; and conducting peer teaching one-to-one or in small groups during the session. These strategies help to break up long class sessions into manageable segments with a variety of activities. Interactivity can be a key component of videoconference instruction. One instructor says, "While I was not at first in favor of teaching via videoconferencing, I did not realize at that time the opportunities that the use of technology provided me in preparing my lessons for instruction. The interactive opportunity especially went far beyond my expectations."

Technical Recommendations for Teachers and Students

Managing the technical environment is an area of concern to potential instructors who may have limited experience using videoconferencing in the classroom. Students who have taken videoconference classes also confirm that the technical skills of the instructor are very important to the quality of their experience. That has implications for the selection of instructors as well as their training and preparation. While the optimum situation is to have a technical consultant available and actively involved at each site, that is not always possible and can become cost prohibitive. At some universities students manage the equipment.

Advance preparation is as critical as having the right support structures in place. Instructors should master the use of equipment at their site (Park & Bonk, 2007). This is best done by conducting a trial run to become familiar with how the equipment works and what the display looks like to remote users. For example, it is helpful to have the camera preset to a small group of participants using the preset function. For small groups of three–four, these can be set to zoom to individuals, which helps to personalize the environment. Nearly every instructor has had something go awry technically at some point in each course. Prior preparation and trial runs can prevent some of these, and having backup systems and technical expertise available can remedy others. A definitive "systems down" plan should be developed in consultation among administrative, instructional, and technical staff as well as with students who may be managing their own site to minimize the loss of class time and the stresses created by breakdowns.

Students are an important consideration also. They need to become familiar with the equipment, with the instructor, and with each other. Meeting with students prior to the first videoconference class and demonstrating to them their options for manipulating the equipment can be helpful. Students are then capable of adjusting the volume and zooming the camera to targeted speakers at their discretion.

Davies (n.d.) recommends dedicating a portion of time during the first meeting for all students to be on camera to help build interpersonal connections. During this time the instructor can build a set of expectations or protocols with students regarding their conduct during class sessions. For example, it is particularly important in this environment not to interrupt or talk out of turn. The establishment of protocols and etiquette for communication between locations can include how students at remote sites will let the instructor know when they have a question or when they wish to contribute to the discussion. Establishing and enforcing a method of gaining recognition is important to the maintenance of a respectful classroom environment.

The following tips for students may be of value as an instructor develops protocols and agreements with them about their participation and interaction during course sessions:

- Sit within view of the cameras and close to the microphones.
- When you have a question, identify yourself and your location so that people at other sites know who is speaking.
- Keep microphones muted until you wish to speak.
- Notify the instructor immediately if you are experiencing any difficulty with audio or visual portions of the course.
- When preparing for presentations in class, post materials ahead of time in the learning management system and arrange for their display during the presentation in a format that is visible to those in another videoconference location.

Guidelines for videoconference instruction at St. Leo University (2008) recommend that instructors keep a list of student names and their site location handy so they can readily call students by name, ask them questions to engage them in the learning process, and involve them in presentations and group collaborations. Keeping a record of student interaction also helps to ensure that all are taking part. One method for gaining attention that has proven effective is to use a visual symbol such as a small flag that the participants can raise in front of them to be recognized. This creates a stronger visual symbol for the presenter than simply raising the hand.

The careful preparation of materials can be a time-consuming but essential element for success. Simple and clear visual content using graphics and large font sizes (36–72) with limited text and easy-to-see colors enhances learning. Landscape view is preferred. Presentations should avoid using too many slides to prevent confusion and any one image source or slide should not be on display for more than five minutes. In videoconference instruction it is particularly important to provide complex material in a step-by-step sequence that is easy to follow (Davies, n.d.; Park & Bonk, 2007).

While appropriate preparation and display of materials are an essential component of effective instruction, an instructor's consideration for his/her personal visual and auditory presentation also influences the student experience. The level of animation and excitement that an instructor conveys contributes to the motivation and engagement of students (St. Leo University, 2008; Park & Bonk, 2007). Varying facial expressions, tone of voice, body movements, and eye contact with the camera can enhance verbal conversation (Davies, n.d.). Long Island University (2006) recommends that instructors consciously adapt their teaching style to the camera. One strategy to accomplish this is to pretend that the camera is a student and to look at it regularly to connect with students at other locations. Making eye contact with the camera helps students feel that they are being communicated with and that they are important.

Visual elements also affect attention and learning. Some skills that can be used and developed include avoiding moving around the room a lot; decreasing gestures; using hands as indicators accompanying speech; and avoiding distracting movements, such as tapping a pencil or swiveling in a chair. Using a pointer on displayed visual material can help focus learners if not overused. Instructors are encouraged to wear solid-color clothing; blues, dark, and neutral colors work well (Long Island University, 2006). Presenters should avoid rapid motions and be aware of the visual range of the camera.

Effective auditory skills include developing the ability to speak naturally, slowly, and clearly, knowing that students at other locations may experience short audio delays. It helps to eliminate noises, such as paper shuffling or finger-tapping (Long Island University, 2006; Saint Leo University, 2008). Clanking jewelry can also be distracting. Instructors should use effective verbal skills, such as taking time to pause, demonstrating enthusiasm for the subject matter, and avoiding speaking in monotones. Instructors should periodically check in with students at other locations to confirm they can hear the discussion and questions that are shared. It may be more important in this environment than in a face-to-face class for the instructor to repeat or rephrase student comments to ensure that all participants have heard them correctly. Active use of the "mute" function enhances engagement when appropriate as long as well-established signals are in place for gaining instructor and student attention when needed.

The importance of the skills and attitude of the instructor in establishing and maintaining a friendly, collegial, and respectful environment cannot be overstated. In an optimal situation, the instructor would teach from rotating sites so that each group has the advantage of face-to-face instruction at some point. When this is not possible, it is especially important to give students opportunities for personal contact with the instructor by telephone, e-mail, or personal appointments.

Lessons Learned

With several dozen courses (including Hawaii) now having utilized videoconferencing at CityU, the body of experience is beginning to inform practice. Additional recommendations from administrative and teaching faculty involved in these courses are helping to inform our future practices. They include:

- Instructors should set their operational protocols ahead of time and do at least one practice session before meeting with the class to test audio and video connections as well as gain personal experience and feedback about their own auditory and visual communication skills.
- Appropriate and effective audio is critical. Having a cordless microphone "unleashes" the instructor. Multiple

microphones should be well positioned among the participant groups.

- Careful selection of instructors is important, with enthusiasm and active engagement perhaps more important that prior experience. Ability to effectively use and manage the learning management system is also very important to students and the success of the class.
- Having backup systems in place is important. At a minimum there should be a telephone contact at each site, whether it is a phone in the room or simply the sharing of cell phone numbers. In the event that a network problem occurs, people need a way to contact each other. In addition, a computer in the classroom or nearby with a printer is desirable.
- Especially when networking with sites external to the system, it is important to identify and involve a network team at each site to test equipment ahead of time. Problems with firewalls can arise and can recur when systems refresh, so permanent as well as temporary solutions need to be put into place.

Future Research Directions

While the experience, the research, and the literature are beginning to inform practice, there are still rich opportunities to contribute to this field. Following are three ideas that may inform future research efforts.

Networking for classroom learning experiences, as well as consultation, decision making, and problem solving in business settings, increasingly links individuals and groups from disparate geographical, cultural, and political settings. To what extent does the utilization of videoconferencing enhance cultural understanding and appreciation for different points of view and experiences over other modes of communication? Is it more effective than an online discussion or a strictly auditory means of communication? What, if any, other advantages accrue to groups who use videoconferencing as a means of communication.

The literature suggests that the success of videoconference instruction may depend somewhat on the number of sites connected for a single section, with the selection of two or three networked sites for course instruction at any one time considered to be the maximum. Additional sites for group setting instruction may lower the participants' impression of personal interaction (Gowan & Downs, 1994). Experience indicates that the number of sites should be limited to four or five, both for instructional and equipment reasons. The downtime interruptions at any one of the sites tends to create disturbances and stresses on both the students and the instructors. It would be helpful to further explore and document the relative success of various numbers of sites.

While the literature and individual experience seem to suggest that the preparation for and conduct of videoconference instruction is more time consuming than face-to-face instruction, what are the particular dynamics and implications of this commitment, and how can they be better managed to attract and retain the best instructors for this environment?

Conclusion

While the utilization of videoconference instruction is relatively new, faculty have and are continuing to learn a great deal about how to utilize it effectively with the belief that it is making a positive contribution to the portfolio of delivery modes. With excellent curriculum and excellent faculty, a university can educate students well anywhere in the world through face-to-face, mixed-mode, online, and now videoconference-supported instruction.

References

City University of Seattle (2001). Academic Model. Retrieved from http://www.cityu.edu/about/profile/academic_model. aspx

Cyrs, T.E., & Conway, E.D. (1997). *Teaching at a distance with the merging technologies: An instructional system approach.* Las Cruces, NM: Center for Educational Development, New Mexico University.

Davies, K. (n.d.). *Designing instruction for ITV.* Port Angeles Community College.

Gowan, J.A., & Downs, J.M. (1994). Video conferencing human-machine interface: A field study. *Information and Management, 27,* 341-356.

Greenberg, A. (2004). Navigating the sea of research on videoconferencing-based distance education. Wainhouse Research, LLC.

Hayden, K.L. (1999, August). Videoconferencing in K–12 education: A delphi study of characteristics and critical strategies to support constructivist learning experiences. Proceeding of the Conference on Distance Teaching and Learning. University of Wisconsin.

Lawson, T., Comber, C., Gage, J., & Cullum-Hanshawl, A. (2010). Images of the future for education? Videoconferencing: A literature review. *Technology, Pedagogy & Education, 19*(3), 295-314. doi: 10.1080/1475939X.2010.513761

Long Island University Office of Academic Affairs (2006). *Video conferencing: Pedagogical strategies and best practices.* Retrieved from http://vpaa.liu.edu/fcit_cwp/documents/VideoConferencing/ VideoConferencingPedagogicalStrategiesandBest%20 Practices.pdf.

Mara, M. (2010). *Video teaching: instructor's guide.* Retrieved from http://www.cityu.edu

Noll, A.M. (1997). *Highway of dreams: A critical view along the information superhighway.* Mahwah, NJ: Lawrence Erlbaum Associates, Publishers.

Olson, F. (2003). Videoconferencing with some life in it. *The Chronicle of Higher Education, 49*(3), A24-A25.

Park, Y. J., & Bonk, C. J. (2007). Is online life a breeze? A case study for promoting synchronous learning in a blended graduate course. *MERLO Journal of Online Learning and Teaching, 3*(3).

Rangecroft, M. (1998) Interpersonal communication in distance education. *Journal of Education for Teaching, 224*(1), 75-76.

Saint Leo University (n.d.). Video teaching & teleconferencing (VTT). Retrieved from http://www.saintleo.edu/Academics/University-Technology-Services/Video-Teaching-Teleconferencing-VTT.

Spooner, F., & Lo, Y. (2009). Synchronous and asynchronous distance delivery experiences from two faculty members in special education at UNC Charlotte. *Rural Special Education Quarterly, 29*(3), 23-29.

Tyler, C. (1999). Beyond the content – Videoconferencing as learning experience. *Speaking English, 32*(2), 15-27.

University of Malta (2007). Guide to videoconferencing: A detailed insight into the technology and pedagogy of two-way communication over distance. Retrieved from http://www.um.edu.mt/itservices/documents/guides/videoconferencing.pdf

Webster, J., & Hackley, P. (1997). Teaching effectiveness in technology-mediated distance learning. *Academy of Management Journal, 40*(6), 1282-1309.

PART THREE

PERSPECTIVES ON TEACHING AND LEARNING

The increasing emphasis on accountability for student learning requires institutions to consider the way in which they assess student learning. Kristin Jones highlights the importance of formative assessment as a productive tool for enhancing learning in student-centered courses. Dr. Elizabeth Fountain presents a proven method for assessing student learning and performance against program and institutional learning outcomes.

Further, colleges and universities are reevaluating their focus and attention on improving teaching. Incorporating information literacy in curricular design is an important way to refine a student's critical analysis skills, and Mary Mara discusses methods of infusing information literacy into academic programs beginning at the earliest design stages. In the final chapter, Dr. Brian Guthrie presents methods for facilitating a transformative learning environment that includes the use of critical self-reflection to help students evaluate their values and beliefs.

Formative Classrooms Shifting the Focus of Assessment in Higher Education

Kristin Jones, MEd
City University of Seattle
Gordon Albright School of Education

Abstract

Over the past decade, as standards-based assessment of student learning has become prominent, ongoing or formative assessment has emerged to the forefront of education and best practices in teaching. The use of formative assessment in classrooms is reaching an all-time high in elementary through high school. However, many in higher education still utilize a more traditional summative assessment so widely used in years past.

Studies are now beginning to show many more productive ways to enhance learning using formative assessment to drive daily instruction. This type of assessment is also referred to as "student-centered," "ongoing," or "evidenced-based" assessment. When teachers use formative assessment in the classroom, they themselves become more effective; students become actively engaged; and both become strategic and intentional learners together. The use of formative assessment in higher education is explained and specific examples are provided.

Introduction

"Formative assessment" has been a leading concept for many years now, staying at the top of the list. What makes this approach so unique is that, even though the term is so commonly used, it is most varied in meaning. Some use the term to mean the use of student information to determine instructional techniques, i.e., pre-assessments or other assessments to establish new learning targets. Others use it as a term meaning the use of smaller, less formal assessments to mark achievement along the way and provide information on progress, i.e., smaller, less imperative summative assessments. Yet others use the term to describe daily interactions with students to determine next steps of instruction, i.e., ongoing conversations, anecdotal notes, and the use of student work in progress to provide information to the teacher on how best to move forward to complete the work. While this term has been highly utilized in educational research and dialogue for over a decade now, it still suffers from lack of understanding by educators at all levels, especially those in post secondary education. Additionally, while research is widespread on the use of formative assessment in K–12, it tapers off greatly with use at the University and post secondary educational levels. It is only now in recent years that higher education has begun to shift from a traditional summative focused assessment system to a more authentic formative assessment system.

Formative assessment is defined as university faculty and instructors actively working together with students through daily

346

interactions, utilizing un-scored assessment tools, to determine next steps of instruction and, thus, setting a student's plan of action to ensure success.

Background

There are two major types of assessment that instructors use to determine the learning that is occurring in their classrooms—formative and summative. Summative assessment is evaluation *of* student's learning and provides a final critique or evaluation of work completed. The assessor evaluates how the student has performed. The student does not typically have a further opportunity to improve. Formative assessment is ongoing evaluation that is not formally critiqued or scored but includes detailed information that is given to the student for the purpose of improving his/her learning.

Formative assessment is the practice of teachers and students actively working together to systematically gather evidence of learning with the intention of continually improving the student's learning. The primary purpose of formative assessment is to improve student learning, not merely audit it. It is assessment *for* learning rather than assessment *of* learning. Formative assessment is both an instructional tool that teachers and their students use while learning is occurring and an accountability tool to determine if learning has occurred (National Education Association, 2003).

Ainsworth and Viegut (2006) explain that when instructors use formative assessment, they are better able to determine what standards students already know and to what degree; decide what changes in instruction to make so that all students succeed; create appropriate lessons, activities, and groupings; and inform students about their progress to help them set goals. It truly aligns teaching with learning using three guiding questions:

- Where am I going?
- Where am I now?
- What strategy or strategies can help me get there?

This continuous process of setting a learning target, assessing present levels of understanding, and then working strategically to narrow the distance between the two is the essence of formative assessment (Moss & Brookhart, 2009).

Ongoing formative assessment has provided teachers with solid platforms to understand "how" students can improve their learning so they can be proficient in each of the standards set. Using this assessment enables teachers and students to work closely together to best determine the learning that needs to occur and the best method in helping them get there, thereby creating critical thinkers who can reach far beyond just completing the requirements. It enables instructors to internalize the principals of formative assessment, making them more powerful teachers themselves. Formative assessment increases teacher quality because it operates at the core of effective teaching (Black & Wiliam, 1998). Furthermore, Black and Wiliam also contend that formative assessment, associated with content areas, knowledge, and skill sets, are effective in virtually all educational settings and at all levels.

There are numerous types of formative assessment that are easy to implement in college classrooms and which provide instructors with quality detailed data to drive instructional practices. Often these are referred to as Classroom Assessment Techniques (CATs) and can be used in both traditional and online learning environments. Formative assessment can be used as a force to improve instruction and enable students to demonstrate real-life application of knowledge and not just recall of facts presented.

Standard Language

Standards are specific targets that state what students should know and be able to demonstrate by the end of a given term. For K–12 education this is by the end of each grade level. In post-secondary education, standards can be set for each course as well as by program. Standards may also be referred to as learning targets, learning outcomes, program goals, or course goals. Proper incorporation of standards is absolutely essential for improving student learning. Often, standards are stated in the course syllabus yet never referenced or intentionally incorporated into learning. Students have even reported not knowing them upon completion of a course. Instructors must not only show the standards but actively use them in their course for optimal results. Instructors should discuss the standards with students and have critical in-depth conversations about what they really mean, not just in direct standard language, which can be unclear, but in everyday language which parallels the language of the students. For students to fully understand standards, they themselves must "speak the standards," understanding and knowing what each term means and represents in their learning. This language must become common everyday language; each class session should have standards clearly identified and posted for all to see. This keeps instruction on target and helps keep student learning focused and directed.

Rubrics and Feedback

Rubrics and feedback clearly go hand in hand when using formative assessment *for* student learning. A rubric articulates the expectations for an assignment by listing the criteria and describes levels of quality from excellent to poor (Reddy & Andrade, 2010). Quality rubrics always include three essential components: evaluation criteria, quality definitions, and a scoring strategy (Reddy & Andrabe, 2010). For any rubric to provide effective data about student learning, it must contain these three components and provide a direct correlation with the standard being assessed. Anyone using the rubric should see key terms stated that are pulled from the standard being assessed. As stated in the previous paragraph, standard language is key. While rubrics are typically used by instructors to evaluate student work, much research reveals that if used by instructors or students to continually evaluate work in progress, rubrics can become a powerful teaching tool, helping students to clearly understand the targets set for their learning and the quality of evidence required for demonstrating this new learning. When using a rubric, students are able to continually monitor their own progress, clearly seeing exactly where their work stands, and what is needed to improve it. Reddy and Andrabe (2010) surveyed over 170 students in both undergraduate and graduate business programs and their research showed that responses were overwhelmingly favorable for the use of rubrics. Students reported a great reduction in completion anxiety and uncertainty, allowing them to focus on what was needed to complete quality work rather than making guesses as to what was expected of them. These results have also been documented in other similar research studies at additional post-secondary institutions. However, it is important to stress that simply handing out rubrics will only provide limited improvement on student work and that rubrics must encompass detailed feedback and cohesive interaction between instructors and students to produce optimal results.

Numerous research studies have found that feedback is crucial to improving student learning and should be embedded in each and every instructional practice. It has been fondly referred to as "feed forward" rather than "feedback" by some in the field of formative assessment. Feedback on performance, in class or on assignments, enables students to restructure their understanding/skills and build more powerful ideas and capabilities (Nicol & Macfarlane-Dic, 2006). In 1998 Black and William reviewed over 250 studies on formative assessment carried out since 1988. While the vast majority were in primary and secondary settings, their meta-analysis clearly showed that feedback resulted in positive benefits to learning and achievement across all content areas and in knowledge and skill types at all levels of education. It was this analysis alone that set the groundwork for all further research on the use and benefit of feedback in post-secondary education. Sadler (1989) closely followed by identifying three conditions necessary for students to benefit from feedback:

1. Possess a concept of the goal/standard or reference level being aimed for;
2. Compare the actual (or current) level of performance with that goal or standard;
3. Engage in appropriate action which leads to some closure of the gap.

Sadler then went on to explain that in many educational settings teachers often give feedback as to how the student performance compares to the standard, yet far too often feedback still falls short of what is actually necessary to close the gap. For example, when using a rubric, the instructor may indicate that the essay was "not sufficiently analytical," which is too vague and difficult for the student to understand and does not provide any information on how to better improve the performance. Detailed feedback must be ongoing and present in each aspect of the educational process to ensure success. Nicol and Macfarlane-Dic (2006) continued this by developing seven principals for good feedback practice. They posited that good feedback:

1. Helps to clarify what good performance is (goals, criteria, expected standards);
2. Facilitates the development of self-assessment (reflection) in learning;
3. Delivers high-quality information to students about their learning;
4. Encourages peer and teacher dialogue around learning;
5. Encourages positive motivational beliefs and self-esteem;
6. Provides opportunities to close the gap between current and desired performance;
7. Provides information to teachers that can be used to help shape teaching.

Figure 1 presents a conceptual model of formative assessment and feedback that synthesizes current thinking by numerous researchers on this topic (Nicol & Macfarlane-Dic, 2006). This figure demonstrates how an academic task, set by the instructor, is the starting point for the feedback cycle to improve student learning. While the student is driving the majority of the elements required to effectively demonstrate learning, it is vital that the *dialogue* aspect, which appears to be subtle, remains at the forefront of the process.

External Feedback

Peer review is a form of evaluation carried out by professional colleagues, peers, and/or other external reviewers. Peers can be experts in the field or classmates who assess the work of other students (Lavy & Yadin 2010). Lavy and Yadin then go on to explain the value of formative assessment in any classroom setting and how this has received large backing from numerous research studies. Using a rubric or a guide when reviewing a peer's paper or project can greatly increase student learning in multiple ways. First, it has been long known that teaching someone to do something truly requires the teacher to understand how to accomplish it first. In peer review, students collaborate to help each other see the strengths and areas for growth in each assignment under review. This type of review requires students to have an understanding of what is expected of them and to use this to evaluate each other's work. It provides an in-depth, hands-on experience with the assignment, in turn increasing understanding and enabling the student to produce a higher quality of work. Second, the use of peer review requires critical analysis of the standard and ways in which students are being assessed on that standard in order for them to adequately demonstrate learning, thus providing students with a rich learning environment which ensures critical thinking beyond the literal level. And lastly, the use of peer review allows students opportunities to reflect and give feedback on each other's work, which in turn helps them to better evaluate their own work, providing a full circle of learning.

Quick CATs

Numerous quick Classroom Assessment Techniques (CATs) are available that instructors can effectively implement into their regular course routine with little additional work. Some CATs are intended to measure learning on a regular basis. One that is particularly effective is a quick write. On a slip of paper, students write one thing they learned that day and one thing they are still unclear about or need more information on. This gives instructors immediate feedback on student learning and provides him/her with an ample amount of information for planning future class sessions. It involves very little planning to implement and requires only a few minutes of class time. However, these few minutes can provide the instructor with an abundance of information about student learning and areas of concern that need to be addressed. Another variation of this CAT is to have students write one thing they learned and one way they plan on immediately implementing this new learning in a different situation. This provides instructors with an immediate sense of understanding, as students must understand new learning to effectively describe how they will implement it. This is particularly useful in a practitioner-based model of learning where students immediately apply what they learned in their personal settings.

Figure 1. *A conceptual model of Formative Assessment*

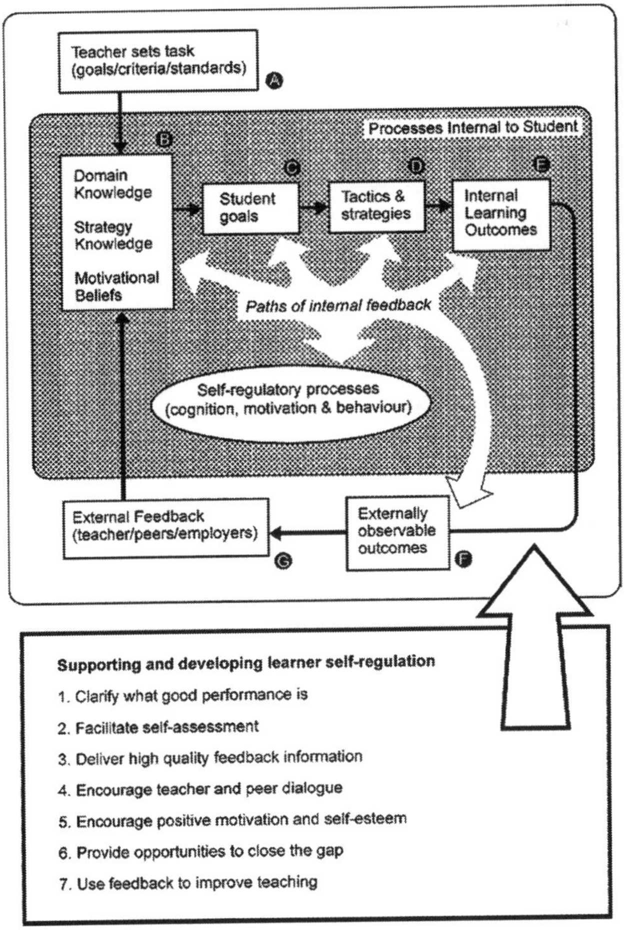
Teacher sets task (goals/criteria/standards)
A
Processes Internal to Student
B
Domain Knowledge
Strategy Knowledge
Motivational Beliefs
C
Student goals
D
Tactics & strategies
E
Internal Learning Outcomes
Paths of internal feedback
Self-regulatory processes (cognition, motivation & behaviour)
External Feedback (teacher/peers/employers)
G
Externally observable outcomes
F
Supporting and developing learner self-regulation
1. Clarify what good performance is
2. Facilitate self-assessment
3. Deliver high quality feedback information
4. Encourage teacher and peer dialogue
5. Encourage positive motivation and self-esteem
6. Provide opportunities to close the gap
7. Use feedback to improve teaching

Formative Blogging

As technology advances, so does the need for its utilization within classroom settings. One emerging area in formative assessment is the use of technology to enhance student learning. Research studies related to either technology or formative assessment have flooded the field over the past decade, especially in recent years. However, research combining these together is less common. Foggo (2007) published a study using blogging as means of formative assessment, particularly in post-secondary education, and her results indicated the use of blogs for formative assessment allowed a more supportive approach to teaching. She then goes on to state that this practice identified what evaluators wanted to achieve and that their expectations were being met. Researchers contend that to meet the needs of the millennial generation in digital information and library research, we must find methods of actively engaging with their social context (Brindley, 2006). Using a blog can allow students greater opportunities for learning, as they are able to add their content and respond to each other at their convenience and are not limited to active classroom time only. This enables them to continue processing outside of the classroom and furthers critical thinking beyond a limited amount of time. Using a blog also increases student interactions and conversations by building community and increasing comfort levels, which in turn can increase student response and participation. Most important, the use of blogs shows a direct response to student needs which in turn will show a direct correlation with student achievement.

Future Research Directions

While research indicates a great amount of growth in the area of formative assessment, it also demonstrates continual evolution. Two areas that would benefit from research are (1) the use of formative assessment in the ever rapidly growing e-learning setting; and (2) the further application of formative assessment in post-secondary education. As more and more educational institutions move away from traditional classroom settings and into more flexible formats such as mixed mode and online, the use of assessment *for* learning rather than *of* learning will need to develop just as rapidly.

Conclusion

Over the years there have been many advances in education to improve student learning; however, many of them do not hold the importance of assessment *for* learning. While incorporating formative assessment in the classroom may require an instructor to become accustomed to new or differing teaching methods and pedagogical beliefs, research strongly indicates that the benefits of incorporating formative assessment greatly outnumber the challenges. Another reason the use of formative assessment is so essential is because of its strong presence and use in primary and secondary education. The use of formative assessment is foundational and currently manifests itself in curriculum at every grade level. As current K–12 students graduate and move into post-secondary educational settings, it is evident that they will expect to receive formative assessment in their work at universities.

References

Ainsworth, L., & Viegut, D. (2006). *Common formative assessments, how to connect standards based instruction an assessment.* Corwin Press.

Andrade, H.G. (2005). Teaching with rubrics: The good, the bad and the ugly. *College Teaching 53*(1), 27-30.

Black, P., & Wiliam, D. (1998). Assessment and classroom learning. *Assessment in Education, 5* (1), 7-74.

Brindley, L. (2006). A world of contrasts: Information literacy in the digital world. In: *LILAC* 2006, 29 March 2006.

Foggo, L. (2007). Using blogs for formative assessment and inter-active teaching. *Ariadne, 51*. Retrieved from http://www.ariadne.ac.uk/issue51/foggo/

Lavy, L., & Yadin, A. (2010). Team-based peer review as a form of formative assessment: The case of systems analysis and design workshop. *Journal of Information Systems Education, 21*(1), 85.

Moss, M., & Brookhart, S. (2009). Advancing formative assessment in every classroom: A guide for instructional leaders. *ASCD*.

National Education Association. (2003). *Balanced assessment: The key to accountability and improved student learning*. Washington, DC.

Nicol, D., & Macfarlane-Dick, D. (2006). Formative assessment and self-regulated learning: A model and seven principals of good feedback practice. *Studies in Higher Education, 31*(2), 199-218.

Reddy, Y.M,. & Andrade, H. (2010) A review of rubric use in higher education. *Assessment & Evaluation in Higher Education, 35*(4), 435-448.

Sadler, D.R. (1989). Formative assessment and the design of instructional systems. *Instructional Science, 18*, 119-144.

CityU's Approach to Outcomes Assessment

Elizabeth Fountain, PhD
City University of Seattle
Associate Provost and Director, Office of Institutional Effectiveness

Abstract

As the higher education community continues to increase its focus on student learning as the essential hallmark of the quality and value of a college education, more outcomes assessment models are being developed. City University of Seattle's model uses its centrally-designed curriculum to embed outcomes at the course, program, and institution level, and to define assessments to provide evidence of student achievement of those outcomes. Program directors ensure this evidence is reviewed annually as part of a continuous improvement process to determine necessary program improvements designed to increase levels of student learning. The model links the outcomes assessment process back to the university's mission and character as a teaching institution, with an emphasis on authentic assessment strategies. The challenges and successes of this model are discussed, along with suggestions for further research.

Introduction

Calls for accountability in higher education continue to increase. All higher education institutions are under pressure to improve their ability to identify and assess student learning outcomes. Policy makers, students, faculty, administrators, and the general public seek ways to judge the quality of a college education not only by the credentials of faculty or their level of research engagement but also by determining what students have actually learned as a result of their education. Over recent decades many educators advocated a change in culture from an emphasis on what teachers teach to an emphasis on what students actually learn (Azeem, Gondal, Abida, Farah, Hussain, & Munira, 2009; Candela, Dalley, & Benzel-Lindley, 2006; Carmichael, Palermo, Reeve, & Vallence, 2001; Chickering, Gamson, & Barsi, 1989; Cuevas, Matveev, & Miller, 2010; Lombardi, 2008; Mancuso, 2001; Pierce & Kalkman, 2003). This phenomenon includes the need for colleges and universities to clearly articulate what students ought to learn in a course or program and to assess whether that learning actually took place. This transition is underway as a result of attempts to improve the value of a student's education and to demonstrate that value to internal and external constituents.

City University of Seattle began its focused efforts to create a robust student learning outcomes assessment system in 2000, placing it squarely in the center of these wider developments in higher education and providing one model for rising to the challenge of increased accountability for student learning. Using its centralized curriculum design and development process, CityU aligns learning outcomes at the institutional, program, and course level, ensures they are effectively embedded in the curriculum, and prescribes assessments that provide direct evidence of student learning in support of those outcomes. This model is most useful for institutions where curriculum design can be coordinated across faculty for an entire program or school. Its applicability is limited for institutions where each course is individually created by a faculty member in isolation from other courses and/or programs. However, even these faculty members can benefit from understanding how to align assessments and learning outcomes inside an individual course, ensuring that the work produced by students gives true evidence of achieving the desired learning outcomes.

Background

CityU's approach to student learning outcomes assessment has as its framework the models developed by Suskie (2004) and implemented in various institutional settings (Barroso & Morgan, 2009; Candela et al., 2006; Chyung, Stepich, & Cox, 2006; Cuevas et al., 2010; Fabry, 2009; Levandar & Mikkola, 2009; MacAskill, Goho, Richard, Anderson, & Stuhldreier, 2008). The basic approach is driven by four questions that can apply to any college or university to assess student learning at any level—institution-wide, in a degree program, or in an individual course.

1. What does the university want students to learn?
2. How does the university enable students to master that learning?
3. How does the university assess student learning?
4. How does the university use the results of assessment to enhance future success for its students?

CityU answers the first question by establishing specific learning outcomes at the course, program, and institutional levels. A learning outcome is a simple, action-oriented statement that describes what a student should know and/or be able to do as a result of the learning that takes place (Suskie, 2004). The second question drives the development of learning activities arranged in course modules that are demonstrably aligned with those outcomes, using the principles of competency-based instruction (Chyung et al., 2006).

To answer the third question, an approach that emphasizes authentic assessment is used. Authentic assessment requires students to engage in learning activities that resemble as closely as possible those they will do in the "real world" of their disciplines and professions (Candela et al., 2006; Cuevas et al., 2010; Lombardi, 2008). These activities then result in direct evidence of student learning, or "tangible, visible, self-explanatory evidence of exactly what students have and haven't learned" (Suskie, 2004, p. 95). Examples include business students producing comprehensive business plans for new or established companies, students in teacher preparation programs being observed in student teaching settings, counseling students providing video tapes of sessions with clients, and technology students completing programming projects. These assessments are then evaluated by faculty using rubrics specially designed to identify the elements that demonstrate achievement of the learning outcomes for the course, program, and/ or institution.

The last question is perhaps the most important. The results of the analysis of student achievement of learning outcomes must be used to improve programs (Barroso & Morgan, 2009; Fabry, 2009; Lombardi, 2008; Suskie, 2004). An annual student learning outcomes assessment process is utilized in which program directors analyze the results in terms of four possible areas for improvement: curricula, instruction, student preparation, and assessment instruments or processes. They identify actions to take as a result of this analysis and determine the impact of those actions on the following year's assessment data.

This basic four-step approach—what should students learn, how will they learn it, how will their learning be assessed, and how will the results of that assessment be used—can be applied in any institution. The next section of this chapter describes in some detail how CityU uses its centralized curriculum development system to support its learning outcomes assessment process.

Learning Outcomes Assessment at CityU

Overview of Outcomes Assessment Practices at CityU

City University of Seattle uses an outcomes-based approach to teaching and learning in alignment with its mission and nature as a higher education institution devoted to applied learning. Because the majority of instruction is delivered by teaching faculty, academically qualified professional practitioners, CityU needs to provide them with a well-designed curriculum that ensures student learning outcomes are embedded in the courses. The curriculum model also needs to allow for the creativity and unique expertise of faculty to construct learning experiences that meet the needs of diverse groups of students.

CityU's Academic Model includes major components that align with CityU's mission and describe the dimensions of a CityU education: a focus on student learning, the use of professional practitioner-faculty, ensuring curricular relevance to the workplace, service to students, accessibility, and responsiveness. The Academic Model provides a framework for ensuring that learning experiences are designed to support clearly articulated outcomes at the course, program, and institutional levels. Educational experiences are carefully designed by faculty to encourage self-directed learning within an appropriately defined structure of expectations. With the focus on applying theory to practical experience, learning activities form explicit links among the crucial abilities of an educated professional: critical thinking, reflection, and ethical practice. Multiple paths to demonstrating each competency are available to learners as appropriate. Students are actively encouraged to define and take responsibility for their own contributions to the learning process, with the understanding that their engagement is critical for substantive learning to take place.

Six CityU Learning Goals describe exit competencies for graduates of all degree programs. All CityU graduates will

1. Exhibit professional competency and a sense of professional identity, bring to the workplace the knowledge and

skills intrinsic to professional success, understand the basic values and mission of the fields in which they are working, use technology to facilitate their work, understand basic technical concepts, and demonstrate understanding through practical application.
2. Employ strong communication and interpersonal skills, communicate effectively both orally and in writing, interact and work with others in a collaborative manner, negotiate difficult interpersonal situations to bring about solutions to problems that benefit all involved.
3. Demonstrate critical thinking and information literacy; think critically and creatively; reflect upon their own work and the larger context in which it takes place; find, access, evaluate, and use information to solve problems; and consider the complex implications of actions they take and decisions they make.
4. Make a strong commitment to ethical practice and service in their professions and communities; take responsibility for their own actions and exhibit high standards of conduct in their professional lives; be aware of the ethical expectations of their profession and hold themselves accountable to those standards; be active contributors to their professional communities and associations, and informed and socially responsible citizens of their communities as well as of the world.
5. Embrace diverse and global perspectives; work collaboratively with individuals from a variety of backgrounds; learn from the beliefs, values, and cultures of others; realize that varied viewpoints bring strength and richness to the workplace; and demonstrate an awareness of the interrelation of diverse components of a project or situation.
6. Commit to lifelong learning, becoming self-directed and information literate in seeking out ways to continue learning throughout their lifetimes.

These institutional-level Learning Goals were designed to align the program learning outcomes already in place with CityU's mission and to ensure consistency across programs. Since 2005

362

the university has engaged in an intensive curriculum design process to ensure students achieve learning outcomes at the course, program, and institutional levels. Administrative faculty who have responsibility for an academic program begin by defining program-level learning outcomes that incorporate the CityU Learning Goals; this process typically involves industry professionals to ensure relevance to the contemporary workplace, a prime value of a CityU education.

Course development also starts with a set of learning outcomes, and those outcomes are carefully aligned to the program-level outcomes. Faculty design the ways in which students will provide authentic evidence of their learning via the use of internships, projects, and other activities that mimic as closely as possible the work required in the profession. A package of information about a course, including its alignment to the program outcomes and place in the program sequence, the major assessments, and a set of recommended learning activities, is provided to the course instructor. This is especially important given the nature of the practitioner faculty at CityU, who are for the most part seasoned professionals who bring real-world experience to their teaching rather than coming from a more traditional academic background. The university takes very seriously its obligation to provide these faculty members with the tools needed to support student achievement of the learning outcomes at the course, program, and institutional level. This has led to a significant investment of time and effort in the curriculum design and outcomes assessment process on the part of its administrative faculty, its curriculum and faculty development office, and its institutional effectiveness office.

All courses at CityU are developed using this process. The university invested in software that "houses" the curriculum development process, using the essential elements of content management to align learning outcomes, assessments, and learning activities. It provides faculty with the means of collaboration on course development as well as providing clear documentation of the linkages between all levels of learning outcomes and means of assessment. It also builds in flexibility to accommodate the different types of students served by the university's programs around the world; as long as outcomes and the means of assessing them are consistent, learning activities are implemented to be responsive to the specific environment and students, and to take advantage of the expertise and creativity of the course instructor.

As faculty design new programs or revise existing programs, they identify appropriate means of collecting direct evidence of student learning related to the program outcomes. Evidence of student learning is analyzed in two ways. First, it is typically graded by the course instructor using a rubric developed to determine how well students achieved the course outcomes. This becomes part of the student's grade for the course and feedback is provided to the student regarding his or her performance. Formative assessments in courses are used to promote learning; summative assessments demonstrate final achievement of the course outcomes.

Second, the evidence of student learning is incorporated into assessment at the program level. Often an additional rubric is used that relates the elements of the student work to the program outcomes rather than to the course outcomes. In many programs this second level of analysis is done blindly by a separate set of evaluators to ensure lack of bias. These data can then be disaggregated by location as well to ensure students at various CityU locations in the US and abroad are achieving at comparable levels. This is also the stage at which the analysis process links back to the CityU Learning Goals. The alignment documented in the program-design phase is used to evaluate how well students are achieving these learning goals. For example, a program outcome is identified as relating to the CityU Learning Goal on diverse and global perspectives; the same evidence of student learning is used to assess both levels.

Once the analysis is concluded, program directors develop action items related to any necessary program improvements. These can include improvement in instruction (better preparation or training of faculty teaching specific courses); improvement in curriculum (adding or deleting content, rearranging course sequences); improvement in student preparation (ensuring the development of writing or quantitative skills); or adjustments in the assessment tools or process itself (redesigning a capstone project or rubric to better align with program outcomes).

Programs provide annual student learning outcomes assessment reports that capture the analysis of evidence, planned improvements, and the impact of any past changes on student learning.

Impact of Assessment Practices

Students can be assured that the courses they are taking are designed to engage them in learning that is relevant to their program outcomes and that the evidence of learning they produce is relevant to their professional ambitions. The intended learning outcomes are transparent to students, providing them with clear understanding of what they must achieve; this goes well beyond information about content that will be covered in a course.

Faculty also benefit from this increased transparency, as they know from the beginning not only the intended outcomes of the course but also how those outcomes support achievement of the program and university level outcomes. They can adjust their instruction far more effectively, using their expertise and creativity to engage students in learning activities that are relevant at all levels.

Issues Related to Assessment Practices

This practice of embedding multiple levels of learning outcomes in curriculum design is made possible by CityU's use of a central curriculum development process. A more common practice in many higher education institutions is to prescribe only the topic or content of a course, leaving the actual course design to the individual faculty member. While this maximizes the faculty member's ability to customize a course to his or her interests and expertise, it makes it much more difficult to align learning outcomes. By using a central process, CityU can provide its practitioner faculty with a fully designed course, one that they can still effectively customize, while using all the resources available to ensure students meet the learning outcomes.

CityU's centrally developed curricula allows for strong alignment of CityU Learning Goals, program outcomes, and assessments. Faculty spend a significant amount of time designing authentic assessments that provide evidence of student learning on program outcomes and CityU Learning Goals. The emphasis on authentic assessment means that summative assessments are generally highly relevant to the professional settings in which students will work. Students invest time and energy in completing the assessments as a result of this relevance. However, this approach also adds complexity to the process of evaluating assessments and distilling results into information that lends itself to program improvements; moreover, it makes comparisons across programs and to national data sets difficult.

The linking of program learning outcomes to the CityU Learning Goals reinforces the emphasis on authentic assessment. Rather than "layering over" another set of learning outcomes and another set of assessment tools, which would risk disconnecting the CityU Learning Goals from the curricula and instruction, this approach requires faculty to emphasize the connections between them. Core skills like critical thinking and information literacy are not afterthoughts in curriculum design; they are intrinsic to the curricula in each program. It is necessary to establish clear, concise, and valid connections between the program learning outcomes and the CityU Learning Goals. In many of the program assessment reports, faculty find this to be quite a challenge. Faculty are refining program and course outcomes, focusing on what it really means to align with the CityU Learning Goals and identifying the best ways to collect and analyze direct evidence of student learning.

The best way to infuse the CityU Learning Goals into program level outcomes is to drill down to the course level, ensure a connection between the course outcomes and the CityU Learning Goals, and then carry that connection forward to the program level. This is done by first establishing a solid link between course outcomes and related CityU Learning Goals. Next, it is important to ensure that the assessments used to measure those outcomes do, in fact, provide evidence of achievement on both the course outcomes and the CityU Learning Goals. This process naturally supports the link between the program outcomes and the CityU Learning Goals once it is properly established at the course level.

Future Research Directions

This technique has allowed the university to build a rich portfolio of data regarding its approach to student learning outcomes assessment. It is in the third year of collecting and analyzing the results of student learning in all its degree programs via annual outcomes assessment reports, and is beginning a more coordinated approach to the collection of evidence of student learning via an e-portfolio and assessment system. Looking forward, the university will seek ways to incorporate the evidence of student achievement as the most important measure of the success and value of its curriculum development system. Over time it should result in improved student learning.

Specific areas of future research include questions related to the linkage of instruction to achievement of student learning outcomes. The university is engaged in defining what it means by "highly effective" faculty, using data from student evaluations and supervisor observations. The ability to link the effectiveness of teaching to actual student learning outcomes data would strengthen this definition significantly. An initial scan of best practices of the faculty receiving the highest ratings from student evaluations was completed two years ago; in the past year the School of Management has also analyzed student comments from poor instructor evaluations. This resulted in a faculty development focus on providing students with developmental feedback to guide their learning; follow-up research in the coming year could help determine the effectiveness of this intervention.

Conclusion

A university's learning outcomes assessment process must be driven by its mission and values. The mission and values are thus incorporated into learning goals established at the institutional, program, and course levels; these goals are integrated into curriculum design and program delivery. The framework provided by the Academic Model informs curriculum design and program delivery as well. The university must then require programs to analyze evidence of student learning regularly, forming the basis for continuous improvement. These improvement plans are then implemented to improve student learning, and their results are captured in the next round of data collection and evidence.

CityU remains committed to refining its learning outcomes assessment strategies, using the direct evidence of student learning to improve programs, and ultimately ensuring that student learning is consistent with the university's mission to change lives for good by providing high-quality and relevant lifelong education to anyone with the desire to learn.

References

Azeem, M., Gondal, M. B., Abida, K., Farah, N., Hussain, A., & Munira, A. (2009). Defining the standards for higher education. *The International Journal of Learning, 16*(4), 234-251.

Barroso, L. R., & Morgan, J. R. (2009). Project enhanced learning: Addressing ABET outcomes and linking the curriculum. *Journal of Professional Issues in Engineering Education and Practice, 135*(1), 11-22.

Candela, L., Dalley, K., & Benzel-Lindley, J. (2006). A case for learning-centered curricula. *Journal of Nursing Education, 45*(2), 59-67.

Carmichael, R., Palermo, J., Reeve, L., & Vallence, K. (2001). Student learning: The heart of quality in education and training. *Assessment and Evaluation in Higher Education, 26*(5), 449.

Chickering, A. W., Gamson, Z., & Barsi, L. M. (1989). *The seven principles for good practice in undergraduate education: Faculty inventory*. Milwaukee,WI: Winona State University.

Chyung, S. Y., Stepich, D., & Cox, D. (2006). Building a competency-based curriculum architecture to educate 21st century business practitioners. *Journal of Education for Business, 81*(6), 307-312.

Cuevas, N. M., Matveev, A. G., & Miller, K. (2010, Winter). Mapping general education outcomes to the major: Intentionality and transparency. *AAC&U Peer Review*, 10-17.

Fabry, D. L. (2009). Designing online and on-ground courses to ensure comparability and consistency in meeting learning outcomes. *The Quarterly Review of Distance Education, 10*(3), 253-261.

Levandar, L. M., & Mikkola, M. (2009). Core curriculum analysis: A tool for educational design. *Journal of Agricultural Education, 15*(3), 275-286.

Lombardi, M. (2008, January). Making the grade: The role of assessment in authentic learning. In D. Oblinger (Ed.), *Educause learning initiative paper one*. Retrieved from *net.educause.edu/ir/library/pdf/ELI3019.pdf*

MacAskill, P., Goho, J., Richard, R., Anderson, K., & Stuhldreier, M. (2008). Creating quality assurance in curriculum: Theory and practice at a Canadian community college. *Community College Journal of Research and Practice, 32*, 939-958.

Mancuso, S. (2001). Adult-centered practices: Benchmarking study in higher education. *Innovative Higher Education, 25*(3), 165-181.

Pierce, J. W., & Kalkman, D. L. (2003, Spring). Applying learner-centered principles in teacher education. *Theory into Practice, 42*(2), 127-132.

Suskie, L. (2004). Assessing student learning: A common-sense guide. San Francisco: Jossey Bass.

Integrated Information Literacy Instruction

Mary Mara, MLIS
City University of Seattle
Department of Library Services

Abstract

In today's ever expanding information environment, the need is increasing for graduate and undergraduate students to develop information literacy skills throughout their academic programs in preparation for the professional work environment. While a variety of information literacy instruction program models exist within higher education, a program that is integrated within the student's chosen discipline can most effectively provide opportunities to learn how to find, evaluate, and use information for both academic and future work environments. Faculty and librarians need to collaborate to design and implement discipline-specific information literacy instruction integrated across academic programs.

Information Literacy in Higher Education

It is not difficult to find a current article or website that refers to the topic of information overload and the importance of building skills to navigate and manage information. Everyone agrees that the amount of information available is expanding rapidly and that much of it can be accessed through the Internet. It is increasingly important for workers to know how to create, manage, and manipulate information to succeed in today's knowledge or information society. While the Internet has increased access to many types and forms of information, the ability to easily find the kind of information needed for a specific task, to evaluate the information found for relevance and credibility, and to use the information effectively and ethically is not guaranteed. Collectively, the ability to find, evaluate, and use information is known as information literacy (IL) (Association of College & Research Libraries, 2011).

Within higher education, the explicit articulation of IL standards by academic accreditation agencies has increased over the past fifteen years. References to IL skill development in academic standards reflects acknowledgement of the increasingly complex information environment as well as the need to develop faculty and students' abilities to find, evaluate, and use information effectively and ethically. The Middle States Commission on Higher Education (MSCHE) has been a leader in these efforts, adopting IL as a concept in 1994 and partnering with the Association of College & Research Libraries (ACRL) in 1999 to shape the definition of IL in higher education (Morse, 2008). MSCHE's 2009 publication *Characteristics of Excellence in Higher Education* recognizes IL "as an essential component of any educational program at the graduate or undergraduate level" (p. 55). The Northwest Commission on Colleges and Universities (NWCCU) has also adopted a standard that addresses the need for faculty and librarians to work as partners to "ensure that use of the library and information resources is integrated into the learning process" (NWCCU, 2010, 2.C.6).

It seems common sense to draw the conclusion that when students know how to find and use top quality information to inform their learning and to support academic assignments, the quality of their learning and academic work will increase. Research confirms that the quality of business students' work increases after receiving context-based IL instruction (Roldan, 2004). Brief course-integrated IL instruction sessions are an effective and engaging method for introducing and reinforcing student skills particularly when related to a specific assignment (Jackson & Durkee, 2008). Lombardo and Miree (2003) take this a step further to integration at the program level stating that

> It is crucial that academic faculty and librarians work together to introduce today's business students to the structure and content of their information environment throughout their academic program so that they will be well prepared to gather the data they need to make effective business decisions upon graduation. (p.19)

Given this, and in light of the necessity for universities to address academic accreditation requirements, the need for IL skill development within graduate and undergraduate programs is clear.

The importance and relevance of IL skills extend beyond the academic setting, relating directly to students' future professional work environments and performance (Katz, Haras, & Blaszczynski, 2010, p. 136; Lombardo & Miree, 2003). In 1993 Peter Drucker spoke to the importance of information literacy when interviewed for the *Harvard Business Review* stating, "In today's organization, you have to take responsibility for information because it is your main tool. But most don't know how to use it. Few are information literate." (Harris, 1993, p.120). More recently, Breivik (2005) affirmed that

> Nowhere is the need for information literacy skills greater than in today's work environment, where efforts to "manage" knowledge are increasingly necessary to keep a strategic advantage within a global market. The list of business leaders calling for information literate workers keeps growing. (p. 23)

The need for an information literate workforce is international. It extends beyond geographic borders as evidenced by *The Prague Declaration,* which states that IL is a key element of the social, cultural, and economic development of individuals, communities, and institutions in the twenty-first century (United Nations Educational, Scientific and Cultural Organization, 2003). Higher education institutions' role in teaching students how to find, evaluate, and use information is increasingly important in the United States and in countries worldwide.

Information Literacy Instruction Models

Traditionally a variety of instructional models have been employed by university librarians and faculty to teach students how to find, evaluate, and use information. Sessions within these models may be recommended to students, or required as a prerequisite to, or limited part of, an academic program. These models include:

- Allowing students to determine their own way to acquire and develop their ability to find, evaluate, and use information (Bruner & Lee, 1970);
- Relying on individual faculty to request IL instruction by librarians for their students;
- Delivering a general research workshop or library tour during new student orientation;
- Designing a specific introductory course within a program that includes an hour-long session on how to use library resources and services that may or may not be designed to support specific assignments (Badke, 2009);
- Designing a stand-alone credit or non-credit-bearing IL course which may or may not be designed to support specific assignments within students' disciplines (Badke, 2008).

While faculty across disciplines generally agree that IL and research skills are important for their students, not all agree on the

374

best model for developing these skills, or even whether students need help becoming information literate. Assumptions are made that students already know how to find information online and don't need additional support to develop these skills. Lombardo & Miree (2003) found that the business faculty they studied "assume that students are already well-versed in business research tools and methods" (p. 20). Faculty who hold this belief often adopt the model of allowing students to determine their own way to acquire and develop IL skills.

However, research reported by McKay (1996) found that graduate and undergraduate business students were unaware of the type of resources available to them from the library and received little guidance from their faculty in how to locate relevant information. Contrary to the belief of faculty who do not feel students need IL instruction, it remains true that students today "are no better prepared in business research than the business students of 35 years ago" (Simon, 2009, p. 260). Today's online research environment, facilitated by easy access to information on the Internet, does not mean that students are able to find the kind of information they need when they need it. Nor does it mean that students know how to recognize whether or not the information they have found is accurate and reliable, both of which are key IL skills (Head & Eisenberg, 2009; Simon 2009).

Students themselves express difficulty finding, evaluating, and using information. In the research report released by Project Information Literacy, *Finding Context: What Today's College Students Say About Conducting Research in the Information Age* (Head & Eisenberg 2009), students state that they have difficulty identifying a topic, knowing and using discipline-specific terminology to locate information effectively, and interfacing between Internet and library resources. Students continue to be overwhelmed by choices, have difficulty finding the kind of information they are seeking, and do not receive adequate orientation on how to find relevant information (Head & Eisenberg, 2009). Thus, allowing students to determine their own way to develop IL skills seems an inadequate response to the need.

The instruction models described that rely on recommended orientations and courses or on faculty-requested IL instruction are also ineffective methods for ensuring that all students have the opportunity to learn how to find, evaulate, and use information ethically. Students who most need IL instruction may choose not to attend a recommended orientation or optional course. Faculty may be unwilling to devote a portion of their instructional time to support the development of skills they perceive students already have or should be able to learn on their own. Recommended IL instruction does not adequately meet accreditation requirements for universities to ensure that all of their graduates are information literate.

Instructional models that require students to complete an orientation, session, or course to develop IL skills are an improvement over recommended instruction, but there are challenges with these models as well. Students introduced to IL skills during new student orientations may not retain these skills and be able to effectively apply them when they encounter their first research assignment weeks or months after orientation. Instruction provided in a single hour-long session can not adequately cover the range of information sources, tools, and skills students need to learn for their academic and future professional work. Stand-alone IL courses are often associated with general education distribution requirements rather than dicipline-specific courses. Given the general nature of these courses, activities and assignments do not provide students with the necessary orientation to information sources, tools, and skills specific to their discipline and profession.

Research in adult learning and motivation originating with Malcom S. Knowles and Raymond J. Wlodowski informs best practices in higher education for instructional design. These best practices, as summarized by Thoms (n.d.), include:

- Presenting new information within the context of the course activities, discipline, and future profession to maintain engagement;
- Presenting information in bite-size chunks that permit mastery;
- Providing opportunities for students to learn by doing through authentic activities and assessments;

- Timing the introduction of new information and skills immediately preceding their need.

Findings from the research in adult learning and motivation that inform best practices in instructional design are also relevant to the design of IL instruction in higher education.

A Path Towards IL Integration

Prior to 2003, City University of Seattle's IL instruction was delivered primarily by staff librarians and adjunct librarians through fifteen–sixty minute sessions at new student orientations and in one–two hour-long sessions in specific courses identified within academic programs. Additional sixty-minute sessions were scheduled at the request of individual faculty members. With academic programs delivered in online, mixed-mode, and face-to-face formats at locations around the world, including the United States, Canada, Mexico, China, and Europe, known gaps existed in IL instructional delivery as well as quality. The IL instruction program prior to 2003 primarily served students at locations in Washington State and Canada, but did not consistently meet the needs of students studying in the variety of delivery formats in locations around the world such as Europe and China.

In addition, CityU librarians were keenly aware that these sessions were their only opportunity to introduce a wide range of skills and resources to students. The time frame allotted was not sufficient for orienting students to the resources within their discipline. Librarians could limit the range of skills they provided instruction on and encourage students to seek additional one-on-one help (which few accepted); or they could rush through instruction on a variety of IL skills using a traditional lecture-style approach, overwhelming students with information they would not likely retain or be able to apply to their assignments. The latter option was out of alignment with best practices in adult learning as well as with the City University Academic Model's (City University of Seattle, 2011) focus on active student-centered learning.

Whenever possible IL instruction sessions were linked to skills needed for specific assignments and were scheduled just prior to students' need to begin their research. More frequently, however, it was difficult to time the instruction appropriately, and by the time librarians were able to meet with students, their need for specific instruction had passed. Success of this program's model was reliant on faculty awareness of and willingness to host sessions. While most faculty acknowledged the importance of IL instruction, each quarter a number of faculty reported concern with the amount of instructional time they lost to the IL sessions, and some faculty refused to schedule the sessions at all.

Internal surveys and anecdotal student and faculty feedback confirmed that the existing models of IL instruction were not effective. Some students reported receiving the same instruction in multiple courses or receiving instruction on how to use tools they were already well versed in, while other students received no instruction at all. A small group of graduates even reported to library staff that they never realized they had access to any library resources from City University.

Librarians grew dissatisfied with their inability to provide consistent, relevant, and engaging instruction to support the development of students' IL skills wherever and whenever CityU programs and courses were offered. It became increasingly clear that the existing instruction program was insufficient and in need of revision.

The move towards program-level integration of IL skill development, designed to reach students and faculty whenever or wherever they were learning and teaching, originated with a plan developed by the library's director of operations at an ACRL Immersion program (Association of College & Research Libraries, 2011). Beginning in 2003, the director of operations led a university-wide initiative to develop a fully integrated IL instruction program designed collaboratively by faculty and librarians. The Information Literacy Task Force, formed in 2003 to design this program, included faculty from each school, a representative from Canadian programs, and the library's director of operations.

The specific goals of the task force were to develop a mission statement, integrate IL into CityU's institutional learning goals, define IL competencies, and develop a rubric based on the ACRL IL model (Salman & Mara, 2009). The work of the IL Task Force, as well as the ongoing collaborations between CityU faculty and librarians to integrate IL instruction throughout the curriculum, was guided in large part by ACRL's *Characteristics of Programs that Illustrate Best Practies* (Association of College & Research Libraries, 2003). Some of the ACRL best practices that are evident in CityU's program include:

- A mission statement aligned with and corresponding to the mission statement of the university;
- Clearly articulated goals and objectives developed with input from relevant consituencies;
- A plan for how faculty and librarians will collaborate to design and integrate student-centered information literacy skill instruction throughout the curriculum;
- Administrative and institutional support for implementing the plan;
- Assessment and evaluation of student achievement of information literacy skills through CityU's program assessment process.

All goals of CityU's task force were achieved by 2005, and the mission statement developed by the task force follows:

> City Univeristy seeks to develop accomplished information users. By infusing information literacy instruction throughout the curriculum, we teach students to recognize when information is required, to find and retrieve it, to evaluate its relevance and authority, and to use it effectively. This supports the university's mission to provide high-qualtiy learning experiences for adult learners and to develop skills for lifelong learning. The ability to use information effectively enriches our graduates' contributions to both academic and professional endeavors.

Two CityU Learning Goals were revised to include IL skills, and the IL rubric developed by the task force was made available to faculty and librarians developing programs and courses at the university.

Work of the IL Task Force was shared in 2005 through workshops attended by program directors and course managers responsible for the design of academic programs and individual course curriculum (Salman & Mara, 2009). With the shift to institutional support of IL skill development and the explicit articulation of IL in CityU's Learning Goals came the acknowledgment that responsibility for IL instruction would be a collaborative venture between faculty and librarians. Task force members faciliated a review of curriculm by faculty and librarians to identify courses and assignments with IL components represented on CityU's IL rubric. Through this work CityU's program to integrate information literacy across academic programs was launched.

CityU's team-based curriculum development process and integration of IL instruction across academic programs continues to evolve through the work of the university's Curriculum Quality Committee. Program development teams consisting of the program director, faculty (domestic and international), subject matter experts, and librarians create program outcomes relevant to the profession that are mapped to university learning goals and existing professional standards. Key assessments for measuring student learning outcomes, and the courses in which they will be offfered, are identified by the team.

With faculty input librarians create IL integration maps to assist in planning which IL skills will be taught within the context of specific courses and required assessments. Faculty and librarians make note of any IL instruction present in required readings and course activities. Gaps between these materials and the information and skills students need to demonstrate mastery of program and course learning outcomes are identified next. Methods for addressing these needs across the academic program are listed on the IL integration map for creation by course design teams (CDTs). Careful planning at the initial design phases of a new or revised program allows multiple opportunities for students to develop from novice to expert users of information specific to their future profession. Students receive small portions of IL instruction at their point of need and within the context of their discipline that lead to mastery (Thoms, n.d.).

Implementation of the program plan for IL integration takes place through CDTs whose membership consists of course managers, faculty (domestic and international), subject matter experts, and librarians. Faculty and librarians serving on CDTs create multiple types of IL instruction materials. To meet the goal of providing IL instruction whenever and wherever students and faculty are learning and teaching, librarians and faculty focus on creating content that is accessible online. Most content is hosted on the library pages in the student portal and linked within the university's learning management system (LMS) to relevant learning activities and assessments.

At the most basic level of IL support, faculty and librarians provide access through the university's LMS to general resources, including a list of online article databases, self-help guides, and the research and reference services provided by the library. In addition, a quarterly system message is posted in the LMS reminding all students of the information resources and services available to them through the university's library. While this may ensure that no future graduates exit their programs without knowledge of the library services available to them, this alone is not an adequate model for teaching students how to find, evaluate, and use information within the context of their profession.

Faculty and librarians focus the majority of their collaboration on developing a range of IL instruction materials that are integrated into specific courses, learning activities, and assessments. The instructional materials are designed for ease of delivery by faculty who know best when and what type of IL instruction students in their course need. Librarians are available on demand to assist faculty with the delivery of any or all IL instruction activities and assessments. The variety of materials developed includes, but is not limited to:

- Course resource pages listing required and recommended resources that are selected by faculty and librarians to meet the needs of required assessments;
- Announcements pre-loaded in the LMS for faculty to use at students' point-of-need;

- Online discussion forums co-facilitated by faculty and librarians on discipline-specific IL topics;
- LMS learning modules on discipline-specific IL topics co-located with required learning activities and assessments;
- Flash-based video and text-based tutorials covering a wide range of topics including how to use APA citation style, how to effectively search specific online databases, how to request or renew library materials, and how to effectively locate discipline-specific information;
- Annotated bibliography activities tailored to meet the needs of required assignments;
- Webinars on discipline-specific IL topics;
- Online office hours for individualized research consultations with a librarian.

Integrated IL instruction is uniquely tailored to each academic program at CityU and may include any combination of the instruction materials and methods listed above.

Integration in Action

The plan for IL integration in City University's Bachelor of Science in Business Administration (BSBA) and Master of Business Administration (MBA) programs began in 2008 during a regularly scheduled review process. Working independently of one another, the MBA and BSBA program development teams started the process by reviewing student assessment data related to existing program outcomes. Subject matter experts and business leaders on the team provided input on the kind of skills business students today need upon graduation to compete effectively for jobs and in the workplace. The MBA and BSBA teams revised graduate and undergraduate program learning outcomes to align with current workplace expectations and university learning goals, and designed authentic summative assessments to demonstrate student mastery of program learning outcomes.

With a clear outline of the needs of each program articulated through program learning outcomes and with key assessments identified, program directors, course managers and the librarian designated to support the BSBA and MBA programs set to work planning how to integrate IL instruction with the goal of providing all students, whenever and wherever they are learning, with multiple opportunities to learn IL skills related to their profession.

While the nature of required assessments for undergraduate and graduate students differ, course managers leading design teams and the business librarian both recognize that the types of information students need to learn how to find, evaluate, and use as they move into new phases of their business careers are similar. For example, students in the BSBA and MBA programs must know how to find information such as:

- Articles by business leaders or professional organizations that inform best practices in the workplace;
- Industry trends and reports;
- Company information (both public and private);
- Industry and company financial data to inform decision making;
- Local, regional, and global market information;
- Local, regional, and global laws governing business practices;
- Domestic or international governmental economic data and reports.

Students in the BSBA and MBA programs benefit from learning how to locate primary source materials on the Internet, such as annual reports and financial statements on company websites, or market demographics from a site such as the US Census Bureau. They also benefit from learning how to locate secondary sources that include some analysis of industry or company data, organizing it in a format within a single source that is more suited for their specific need. While some secondary sources can be found on the Internet, full text access may be limited or reports (such as specialized marketing data) may be prohibitively expensive for students to purchase. To access these kind of resources, students need to learn how to use tools such as subscription business databases provided through academic library sites.

In a cohort-based program, one in which a group of students take courses in a prescribed order, faculty and librarians can be very specific in the design of a sequenced integrated IL instruction program. Pretesting in one of the first classes in the sequence would identify the IL skills students bring with them. Learning activities could be modified to place more or less emphasis on developing certain skills depending on the results of the pretest. Based on the plan articulated on the IL instruction map, faculty teaching individual course sessions would know with certainty the courses in which IL skills are taught and would not repeat skill-based instruction unless they recognize that their students need to have these skills refreshed for their course's required assessments.

In non-cohort-based programs, programs in which there is flexibility in the order in which students take courses, it is more challenging to design a sequenced integrated IL instruction program. CityU's BSBA and MBA programs are non-cohort based. While there is a recommended sequence for moving through each program, students may take courses in nearly any order. It is more challenging for faculty to know whether or not students have taken courses in the recommended sequence that would build the IL skills they need for the courses students are currently enrolled in. For this reason, CityU faculty and librarians designed integrated IL instruction programs for BSBA and MBA students that include required, recommended, and on-demand instructional materials linked within the LMS at students' point-of-need.

While CityU's MBA program is non-cohort based, the program director and faculty know that the majority of students begin their program by taking Essentials of Business Management, and Business Communications. Required readings in these courses introduce students to primary and secondary research sources and to methods for evaluating websites. In addition, textbook readings cover specific sources recommended for business news and trends, company and industry information, US Government data, and international trade information. Tools used to locate business information that are introduced include subscription article databases available through public or academic libraries, and search engines such as Google.

Faculty and the MBA librarian extend students' learning in these courses through instructional materials and activities that include learning units on how to locate company and industry information using CityU's online business article databases (*Business Source Complete* and *ABI-Inform Industry/Trade*), co-facilitated webinars and discussion forums designed to support students' first attempts using these tools, and research tips posted as announcements in the LMS course shell and e-mailed to students. Students also receive instruction on the American Psychological Assocation's style for writing and correct citation of resources. Student skills in finding, evaluating, and using business information sources are measured through assessments such as the *Company Competitive Analysis, Personal Learning Journal, Capsim Simulation Rounds,* and writing activities in which students practice incorporating business research found in scholarly sources with practical applications in the workplace.

Intermediate-level instruction, focusing on how students can improve search results in online databases, is delivered during the MBA's Project Management and Priortization course in the form of learning units on executing research for a business plan and locating data for the interview and narrative sections of a business plan. Students explore resources available at no cost on the Project Management Institute's website, comparing and contrasting these resources with those available through subscription databases hosted by the library. In the event that individual students have enrolled in this course outside the program's recommended sequence, learning units that teach students introductory search skills are also linked within the LMS course shell.

Intermediate and advanced IL skills are further developed through courses MBA students typically take later in their program. Focused instruction through discussion forums and learning units on how to locate and evaluate market research data through *Global Market Information Database* is integrated in the Applied Marketing course. In Evaluating Financial Information, IL learning activities introduce students to how to locate industry and company data and financial ratios using specialized business databases such as *Morningstar, MintGlobal,* and *Standard & Poor's NetAdvantage*. In Managerial Accounting, students are taught how to navigate the *FASB Codification Database* to locate current accounting regulations, and in Law and Economics for Global Business the MBA librarian and faculty teach students how to locate business information for specific countries.

Having learned of multiple authoritative sources for business information and having practiced the skills needed to access information from tools such as subscription business databases through earlier coursework in the MBA program, students are well equipped to complete the program's summative *Practical Business Application* assessment and to demonstrate mastery of program outcomes, including outcomes related to IL skills. At this point in the program, the MBA librarian is available on demand to students for small-group or one-on-one research consultations, and students are provided with information on how to access similar subscription business databases through community resources such as public library systems.

Instruction in the BSBA non-cohort-based program follows a similar pattern to that provided to MBA students. Most students begin the BSBA program by enrolling in the Critical Thinking, and Professional Communication courses. Introductory-level IL instruction materials are integrated and aligned with required assessments, teaching students how to locate professional and scholarly business sources through the Internet and online article databases provided by academic and public libraries. Faculty and the BSBA librarian begin the program with an introduction to *Business Source Complete* and *ABI/Inform Trade & Industry*. Intermediate instruction in the use of tools such as *MintGlobal, Global Market Information, Morningstar,* and *Standard & Poor's NetAdvantage* is integrated in courses such as Interpretation of Financial Accounting, Legal Issues in the Workplace, and Business Economics. When students complete their program through a capstone assessment course such as Business Strategy, the BSBA librarian is available on demand to students for small-group or one-on-one research consultations.

Future Directions for Information Literacy Integration

Evaluation of student achievement of BSBA and MBA IL program learning outcomes is in the beginning phases at CityU. Assessment data for program outcomes related to IL skills was not included in the 2010 program assessment report due to lack of comparative data from previous years. Qualitative feedback from course managers and students indicates that the integerated IL instruction program is more effective than CityU's previous model of providing a single, hour-long session in the courses Critial Thinking (BSBA), and Essentials of Business Management (MBA). Course managers feel that the librarian assigned to course design teams adds value to the development of required and recommended resources, IL learning activities, and the design of authentic assessments that include deliberate research components. Students' access to IL instruction at their point-of-need has improved in the revised BSBA and MBA programs with the development of online tutorials and learning units available whenever and wherever students and faculty are learning and teaching. Quantitative data on the use of business databases available through CityU's library confirms that students are accessing these resources 10–30 percent more frequently in the 2009–2010 academic year than in the same time period during the 2008–2009 academic year.

As BSBA and MBA courses are reviewed by course mangers, feedback from faculty teaching individual sessions of each course is gathered and used to inform improvements to course materials, including the integrated IL instruction materials. The business librarian adds data collected through an analysis of reference questions posed by BSBA and MBA students, illustrating gaps in their ability to find, evaluate, and use information for required assessments. In collaboration with course managers, the business librarian will continue to develop new materials, to increase the differentiation of existing IL instruction materials to meet the needs of graduate and undergraduate students, and to strengthen the ties between IL learning activities and required assessments.

Quantitative research designed to demonstrate the impact of integrated IL instruction on BSBA and MBA student learning should be conducted by CityU faculty and the business librarian. While IL instruction materials are integrated into CityU's curriculum document and may be listed as required, neither the BSBA or MBA programs have measured whether faculty teaching individual course sessions are using these materials with their students. If the results of quantitative research confirm improved student achievment of course and program learning outcomes when IL instruction materials are used, faculty teaching individual courses will be more likely to follow course guidelines and use materials designated as required in the curriculum.

The library should also collaborate with the university's Department of Training, Curriculum, and Faculty Development to provide faculty with professional learning opportunities to enhance their own IL skills. Professional learning opportunities for faculty would increase awareness of the specialized business databases available through CityU's library and increase faculty comfort levels using these resources. Students will benefit from faculty's increased knowledge of current tools for finding information.

City University of Seattle will continue to combine the discipline-specific knowledge of program directors, course managers, and faculty in the classrom with the business librarian's knowledge of information tools and sources to improve student learning and achievment of program learning outcomes.

References

Association of College and Research Libraries (2003). *Characteristics of programs of information literacy that illustrate best practices.* Retrieved from http://www.ala.org/ala/mgrps/divs/acrl/standards/characteristics.cfm

Association of College and Research Libraries (2011). *Immersion program.* Retrieved from http://www.ala.org/ala/mgrps/divs/acrl/issues/infolit/professactivity/iil/immersion/programs.cfm

Association of College and Research Libraries (2011). *Introduction to informaton literacy.* Retreived from http://www.ala.org/ala/mgrps/divs/acrl/issues/infolit/overview/intro/index.cfm

Badke, W. (2009). Ramping up the one-shot. *Online, 33*(2), 47-49.

Badke, W. (2008). Ten reasons to teach information literacy for credit. *Online, 32*(6), 47-49.

Breivik, P. S. (2005). 21st century learning and information literacy. *Change, 37*(2), 21-27.

Bruner, J. M., & Lee, J. W. (1970). Fact, fallacy, and the business library. *Improving College and University Teaching, 18*(4), 292-293.

City University of Seattle (2011). *Academic model.* Retrieved from http://www.cityu.edu/about/profile/academic_model. aspx

Harris, T. G. (1993). The post-capitalist executive: An interview with Peter Drucker. *Harvard Business Review, 71*(3), 114-122.

Head, A. J., & Eisenberg, M. B. (2009). *Finding context: What today's college students say about conducting research in the digital age.* Retrieved from http://projectinfolit.org/pdfs/PIL_ ProgressReport_2_2009.pdf

Jackson, S., & Durkee, D. (2008). Incorporating information literacy into the accounting curriculum. *Accounting Education, 17*(1), 83-97. doi: 10.1080/09639280601026063

Katz, I. R., Haras, C., & Blaszczynski, C. (2010). Does business writing require information literacy? *Business Communication Quarterly, 73*(2), 135-149.

Lombardo, C. V., & Miree, C. E. (2003). Caught in the web: The impact of library instruction on business students' perceptions and use of print and online resources. *College & Research Libraries, 64*(1), 6-21.

McKay, P., & Diamond, W. (1996). Investment information in academic libraries. *RQ, 35*(3), 375-392.

Middle States Commission on Higher Education (2009). *Characteristics of excellence in higher education.* Retrieved from http://www.msche.org/publications.asp

Morse, J. A. (2008). *General education and essential skills.* Retrieved from http:// www.msche.org/publications/General-Education-and-Essential-Skills.ppt

Northwest Commission on Colleges and Universities (2010). *Standard two: Resources and capacity.* Retrieved from http://www.nwccu.org/Standards%20and%20Policies/Standard%202/Standard%20Two.htm

Salman, T., & Mara, M. (2009). City University: Information literacy and the push for integration. *ACRL Washington Newsletter.* Retrieved from http://www.lib.washington.edu/acrl-wa/News/spring2009/cuinfolit.html

Simon, C. (2009). Graduate business students and business information literacy: A novel approach. *Journal of Business & Finance Librarianship, 14,* 248-267. doi:10.1080/08963560802361981

Thoms, K. J. (n.d.). *They're not just big kids: Motivating adult learners.* Retrieved from http://frank.mtsu.edu/~itconf/proceed01/22.html

United Nations Educational Scientific and Cultural Organization (2003). *The Prague declaration: Towards an information literate society.* Retrieved from http://portal.unesco.org/ci/en/files/19636/11228863531PragueDeclaration.pdf/PragueDeclaration.pdf

26

Facilitating a Transformative Learning Environment: A Case Study of Its Use in a Graduate-Level Psychology Course

Brian Guthrie, PhD
City University of Seattle
Division of Arts and Sciences - Canada

When we are no longer able to change a situation, we are challenged to change ourselves. ~Victor Frankl (2004)

Abstract

This chapter will describe the principles and practices of transformative learning that have been applied to a graduate-level course in the psychology of addictions. It will illustrate specific pedagogic and assessment strategies intended to promote transformative learning. In addition, it will detail how students were engaged in a transformative learning environment; how they were challenged to critically evaluate their values and beliefs, to become conscious of their biases, and to acquire ethical reasoning. The chapter will conclude with a discussion of steps involved in facilitating a transformative learning environment and the components that promote transformative learning.

Introduction

<u>The human experience involves change.</u> Navigating one's way in a modern world involves the interpretation and understanding of dramatic, often rapid, change. In addition, negotiating relationships involves interpreting and understanding diversity in values, beliefs, and social norms. When individuals experience change in their lives or are confronted by a dilemma or engage new information that contradicts what they have always believed, they may have to revise their traditional beliefs and norms (Cranton, 1998).

Mezirow (1985 , 1991, 2000, 2006), who first introduced the concept of transformative learning in his 1978 paper titled "Perspective Transformation," believed that being confronted with a change that contradicts what one has always believed poses contradictions in meaning for the individual. This contradiction confronts the individual with a disorienting dilemma. In the face of this dilemma, the individual can choose to reject the competing belief or to reflect and to critically question the meaning of this new perspective. To deal effectively with life changes, "rather than merely adapting to changing environments by more diligently applying old ways of knowing," Mezirow theorized that individuals "discover a need to acquire new perspectives in order to gain a more complete understanding of changing events and a higher degree of control over their lives" (Mezirow 1991, p.3). Mezirow applied this belief to adult education and developed a theory of transformative learning that can explain how adult learners make sense or meaning of their experiences, the nature of the structures that influence the way they construe experience, the dynamics involved in modifying meanings, and the way the structures of meanings themselves undergo changes when learners find them to be dysfunctional (Mezirow 1991, p. xii).

As an educational philosophy, *it* has become a lens to inform the practice of teaching by explaining the way students reinterpret prior learning experiences.

As an outcome of his 1978 research on women returning to college following a significantly long period away from formal education, Mezirow (1991) conceptualized transformative learning as "a constructivist theory of adult learning" (p. 31) that is intended "to be a comprehensive, idealized and universal model consisting of the generic structures, elements and processes of adult learning" (Mezirow, 1994, p. 222). As a constructivist theory of adult learning, knowing is conceptualized as an active process of constructing meaning or making sense of experience. Glaserfield (1995), a proponent of radical constructivism, defines knowledge construction as an adaptive activity requiring interaction with experience. Therefore, knowledge is not passively received but rather developed actively by the individual. Mezirow (1991, 1994) was influenced by Thomas Kuhn's work on "paradigms" (1962), Freire's concept of conscientization (1970), Habermas's emancipatory action domains of learning (1971), and the consciousness raising women's movement in adult education in the 1970s (Ketchenham, 2008).

Mezirow (1990) further defines transformative learning as a process that "involves reflectively transforming the beliefs, attitudes, opinions, and emotional reactions that constitute our meaning schemes or...meaning perspectives" (p. 223). This occurs through critical reflection of existing frames of reference in contrast to new knowledge and experience (Brookfield, 1995; Cranton, 2002). It involves a process of becoming conscious of new patterns, deconstructing and reconstructing old schemas, and creating new frames of reference. These new schemas or cognitive frameworks help organize concepts and actions and, in turn, can be revised by new information about the world.

At the core of Mezirow's (1991) theory of transformative learning is the process of making meaning from one's experiences through reflection. Mezirow defines reflection as "the process of critically assessing the content, process, or premise(s) of our efforts to interpret and give meaning to an experience" (p. 104). According to Mezirow when individuals engage in critical self-reflection the outcome will be a deep shift towards a more open, permeable, and congruent way of seeing themselves and the world around them. This questioning or critical self-reflection can then lead to a revision of a value, belief, assumption, or even a broader perspective. If this happens, transformative learning has taken place.

Certain principles and practices of transformative learning can be adopted and applied to a graduate level education. There are also specific pedagogic and assessment strategies intended to promote transformative learning. These principles were applied to a master's level counselling psychology course that included four assessment strategies: (a) a critical reflection journal; (b) a case study which involved a psychosocial substance abuse assessment; (c) a class presentation of an evaluation of a treatment program; and (d) class participation in the form of rational discourse groups. These examples will detail how students were engaged in a transformative learning environment, how they were challenged to critically evaluate their values and beliefs, to become conscious of their biases, and to acquire ethical reasoning.

Transformative Learning Theory

It is a common experience that students come to learning with their own frame of reference based on assumptions about themselves and their world and grounded in earlier life experiences. One's frame of reference is comprised of sets of beliefs, values, and assumptions that provide a definition of oneself and a sense of meaning to one's experiences and worldview. It is equally as common for educators to want students to question the presuppositions of their lived experience by considering the alternative perspectives of peers, by critically examining the literature in the field of study, and by challenging the frame of reference presented by the educator. There is a consensus that it is important that university students, especially those engaged in graduate level studies, develop the ability to engage critically with the course content presented to them and to translate that material into real-world contexts (Bruce & Candy, 2000; Spronken-Smith, 2005).

Mezirow (1991) believes that transformative learning "occurs when individuals realize how and why assumptions have constrained the way they understand the world and begin to consciously use other strategies to rethink issues and define their worlds differently" (Tower & Walker, 2007, p. 305-306). O'Sullivan, Morrell and O'Connor (2002) further define transformative learning as a process that

> involves experiencing a deep structural shift in the basic premises of thought, feelings, and actions. It is a shift of consciousness that dramatically and permanently alters our way of being in the world. Such a shift involves our understanding of ourselves and our self-locations; our relationships with other humans and with the natural world; our understanding of relations of power in interlocking structures of class, race and gender; our body awareness, our visions of alternative approaches to living; and our sense of possibilities for social justice and peace and personal joy. (p. xvii)

Transformative learning changes the way adult students understand themselves and their perception of the world. It provides an explanation of how their expectations, framed within cultural assumptions and previous life experience, directly influence the meaning they derive from their experiences. It explains the learning process of constructing and appropriating new and revised interpretations of the meaning of an experience in the world (Taylor, 2008). The practice of transformative learning focuses on changing the ways in which students learn by engaging them in a conscious process of discovering the meaning of knowledge to their worldview rather than just the acquisition of knowledge. The goal is to create more critically reflective and autonomous thinkers. Students are challenged to evaluate the concepts and premises of their learning and not accept knowledge as a fact or truth without critical self-reflection on how what is being learned is meaningful for them.

Transformative learning theory posits the premise that the majority of individuals are not conscious of the origin of the meaningful structures that make up their worldview (Mezirow, 1997). Mezirow observed that individuals learn what they seek to learn by transforming their frames of reference, that is, challenging assumptions and one's taken-for-granted beliefs about reality. In transformative learning, individuals "reinterpret an old experience (or a new one) from a set of expectations, thus giving a new meaning and perspective to an old experience" (Mezirow, 1991, p. 11). These sets of expectations are unconsciously embedded in what Mezirow (1990) initially termed *meaning perspective*. Replacing the term meaning perspective with the term *frame of reference* (Mezirow, 1997; 2000), Mezirow (1997) defines "frames of reference" as the "structures of assumptions through which we understand our experiences" (p.5). They selectively shape and delimit expectations, perceptions, cognition, and feelings. They set "our line of action" (p. 5). Taylor (2008) reiterates the definition that frames of reference:

> are structures of assumptions and expectations that frame an individual's tacit points of view and influence their thinking, beliefs, and actions. It is the revision of a frame of reference in concert with reflection on experience that is addressed by the theory of perspective transformation—a paradigmatic shift. (p.5)

Mezirow (2000) views learning as " the process of using prior interpretation to construe new or revised interpretation of the meaning of one's experience as a guide to future action" (p. 5). He outlines three steps in transformative learning:

1. Becoming critically aware of assumptions and limitations.
2. Changing habits of mind to be more inclusive.
3. Acting upon these new understandings.

Mezirow's (1991, 2000) theory of transformative learning involves a process in which the student goes through stages of cognitive restructuring that include the integration of experience, action, and reflection. He initially (Mezirow, 1978) identified ten phases of meaning in the process of transformative learning, but added an eleventh phase in 1991, which emphasized the importance of altering present relationships and forging new relationships (Mezirow 2000). He asserts that "transformations often follow [when] some variation of the following phases of meaning becoming clarified" (Mezirow, 2000, p. 22). The following table lists Mezirow's phases of meaning.

Table 1

Mezirow's Phases of Meaning in Transformational Learning

Phases

1. A disorienting dilemma.
2. Self-examination with feelings of shame, fear, guilt, or anger.
3. A critical assessment of assumptions.
4. Recognizing that one's discontent and the process of transformation are shared.
5. Exploration of options for new roles, relationships, and actions.
6. Planning a course of action.
7. Acquiring knowledge and skills for implementing one's plan.
8. Provisional trying new roles.
9. Building self-confidence and competence in new roles and relationships.
10. Re-integrating into one's life on the bases of conditions dictated by one's new perspective.
11. Altering present relationships and forging new relationships.

Mezirow (1991) suggests that as the student moves through the series of stages the change in perspective can be gradual or immediate and is contingent upon the student experiencing cognitive restructuring and a reorganization of experience and action. The transformative learning experience begins with a disorientating experience that causes students to become critically aware of their assumptions and how these assumptions constrain the way they perceive, understand, and feel about the world. Transformative learning evolves as the student changes the

> taken for granted frame of reference (meaning perspectives, habits of mind, mind-sets) to make them more inclusive, discriminating, open, emotionally capable of change, and reflective, so that they may generate beliefs and opinions that will prove more true or justified to guide action. (Mezirow & Associates, 2000, pp. 8-9)

The transformation is seen as complete when students make choices or act upon the new understanding (Mezirow, 1991). Merriam, Caffarella and Baumgartner (2007) emphasize that transformation is the result of critical thinking, reflective discourse, and ultimately an action or change of some sort.

Certain principles and practices of transformative learning can be adopted and applied to a graduate level education. There are also specific pedagogic and assessment strategies intended to promote transformative learning. These principles were applied to a master's level counselling psychology course that included four assessment strategies: (a) a critical reflection journal; (b) a case study which involved a psychosocial substance abuse assessment; (c) a class presentation of an evaluation of a treatment program; and (d) class participation in the form of rational discourse groups. These examples detail how students were engaged in a transformative learning environment, how they were challenged to critically evaluate their values and beliefs, to become conscious of their biases, and to acquire ethical reasoning.

An example of how the students in the course described in this chapter experienced being engaged critically with the course content and how they translated the material into real-world contexts is highlighted by a reflective journal entry of one of the students:

Prior to registering in the addictions course the thought of working with people with addictions made me nervous, angry and hopeless. Much has changed for me. I believed addicts were making a conscious choice to participate in risky activities. I had a sense that addicts were in some way rebels choosing to participate in illegal activities. For me, that way of thinking lent itself to the belief that people who do illegal drugs are selfish, not concerned about potentially harming others through their actions and truly not willing to change. When I imagined working with addicted clients, I imagined that many would REFUSE to change. Even the thought of working with addicted clients angered me. I had a sense that efforts to facilitate change in these types of situations would be hopeless. There were times I did not believe I would be capable of helping addicted clients.

The classroom lectures, readings, journals and student participation component of the class helped flip my perspective about addictions. I see how easy it is to believe and continue the social stigma attached to people who are addicted to illegal substances. The biggest influence this course had on me personally was to help me develop a sense of empathy toward people who are addicted. Professionally I moved from being opposed to working with addicted clients to feeling a sense of urgency to help them.

I am grateful for the drastic change in my perspective. I can honestly say that this course has changed my beliefs about addictions and addictions treatment which will positively influence my interactions with future clients. As a psychologist I will be more understanding about my client's experience with addictions, I will be more patient, less critical and less angry toward my client for their behaviour.

This student's entry not only demonstrates critical reflection of the course content, but also details how the course challenged prior personal beliefs and ultimately led to the development of a new view of those struggling with addictions along with anticipated changes in behaviour as a result of the shift. Cranton (2002) would describe this student's experience as transformative learning since it involved a fundamental change in perspective as a result of the student changing something about how he or she constructed meaning about the world.

Critical Reflection, Rationale Discourse, and Action

Reliance on adult learning theory and Habermas's (1984) communicative theory, experience, critical reflection, and rational discourse are central themes in Mezirow's transformative learning (Boyd, 1991; Cranton, 1994; Kegan, 1994). Mezirow (1990) described the process of critical reflection on one's own experience and engaging in rational discourse as:

> From this vantage point, adult education becomes the process of assisting those who are fulfilling adult roles to understand the meaning of their experience by participating more fully and freely in rational discourse to validate expressed ideas and to take action upon the resulting insights...Rational thought and action are the cardinal goals of adult education. (p. 354)

Critical reflection is a central process in Mezirow's (2000) conceptualization of transformative learning (Cranton and Corusetta, 2004). Critical reflection, according to Brookfield (1995), focuses on three interrelated processes:

1. The process by which adults question and then replace or reframe an assumption that up to that point has been uncritically accepted as representing commonsense wisdom.
2. The process through which adults take alternative perspectives on previously taken-for-granted ideas, actions, forms of reasoning and ideologies.
3. The process by which adults come to recognize the hegemonic aspects of dominant cultural values. (p. 2)

Mezirow (1991) defines reflection as "the process of critically assessing the content, process, or premise(s) of our efforts to interpret and give meaning to an experience" (p. 104). He divided critical reflection into two components, non-reflective action and reflective action. The process of non-reflective action includes two types of action, habitual action and thoughtful action. Habitual action results from previous learning related to psychomotor tasks and can be performed while one's attention is focused some-where else. Habitual action is often considered to be the product of rote learning. Thoughtful action, on the other hand, depends on higher-order cognitive processes that guide individuals in tasks that involve things like analyzing, discussing, or evaluating. Similar to habitual action, thoughtful action also depends on prior learning and remains within preexisting meaning schemes and perspectives.

Reflective action is the outcome of insights that were gained from the process of reflecting. Reflective action is considered to be mindful and purposeful as opposed to the repetitive pre-scriptive behaviour of non-reflective action. Mezirow (1991) considers reflective action or mindfulness as transformational because it is associated with "greater accuracy of perception of the unfamiliar and deviant, avoidance of premature cognitive commitments, better self-concept, greater job productivity and satisfaction, flexibility, innovation, and leadership ability" (p. 117).

Reflective learning strategies. Both the critical reflective jour-nal and the rational discourse groups in this course were consid-ered reflective learning strategies. The two other assignments, the case study and the evaluation of a treatment agency, were consid-ered action-learning strategies and are described in a subsequent section.

Mezirow (1998) posited that adult learning occurs in four ways:

1. Elaborating existing frames of reference.
2. Learning frames of references.
3. Transforming points of view.
4. Transforming habits of mind.

He applies critical reflection as a component of all four and argued that the overall purpose of adult development is to realize one's agency through increasingly expanding awareness and critical reflection.

One of the major dilemmas often experienced by students entering the helping professions is that their lived experience and frames of reference are challenged by the theories of practice. These theories are also seen as describing competing principles and premises which can lead to a sense of confusion as to what is right. Sometimes students may gravitate towards a theory that fits their frame of reference and adopt the premises of that theory because the knowledge is comfortably familiar, that is, the philosophical underpinning of the theory supports their presuppositions, their world view, and their lived experience. They adopt the theory as a truth without critical evaluation. Critical reflection challenges students to explore their biases and assumptions and to contrast these with the premises and principles that support the theory in order to examine how the theory relates to professional practice rather than personal preference.

One student's reflection at the end of the course highlights a personal transformation in relation to a bias she held about individuals struggling with addiction.

> I have gotten over the notion that most addicts (a) will never permanently change, and (b) it is a rather hopeless endeavour to attempt to help them. I held this belief because I think that in the work I have done to date with this population, I saw very little response or recovery that was maintained for a long period of time (months, years). This was especially true for the hard core drugs. Addicts were disappointing to me as clients because most of them did not want to change, were forced to come to treatment, or just wanted to get it over with and be back to their use. This is not the truth.

For this student to develop into a critically reflective professional, she would need to continue to evolve this capacity for critical inquiry and self-reflection (Larrivee, 2000; Schon, 1987).

Course assignments emphasized the process of critical inquiry, which involved the conscious consideration of the moral and ethical implications and consequences of practice with clients. Each assignment incorporated two components. Students began with self-reflection of personal assumptions, values, and beliefs, and their current frame of reference. This was followed by critical inquiry, which contrasted and compared their personal and professional belief systems. As one student's reflective journal entry highlighted:

> *I am now open to the range of approaches in addiction treatment. I know now that tailoring treatment to suit the client will realize the best results. My role is to advocate for the client so that they have access to the best support available, including treatment centres, medication, or other therapeutic interventions. It matters not whether I align myself with the disease, biopsychosocial or the harm-reduction model; what matters is what is best for the client.*

Reflective journal assignment. Reflection is a primary component of transformative learning. The development of critical thinking requires what Dewey (1910) described as the willingness to suspend "judgement: and the essence of this suspense is inquiry" (p. 74). The intent of the reflective journals was to provide the students with a vehicle to contemplate their personal thoughts and feelings based on their current frame of reference. Journals served the purpose of assisting students in articulating and clarifying their thoughts, emotions and beliefs about issues raised in class dialogue and course readings. The expected outcome of the journaling experience was to promote insight into self and issues, the discovery of connections in theory and practice, and the generation of new knowledge through critical inquiry of existing knowledge.

The critical reflective journal became the foundation for class dialogue and interaction. Students completed their journal entries in two stages: (a) upon completion of assigned reading; and (b) following the completion of class dialogue. The journal tasks were structured to promote the development of critical reflection of self, critical reflection of others, and development of self as a professional. Journal entries, although private between the student and the educator, were intended to provide content for class group dialogue. Students chose to what degree they would disclose personal thoughts and beliefs contained in their journal. To promote reflexivity and reflection, the journal assignment was designed based on research by Stamper (1996) and Gustafson and Bennett (1999) who investigated the barriers that inhibit deep reflective journaling. Their four recommendations were incorporated into the development of the course reflective journal assignment. Their recommendations included:

1. Designing appropriate learning experiences enabled students to develop reflective skills. Each journal assignment was based on the assigned course reading for the class and the class dialogue and posed questions that required the students to provide reasons for their thoughts and ideas, taking into account the broader historical, social, and political contexts highlighted in the course content.

2. The ability to reflect on a specific topic is directly proportional to how much one already knows. To assist the student to become more conscious of his/her existing frames of reference, each journal entry began with a reflection on the student's own perspective prior to his/her critical inquiry of course content.

3. Both internal and external sources of motivation affect the quality of reflection. In the reflective journal assignment, internal motivation was fuelled by the acquisition of insight into the meaning of one's values and beliefs. Although dialogue was not specifically recommended by Gustafson and Bennett (1999), it was incorporated into the journal assignment as a method of encouraging external motivation. Bandura (1977), who developed social learning theory, believed that environments that promote interpersonal interaction result in greater reflection.

4. Confidence in the professionalism and integrity of the educator enhances the quantity and quality of reflection. Trust in this educator was enhanced by the emphasis on con-

fidentiality of journal entries. Each student was assigned a secure electronic posting log. Confidence in the professionalism and integrity of the educator was also enhanced by providing positive feedback that acknowledged the work the student had done, by adding additional information to reinforce his/her understanding of the concepts, and by encouraging deeper self-reflection on the meaning of what was being learned to his/her frame of reference.

The process of reflective journaling. Cranton (1996, 2006) emphasized three levels of reflection that she viewed as especially effective at promoting critical self-reflection and self-knowledge. These, as originally distinguished by Mezirow (1991), are content reflection, process reflection, and premise reflection. Content reflection occurs when an individual reflects on the content or description of the problem (Cranton 1996). Process reflection involves thinking about the strategies used to solve the problem rather than the content of the problem itself and is considered to be rational rather than intuitive. Premise reflection is the process that leads one to question the relevance of the problem itself in the context of one's assumptions, beliefs, or values (Cranton, 1996). The goal of including these types of reflection into the reflective journaling process is to establish "an environment where people can figure things out for themselves." (Cranton, 1996, p.138).

The critical reflective journal assignment for this course was developed to incorporate the three levels of reflection recommended by Cranton (1996). The first task of each journal assignment introduced content reflection. Based on the assigned reading and the subsequent class dialogue, students incorporated the process of focus-free writing, which is nonstop writing on a specific subject and is intended to help them crystallize their ideas and feelings. They were coached in the process of allowing their thoughts and feelings to surface for a minimum of ten minutes as they began to record their understanding and interpretation of the class dialogue and course reading. Content reflection "serve(s) to raise learner awareness of assumptions and beliefs" (Cranton, 1996, p. 139). Content reflection relates to knowledge and the way it is obtained.

The second task of each journal assignment required students to engage in process reflection. Students were asked to contemplate the following questions:

Question one: This is what I know that was confirmed in class or in the course reading. How was this confirmed for you?

Question two: This is what I did not know. Discuss what was unclear or confusing.

Question three: This is what surprised me.

Process reflection "address(es) how a person has come to hold a certain perspective" (Cranton, 199, p. 140). These questions where intended to assist learners to reflect on the source of their assumptions and beliefs. In addition, these questions where intended to prompt learners to critically reflect on their current frame of reference and to critically evaluate their values and beliefs in light of new knowledge.

The last journal task was to answer the following premise reflection question: This is what I found myself thinking differently about _____. Premise reflection "get(s) at the very core of belief systems." (Cranton, 1996, p. 141). It raises questions about the most foundational aspects of thinking and belief.

One student's reflective journal entry summarizes a change in perspective:

> I was surprised to see myself typing the idea that some people are more prone than others (to addiction) because of a "weak will." This is basically the weak moral argument and it is an age old one. I didn't know I held this belief quite as strongly as I did when I started this class. I see the pros and cons of the argument that the environment and genetic loading really can make some people more susceptible to substance use. I had this thought lurking around at the beginning of this class that it's got to be decently easy to quit smoking or drinking if you really wanted to, right? I think I fell on my own face here, because I did not realize that the same bias I held before, about addicts being "weak willed" was flipped on its side by the "strong willed" person who can quit without hesitation.

Rational Discourse. According to transformative learning theory (Mezirow, 1991), rational discourse is a means for testing the validity of one's construction of meaning. It is considered to be the catalyst through which transformation is promoted and developed. Rational discourse requires adequate time to accommodate extended and repeated conversations that evolve with time. The time invested into rationale discourse helps to foster a culture of respectful listening and openness to new perspectives. The goal is not a shared understanding in the sense of consensus but rather a conscious understanding of one's own biases as well as how others in the learning group construct their frames of reference. The dialogue involves the purposeful weighing of current knowledge, the examination alternative perspectives, and the critical inquiry of assumptions.

At the beginning of every class, students entered into different groups of three. The groups were given the task of sharing their experience of critically reflecting on the previous class content, class dialogue, and assigned course reading. Students were encouraged to refer to their previous reflective journal entry to contribute to the group dialogue. Group members assumed the role of either facilitator, recorder, or moderator. Each role had specific assigned duties. The facilitator's role was to evoke critical dialogue grounded in the three journal questions and focus the group on weighing supporting evidence from class reading and lectures. The recorder's role was to capture what was clear, what was unclear, and what was surprising to learn as well as to record the group's experience of examining alternative perspectives. The moderator assumed the role of group conscience, keeping the group on task and focusing the dialogue on critically assessing assumptions. The last component of the group dialogue exercise was for each group to present its response to the class group to the final journal question, "This is what we found ourselves thinking differently about _____."

Similar to the journal tasks, the group dialogue was structured to incorporate the three levels of reflection described by Cranton (1996). This structure provided the students with what Yip (2006) has described as "flexibility of content and more importantly a multiplicity of thinking" (p. 253). Yip describes the process students' experience in reflection and rational dialogue as being "on the one hand involved in intervention and action and on the other being aware of their personal feelings and thinking in action" (p. 253).

As a foundation exercise for each class the journal/group dialogue exercise was intended to help students to develop their skills for critical reflection by acknowledging the importance of meaningful dialogue. The combination of internal individual reflection and dialogue in a shared group experience was intended to provide a bridge of understanding among students and, also, between students and the course content. It also served the purpose of empowering the students by recognizing and validating their experience, promoting a safe starting point for indentifying the dilemma they are being confronted with, and for engaging in critical reflection.

The overall intent of rational discourse is to validate meaning by comparing and contrasting differing perspectives. In this course it involved the critical evaluation of research and theory, the examination of alternative perspectives on treatment, and the critical assessment of practice assumptions. Through the connection between the reflective journal and the class dialogue, students reported that they were able to find their voice in constructive dialogue with others.

Action. *Praxis* is a Greek word that means moving back and forth in a critical way between reflecting and acting on the world. It is the process of learning through the reconstruction of experience. Praxis involves taking time to deepen one's understanding of the implications and longer-term impact before taking action. Because reflection alone does not produce change, Freire (1970) advocated for the necessity of action based on reflection. When action and reflection are integrated, actions should be considered not in light of the how do we do this, but rather what do we believe taking this action will do; why are we choosing this action; and what alternatives are there that we have yet to consider. According to Cranton (1992), action is the litmus test of transformative learning; it is evidence of changed perspectives.

In addition to the reflective journal assignment and the in-class rational discourse, the course incorporated two additional assignments. Students are required to use a case study to complete a psychosocial substance abuse assessment and also present their evaluation of a substance abuse treatment program. These two assignments focus learning on the production of action, that is, putting their theoretical understanding into practice. They also serve the purpose of providing a transition for students to move from critical reflection on theory to critical reflection on practice.

Based on their work in their reflective journals and in group dialogue sessions, students were asked to declare the theory that they believe provides them with the clearest conceptual understanding of substance abuse. Given that the course content focused on the Disease model, the Biopsychosocial model and the Harm Reduction model, students aligned with the theory they believed was the closest fit to their world view of substance abuse/addictions. Students were then asked to identify the theory that they believed was the most challenging to their current beliefs. Students were given four case study examples to choose from. Their task was to formulate a psychosocial substance abuse assessment congruent with the theory that they identified as most challenging to their current beliefs. The purpose of the assignment was to introduce a disorienting dilemma to the students. The dilemma that confronted students was, Is there a right way to conceptualize, assess, and treat substance abuse? One student commented on the experience of completing the psychosocial substance abuse assessment in their reflective journal with the following comment:

> Although I have taken many courses in addictions, I had not evaluated the different approaches each model would take when presented with a specific case. Personally, I like the idea that depending on the stage of change, different approaches would be appropriate. I am more comfortable in knowing where to start when someone presents with substance abuse. I can identify whether they fall into use, abuse or addiction.

The second action strategy assignment continued the focus on action as an outcome of learning. Students presented their evaluation of a substance abuse treatment agency. In addition to identifying the mandate, mission, and agency's theory of treatment, students provided a critical evaluation of the agency's statements of effectiveness. The purpose of the assignment was to engage students in the critical evaluation of practice. As one student reflected on the experience of evaluating a community treatment agency:

> I have learned that the barriers to successful addictions treatment are numerous while supports are limited. Subsequently, as professionals, we have an ethical responsibility to challenge negative social responses, advocate for support and lobby for changes to access to treatment. Finally I found it helpful to evaluate the community resources. In the future we may relay our criticism to improve services in the community.

The constructivist orientation underpinning transformative learning argues that knowledge is not an entity waiting to be discovered and consumed by the learner but rather is created by the learner through interpretation and reinterpretation of experience. As Mezirow (1991) states, " ... it is not so much what happens to people but how they interpret and explain what happens to them that determine their actions, their hopes, their commitment and emotional well being, and their performance" (p.xiii). Action then is the foundation for transformation. Acting upon knowledge is the way that new experiences, and particularly significant disorienting experiences, are dealt with, and it is critical to the process of transformation. As Mezirow (1990) states, simply reflecting on or even changing ones meaning perspective is not sufficient for transformative learning to have taken place. Action is also required, in the sense of the enactment of the altered perspective in the social world. The evolution from reflection to dialogue to action was reflected in another student's final journal entry:

> Before entering the program I was baffled by why people would choose to destroy their body, mind and soul with toxic substances. In addition, my personal experiences and the social stigma associated with addicts accounted for most of my negative attitudes and beliefs towards addicts. However,

the knowledge that I attained from the lectures, discussions, case study assessment and the agency presentation has made me realize that addictions are much more complicated than I thought. On a professional level I have grown to appreciate the addictions field. This is surprising insight as I never had an interest to work with addicts prior to the course. Thanks to this course I feel that I am more prepared to face this challenge.

Facilitating Transformative Learning

Facilitating transformative learning as a teaching practice is "predicated on the idea that students are seriously challenged to assess their value system and worldview and are subsequently changed by that experience" (Quinnan, 1997, p. 42). Mezirow (1997) describes a transformative learning environment as one in which those participating have full information, are free from coercion, have equal opportunity to assume various roles, can become critically reflective of assumptions, are empathetic and good listeners, and are willing to search for common ground or a synthesis of different points of view. He sees the role the educator plays as crucial in the process of facilitating transformative learning. According to Mezirow, the role of the educator is to assist learners in assessing their previously unexamined frame of reference and critically evaluating the way in which the resulting beliefs, feelings, and actions have shaped their lives. The educator then fosters transformative learning by assisting students to explore alternative ideas and to test their validity in reflective dialogue with their peers (Mezirow, 1991).

Taylor (1998; 2000), in his review of the research on transformative learning theory, identified a number of strategies that educators can employ that foster transformative learning, including (a) individual experience; (b) critical reflection; (c) dialogue; (d) holistic orientation; (e) awareness of context; and (f) authentic relationships. For these strategies to begin to foster transformative learning in the classroom environment, Cranton (2002) identified a number of conditions and processes she believed are required to support a revision of underlying assumptions, the adoption of a new paradigm and the application of the new paradigm. They are (a) an activating event that exposes the limitations of a student's current knowledge/approach; (b) opportunities for the student to identify and articulate the underlying assumptions in the student's current knowledge/approach; (c) critical self-reflection as the student considers where these underlying assumptions came from, how these assumptions influenced or limited understanding; (d). critical discourse with other students and the instructor as the group examines alternative ideas and approaches; and, (e) opportunities to test and apply new perspectives.

Taylor (2008) describes the teaching practice of transformative learning as not simply incorporating additional instructional strategies into the course curriculum. He views transformative learning as "first and foremost about educating from a particular worldview, a particular educational philosophy" (p. 13). According to Taylor (1998), ideal learning conditions that facilitate a transformative learning environment promote (a) a sense of safety, openness, and trust; (b) effective instructional methods that support a learner-centered approach; (c) student autonomy, participation, and collaboration; (d) activities that encourage the exploration of alternative personal perspectives, problem-posing, and critical reflection. His research also highlighted several attributes of the educator and the teaching philosophy that helps to foster a quality learning experience congruent with transformational learning. Some of the attributes that he identified as significant include being "trusting, empathetic, caring, authentic, sincere, and demonstrating a high degree of integrity" (Taylor, 1998, p. 54). In addition, Taylor (1998) emphasized that effective educators who practice transformative learning should (a) encourage students to reflect on and share their feelings and thoughts in class; (b) are holistically oriented, aware of body, mind, and spirit in the learning process; (c) become transcendent of their own beliefs and accepting of others' beliefs; (d) cultivate awareness of alternate ways of learning; (e) establish an environment characterized by trust and care; (f) facilitate sensitive relationships among the participants; (g) demonstrate ability to serve as an experienced mentor reflecting on their own journey; and (h) help students question reality in ways that promote shifts in their worldview.

Teaching from a transformative perspective is aimed at helping students "gain a crucial sense of agency" over themselves and their world (Mezirow and Associates 2000: p. 20). Freire (1997) emphasizes the importance of cooperation between teachers and students as a critical factor in evaluating the world in a reflexive manner. He believed that the educator's own philosophy and teaching approach can facilitate reflective thinking and meaningful change by reducing the polarity between the roles of the student and the educator. Cranton (2006) reiterates that "fostering transformative learning in the classroom depends to a large extent on establishing meaningful, genuine relationships with students" (p. 5). She recommends that the educator move from being an expert and manager to an advocate, co-learner, provocateur, challenger, and facilitator.

The journey of adapting and adopting transformative learning theory as a teaching practice involves a number of challenges as articulated by Taylor (2008). Specifically he identifies two inherent challenges for the educator who is intrigued by the potential benefits of the transformative learning process for his/her students. His first challenge emphasized that to incorporate transformative learning into teaching one needs to integrate transformative theory into practice, and this involves adopting a particular worldview and a specific educational philosophy. This challenge involves moving away from a classroom environment that was grounded in instrumental learning—which Habermas (1971) describes as learning to control the environment—to a classroom environment that promoted reflection, dialogue, and action. That is, fostering a learning environment that encouraged exploration by students as to why they think in a certain way, critical evaluation of theory and research, and critical reflection that evolved to deeper and deeper understanding of one's values and beliefs.

Taylor (2008) identified the second challenge as accepting a belief and position that the facilitation of transformative learning is treated as a commitment to the development of each individual student. This means abandoning the belief that there are good students and there are poor students and that not every student is in class to learn. Challenging this frame of reference means a commitment to acknowledge each student's passion for learning and to validate each student's progress in acquiring knowledge.

Facilitating an environment where the student feels validated involves engaging every student in a more authentic relationship. To develop an authentic relationship with students, classroom relationships are defined by the expectation of mutual respect and developed by demonstrating a sense of care for learners and an ethic of care in the classroom. Goodfellow and Sumsion (2000) identify a number relational qualities that promote a culture of care that in turn promotes transformative learning. They cite these qualities as (a) reciprocity, or an exchange within which there are shared understandings; (b) responsiveness, or concern for and commitment to the other, and a shift in focus from self to the other; (c) respectfulness, or high regard for the other; (d) empathy or conscious effort to convey to the other an understanding of what the other is thinking and feeling; (e) attunedness, or an awareness of the climate within the context, and an ability to act in harmony within that context; and, (f) a consciousness of self and of self in relation to others.

Incorporating the relational qualities recommended by Goodfellow and Sumsion (2000) into interactions with students results in relinquishing the position of authority figure and gaining a position of trust where the relationship with the adult learners in this course becomes a journey of collaborative and cooperative learning. The role becomes, as Cranton (1996) recommended, one of advocate, co-learner, provocateur, challenger, and facilitator.

Conclusion

"Every adult educator has the responsibility for fostering critical self-reflection and helping learners plan to take action" (Mezirow, 1990, p. 357). In learning about themselves and others, students are challenged to think independently, to observe, to experience, to reflect, to learn, and to dialogue. Students are encouraged to think beyond their taken-for-granted frames of reference and consider how things might be different (Brookfield, 2000; Mezirow, 1990).

This journey into transformative learning theory involves what Brookfield (1995) describes as the most difficult challenge of becoming a reflective educator, stepping outside oneself. He writes that to become a critically reflective educator one must examine his/her teaching through the following critical reflective lenses: (a) autobiographies as learners and educators; (b) students' eyes; (c) colleagues' experiences; and (d) theoretical literature. Critical self-reflection of teaching practice and adoption of transformative learning theory reinforces that adult learners bring to the classroom a passion for learning, a wealth of lived experience, and a willingness to challenge their world view.

Critically reflective educators must become congruent with the process of transformational learning. This involves a commitment to questioning assumptions, beliefs, and values and being critically reflective of one's teaching philosophy.

Transformative learning theory offers a framework for practice that confirms that learning has the potential to transform one's world view. It is a reflective process that results in a change in the frames of reference through critically reflecting on assumptions and beliefs and by consciously making and implementing plans that bring about new ways of defining the practice of teaching. It is an educational philosophy that has provided a lens to inform the practice of teaching by explaining the way students reinterpret prior learning experiences. Apte (2009) captures the essence of the educators' experience in transformative learning in her comment, "we are not only an audience for participant's current frames of reference. We are the audience for emerging knowledge and capability" (p. 186).

References

Apte, J. (2009). Facilitating transformative learning: A framework for practice. *Australian Journal of Adult Learning*, 49(1).

Bandura, A. (1977). *Social learning theory*. Englewood Cliffs, NJ: Prentice-Hall.

Boyd, R. (1991). *Personal transformations in small groups*. London: Routledge.

Brookfield, S. D. (1995). *Becoming a critically reflective teacher*. San Francisco: Jossey-Bass.

Bruce, C., & Candy, P. (2000). *Information literacy around the world*. Charles Stuart Uni Press.

Cranton, P. (1992). *Working with adult learners*. Toronto, Canada: Wall & Emerson.

Cranton, P. (1994). *Understanding and promoting transformative learning: A guide for educators of adults*. San Francisco: Jossey-Bass.

Cranton, P. (1996). *Professional development as transformative learning: New perspectives for reachers of adults*. San Francisco: Jossey-Bass.

Cranton, P. (2006). *Understanding and promoting transformative learning: A guide for educators of adults*. (2nd Ed.). San Francisco: Jossey-Bass.

Cranton, P., & Carusetta, E. (2004). Perspectives on authenticity in teaching. *Adult Education Quarterly, 55*(1), 5-22.

Dewey, J. (1910). *How we think: A restatement of the relation of reflective thinking to the educative process* Boston, New York & London:Heath.

Frankl, V. (2004). *Man's search for meaning: An introduction to logotherapy*. Boston: Beacon and Random House/Rider. London.

Freire, P. (1970). *Pedagogy of the oppressed*. London: Penguin.

Freire, P. (1995). *Pedagogy of hope: Reliving pedagogy of the oppressed*. Continuum. New York.

Glaserfield, E.von. (1995) *Radical constructivism A way of knowing and learning.* Falmer Press: London.

Goodfellow, J., & Sumsion, J. (2000). Transformative Pathways: field-based teacher educators' perceptions. *Journal of Education for Teaching, 26*(3), 245-257.

Gustafson, K., & Bennett, W. (1999). *Issues and difficulties in promoting learner reflection: Results from a three-year study.* http://it.coe.uga.edu/~kgustafs/document/promoting.html

Habermas, J. (1971). *Knowledge and human interests.* Boston: Beacon Press.

Habermas, J. (1981). *The theory of communicative action: Vol. 1. reason and rationalization of society.* (T. McCarthy). Cambridge: Polity Press.

Kegan, R. (1994). *In over our heads.* Cambridge, MA: Harvard University Press.

Kitchenham, A. (2008). The evolution of John Mezirow's transformative learning theory. *Journal of Transformative Education.* London. Sage, 6(2).

Kuhn, T. (1962). *The structure of scientific revolutions.* Chicago: University of Chicago Press.

Larrivee, B. (2000). Transforming teaching practice: Becoming the critically reflective teacher. *Reflective Practice, 1*(3), 293-307.

http://tecfa.unige.ch/themes/sa2/act-app-dos2-fic-component.htm

Merriam, S. B., Caffarella, R. S., & Baumgartner, L. (2007). *Learning in adulthood: A comprehensive guide* (5th ed.). San Francisco: Jossey-Bass

Mezirow, J. (1978). Perspective transformation. *Adult Education Quarterly, 28*(2), 100-110.

Mezirow, J. D. (1981). A critical theory of adult learning and education. *Adult Education Quarterly, 32*(1), 3-24.

Mezirow, J. (1985). A critical theory of self-directed learning. *New Directions for Adult and Continuing Education, 25,* 17-30.

Mezirow, J. D. (1990). *Fostering critical reflection in adulthood: A guide to transformative and emancipatory learning.* San Francisco: Jossey-Bass.

Mezirow, J. D. (1991) *Transformative dimensions of adult learning.* San Francisco, CA: Jossey-Bass.

Mezirow, J. D. (1994). Understanding transformation theory. *Adult Education Quarterly, 44*(4), 222-232.

Mezirow, J. D. (1997). Transformative learning: Theory to practice. *New Directions for Adult and Continuing Education, 74,* 5-12.

Mezirow, J. D. (1998). On critical reflection. *Adult Education Quarterly, 48*(3), 185-198.

Mezirow, J. D. (2000). *Learning as transformation: Critical perspectives on a theory in progress.* San Francisco: Jossey-Bass.

O'Sullivan, E. (2003) Bringing a perspective of transformative learning to globalized consumption. *International Journal of Consumer Studies, 27*(4), 326–330

O'Sullivan, E., Morrell, A., & O'Connor, M. A. (2002). *Expanding the boundaries of transformative learning.* New York: Palgarave.

Quinnan, T. (1997). *Adult students at risk: Cultural bias in higher education.* Bergin & Garvey. Westport. Conn.

Schon, D. (1987). *Educating the reflective practitioner*. San Francisco: Jossey-Bass.

Spronken-Smith, R. A. (2005). Implementing a problem based learning approach for teaching research methods in geography. *Journal of Geography in Higher Education, 29*, 203-221.

Stamper, C. (1996). *Fostering reflective thinking through computer mediated journaling*.

Unpublished doctoral dissertation. Tempe: Arizona State University.

Taylor, E. W. (1998). *The theory and practice of transformative learning: A critical review*. (Information Series No. 374). Columbus, OH: ERIC Clearinghouse on Adult, Career, & Vocational Education, Center on Education and Training for Employment, College of Education, the Ohio State University.

Taylor, E. W. (2000). Analysing research on transformative learning theory. In Mezirow & Associates (Eds.). *Learning as transformation: critical perspectives on a theory in progress*. San Francisco: Jossey-Bass.

Taylor, E. W. (2006). The Challenge of Teaching for Change. In E. W. Taylor (eds.),

Teaching for change: Fostering transformative learning in the classroom. New Directions in Adult and Continuing Education, no. 109. San Francisco: Jossey-Bass.

Taylor, E. W. (2008). Transformative learning theory. *New Directions for Adult and Continuing Education, 119*, 5-15.

Yip, K. (2006). Reflectivity in social work practice with mental-health illness: Promise and challenge in social work education. *International Social Work, 49*, 245-255.

Made in the USA
Charleston, SC
01 November 2014